Telling Tales Out of School

Eurunderee Public School, c.1879 , the teacher is John Tierney with his wife Elizabeth. This John Tierney was the father of John L.Tierney (pen name Brian James) quoted in this book (see pp. 136–138). (NSW Dept of School Education)

Telling Tales Out of School

Compiled by

Mary McPherson
History Information Officer
New South Wales Department of School Education Library

Kangaroo Press

This book is dedicated to the people
from whose lives these stories are drawn.

Teacher John Lewis and pupils at Moonahcullah Aboriginal School, c.1912 (see p. 138)
(Photograph courtesy of Sue Haw)

© New South Wales Department of School Education Library 1996

First published in 1996 by Kangaroo Press Pty Ltd
3 Whitehall Road Kenthurst NSW 2156 Australia
PO Box 6125 Dural Delivery Centre NSW 2158
Printed in Hong Kong through Colorcraft Ltd.

McPherson, Mary.
Telling tales out of school.
ISBN 0 86417 807 7

Bibliography.
Includes index.
1. Public schools - New South Wales - History.
2. Education, Primary - New South Wales - History.
3. Education, Secondary - New South Wales - History. I. Title.

379.944

Cover photograph: Kerry and Co. *Off to School* 1893–1910; gelatin silver
photograph, 15.9 x 20 cm. *(The Art Gallery of New South Wales)*

Contents

Preface

I have selected these documented historical tales of life in New South Wales government schools (c.1850s-1950s) for their human interest and/or for their illustration of some interesting aspect of school life. Wherever possible I have presented the material in the participants' own words and arranged it chronologically within the chapters.

The material is mostly from the archival records of what is, in 1996, the New South Wales Department of School Education. Being mostly from this source, it deals mainly with situations where school life was not proceeding smoothly as only such situations produced detailed reporting on what the day-to-day lives of those associated with schools were like.

Mary McPherson
History Information Officer
New South Wales Department of School Education Library
January 1996

Author's note: Every effort has been made to trace the owners of the original copies of documents and photographs used in this book in order to seek permission for their use. Apologies are offered to any such owner unable to be traced.

1

Reasons for Wanting a School

Poor but respectable parents of 80 or 90 children deserving assistance

On 20 September 1867 James Breckenridge, the manager of the saw mill at Tucki Tucki (later Wyrallah) near Lismore, requested the establishment of a Public School there, asking the authorities

to take our case into immediate consideration as one in every respect deserving assistance. I may state that within a radius of two miles there are between 80 and 90 children destitute of the means of education, the parents of whom are poor but respectable.[1]

Danger to children of abandoned shafts on the way to Pipeclay Creek

In recommending the establishment of a school at Eurunderee near Mudgee on 2 August 1876, Inspector O'Byrne wrote of the two nearest schools to which the children could go at that time:

The Wilbertree Public School is about 4° miles from where the school is proposed to be established at Eurundery [note different spelling]. The road from Eurundery to Wilbertree is good, whilst that to Pipeclay [Creek] Pub. [about three miles away by public road] is a bush track, and leads through abandoned Shafts. It is not safe for children to travel.[2]

Wheat-growing at Pipeclay Creek (later Buckaroo) Public School (From Report of the Minister of Public Instruction, *1909, p. 92)*

Newrybar Public School (see p. 9) 1910 (NSW Dept of School Education)

Bungawalbyn Public School (see p. 9) photograph undated, 1892 building (NSW Dept of School Education)

Not safe for Newrybar children to walk through scrub

William Hayter, a promoter of the school at Newrybar near Ballina, wrote to the Minister in May 1889 that the proposed school, if established, would not deprive other schools of their pupils as none of the children could attend other schools because 'it is not safe to send children through dense scrub three miles on tracks that the residents have made themselves.'[3]

Children two at a time at Bungawalbyn

Requesting enlargement of the proposed new building for Bungawalbyn Public School near Woodburn in 1892, a resident, J. Olive, wrote to the Minister: 'If the Minister only knew the rate at which the population was increasing he would not hesitate ... to grant our request. There are several women here who have children two at a time.' [4]

Fear of tramps at Buxton

In a letter accompanying the application for a school at Buxton near Picton in December 1893, J. R. Holmes, secretary of the Buxton Progress Association, wrote of the proposed school:

We want it badly enough as none of the girls are going to school yet owing to the nearest school being so far away & there being so many tramps on the road that it is really unsafe to send the girls. Three of the boys go to Balmoral but it is too far, they have over ten miles a day to walk.[5]

Winter journey to Luddenham too cold for Badgerys Creek children who are poor

On 7 May 1894 local member of parliament, Samuel Lees, in a letter to the Department urging the establishment of a school at Badgerys Creek, wrote:

I shall be very thankful if this school is established as Luddenham is a cold climate in winter and many of the children are poor, and the long journey they have to make [is] very trying to their health and comfort.[6]

The need to prevent Mulwee children becoming dunces

On 5 November 1898, forwarding an application for the re-establishment of a school at Swan Bay, Port Stephens, parent Samuel Lilley urged the Department to provide the school at once to 'Put our children past the possability [sic] of becoming dunces'. The school was re-established with the name 'Mulwee' because the Department already had a school called Swan Bay on the Richmond River.[7]

Fear of children being washed overboard on the way to Point Danger School

In February 1901 the residents of Cave Point (later Fingal Head) unsuccessfully petitioned for the re-opening of the school there. At that time their children were attending Point Danger (later Tweed Heads) Public School. The petitioners wrote:

We have 34 children over 6 years and under 14 years and the only way we have at present of having them educated is to send them to the Tweed Heads school by the mail launch.

The Captain of the launch has already twice refused to take them, owing to the danger of some of them being washed overboard when passing the bar, where there is always a heavy swell on, even during the finest weather.

Owing to the danger we cannot send the young children and their education is neglected.[8]

Children going wild near Gravesend

A promoter of the school which was named Macarthur near Gravesend, Phillip Wells, wrote to the Department in November 1905 with regard to the proposed school that

the residents is [sic] too poor to assist

trusting you will look the matter up has [sic] the children going wild.[9]

Fear of children getting lost in the bush at Tullamore

The re-opening of a school at Tullamore had been approved but was taking too long for the satisfaction of the residents when, in September 1911, Mabel Innes, a new resident who was also a parent, wrote to the Department that

it grieves me to see the children missing their schooling and wandering about and fearing they will get lost in the bush if they go far. The children I have seen so far here are bright and promising looking and it seems a great pity to see them learning nothing.[10]

Children running about like heathens at Willala

In order to hasten the already approved re-opening of Willala Provisional School near Boggabri, William Jones wrote to the Department on 7 December 1914:

I would be glad if you would let me know when it will be started as the people here are continually hectoring me about it as those children that can are going six or seven miles to school & those that can't are running about the bush like a lot of heathens and its about time something was done in the matter we live in an age now when Education is a person's mainstay.[11]

Bike ride to Williamtown Public School plays on the nerves of Medowie children

Daniel James of Medowie wrote to local member of parliament, Charles Bennett, on 1 October 1936 requesting the re-opening of the school at Medowie. He wrote:

There are 15 children from Medowie attending Williamtown School and most of them on bikes and some of [them have] over 6 miles to travel. The matter of fact [is], it is cruel to ask children to travel on bikes [in] cold and showery weather, and now the summer is coming the children will be overheated and perspire and have to sit in damp cloths [sic] and then ride home on a bike over the rough New mettaled [sic] road that would play on the nerves of even a grown up person.[12]

2

Location Difficulties

Inspector needs a blacktracker to locate Putty House to House School

The locality containing Putty House to House School (between Singleton and Windsor) was described by Inspector John Murray on 20 October 1885 as being 'very difficult to reach from the South and no stranger could go to it without a guide. A constable who went there [to Putty] three times told me he always had a black tracker with him: that alone he could never have found it.'[1]

Neither of two inspectors wants Warge Rock House to House School in his inspectorate

Warge Rock House to House School near Tullamore was the subject of argument between two inspectors, neither of whom wanted it in his inspectorate. Inspector W. George Thomas of Forbes, who had visited the area and reported before the establishment of the school, believed that the school should be under Inspector John Smith of Dubbo. Inspector Smith, however, did not want Warge Rock in his inspectorate and in his defence against its placement under his supervision he wrote in February 1890:

This place is situated near Dandaloo and would be most inconvenient for me to reach in as much as there is no coach from Dandaloo to Warge Rock and very little possibility of my being able to hire a trap to take me to Warge Rock from Dandaloo. I have hitherto taken the coach from Trangie to Dandaloo and returned in the same vehicle.

A new large Public School at Peak Hill has recently been opened and placed under my supervision, and I hope I may be excused from visiting Warge Rock.[2]

Inspector Thomas did not want Warge Rock School foisted upon him just because it was inconvenient for Inspector Smith to get to. Thomas suggested that

starting from Dubbo, Mr Smith could form a chain of inspections by visiting in order Tomingley, Peak Hill, Genanaguy, Warge Rock and Dandaloo. As a matter of fact Warge Rock can be reached from Narromine on the Western Railway, and settlers in the district think nothing of driving either to that Station or even to Mr Smith's headquarters—Dubbo—in a day.[3]

But Inspector Smith definitely did not want to have to supervise Warge Rock School. In March 1890, obviously exasperated, he wrote:

I have just returned from my visit to Dandaloo, and made inquiries respecting this place [Warge Rock]. I could not hire a conveyance to take me to Warge Rock, and Mr Richardson, the oldest living resident informed me that neither he nor anyone else could direct me there, and it would be quite impossible for any stranger to find out the place and the country at present is under water, and my horse would not take me to Trangie or Dandaloo. Warge Rock cannot be reached from <u>Narromine</u> as Mr Thomas alleges, <u>without changing horses</u>, and under no circumstances without a guide—and there is not a person in Narromine that has heard of such a name [as Warge Rock] ... I have but the one horse and it would not take me to Trangie in a month and I could not find my way to Warge Rock, and there is no one to direct the way.[4]

The district inspector made the final decision that Inspector Thomas rather than Inspector Smith would supervise Warge Rock.

Frank Cahill at Wedallion Half-Time School unable to find 'Thuddur'

Having received his notice of appointment to Wedallion and Bribbaree Half-Time Schools near Young on 6 May 1899, Frank Cahill, aged 23, entered on duty as teacher on 15 May.[5] Inspector Friend considered that Cahill could have taken up his duties a day or two earlier than he did. Cahill was called upon to explain and on 1 June he wrote of his actions after receiving his appointment:

Having my own horse and sulky and being unable to dispose of them, and a horse being necessary in the working of Half Time schools, I drove from my former school Sandy Creek [10 miles from Molong] to Wedallion. Monday the 8th May I spent making out the books and returns of the school, and going to Molong to post my returns and forward some of my luggage to Young. I left for my present schools on Tuesday morning and arrived at Thuddungra on Thursday night. Friday I spent visiting the parents of the children attending Bribaree [note different spelling] & Wedallion. [6]

Inspector Friend was not satisfied with this account and Cahill was required to be more detailed in his explanation. On 14 June he wrote that among other causes of his delay was the fact that 'notice of my removal informed me to proceed to Wedallion & Bribaree Half Times Via Thuddur, Young. Could not find the whereabouts of Thuddur. So came to Young and inquired at Post Office and was informed that the Post Town of my present schools was Thuddungra.'[7] Inspector Friend made the successful recommendation that Cahill 'be informed that his explanation concerning his delay in entering upon duty at Bribaree & Wedallion is not considered fully satisfactory & that he will require to be more prompt in future, otherwise he will be severely dealt with'.[8]

Inspector Smith in search of Macarthur Provisional School locality

In July 1905 Inspector Stephen Smith abandoned his proposed visit to where Macarthur Provisional School was to be established near Gravesend. On 15 August he reported:

I wrote to the people concerned in the question [of establishing the school] asking them to meet me at Mosquito Creek on 27th July, to guide me to the locality,—which is said to be a difficult spot for a stranger to find. Though I had written separately to Messrs Wells & Andrews, neither of them met me at the appointed time & place. [9]

As it would have been many weeks before he could get back there, Inspector Smith asked the teacher at Gravesend Provisional School to do what he himself had intended to do towards deciding the best site for the school.

Conscientious young teacher gets lost and spends a night in the bush

In April 1930 James Whittaker, aged 22, who had been appointed to Ross Hill Public School at Inverell at the beginning of that year, was absent from school for the morning of the 23 April and sought leave for this time. Inspector Keller wrote: '[Whittaker] left Armidale at 11.30 a.m. on Tuesday, was mis-directed and, as is quite a likely happening for anyone, missed his way and spent the night in the bush. He is a conscientious young teacher and should not, in this instance, be penalised. I recommend that leave of absence be granted without penalty.'[10] Nevertheless Whittaker lost a half-day's pay for his absence. (After two years at Ross Hill, Whittaker taught at various other schools before enlisting in the AIF in 1941. The last two entries on his teacher card are 'Missing Cas List 13.8.42' and 'Presumed to be dead 9.5.46'.[11])

* * *

3

Teachers' Travel

Ellen Johnson's journey to Eringonia Public School

Ellen Johnson was appointed to Eringonia (later Enngonia) Public School, 70 miles north of Bourke in May 1884.[1] She then travelled there from her previous school at Goodooga with her husband and four children in a 168 mile journey which took three weeks. She wrote:

We started the journey with six horses, and finished it with four [through injury] ... My husband drove myself and family, but he had to pay a man £1 per week and rations, to drive another vehicle, which cost him £30, as one was not strong enough to carry us and our luggage, bedding, rations etc. which was necessary for camping out on our long journey ... We started from Goodooga to New Gnomery, Mina West, Old Gnomery, Tatala, Toulby Springs, Toulby Saw Mills, The Boundary, Moutton Plains, Garah Springs, from thence to Eringonia.[2]

Assistant Inspector Fletcher initially supported Johnson's claim for £15 10s. travelling expenses but the amount was reduced to £8 14s. when Fletcher was

Eringonia (later Enngonia) Public School, teacher Ellen Johnson, 1892 (Original photograph lent to Dept of School Education)

informed that 'The Department does not undertake to defray the cost of removing teachers' furniture &c.'[3]

During her time at Eringonia School Ellen Johnson was highly thought of as a teacher. In her nine years at the school she had frequent short periods of accouchement leave, and had cause to complain of the high cost of provisions at Eringonia. She resigned in May 1893 to go into business in the town with her husband in his butchery (he had previously been a carrier). In 1898 she tried, probably unsuccessfully, to have her two eldest daughters become teachers. From 1905 to 1911, after the government school at Enngonia was closed (although it later re-opened), Ellen Johnson herself taught at a Subsidised School there.[4]

Jane Hackett at Aliceton and Swan Bay Half-Time Schools, Port Stephens

In May 1889 Jane Hackett opened the Half-Time Schools at Aliceton (later Karuah) and Swan Bay (later Mulwee) near Port Stephens which were four miles apart by water and six miles apart by land. Notifying her entry on duty she wrote that she intended to teach at the schools in alternate weeks 'as the evenings are at present too short to ride from one place to another after the school is dismissed, and I cannot make it convenient to go by water which is the quicker way'.[5]

William Thompson's wet walk to Narara Public School

William Thompson, the teacher at Narara Public School near Gosford in 1890, complained to the Department that there was no private place at the school for him to change his clothes when he arrived at school wet after walking from his lodgings. In March 1891 he applied without success 'to be provided with a waterproof coat and leggings to enable me to go to and from my duties'.[6]

A young man who can ride would suit Megalong

Reporting on an application for a school at Megalong made at the end of 1891, Inspector Kevin wrote:

There are two entrances to the place
1. a dray track from Katoomba round by Mt Victoria, Little Hartley, and Kanimbla, a distance of over 30 miles, and
2. a bridle track through Nellie's Glen—3 miles of which is the vilest on the face of the earth. The distance by this route is only 7 miles.[7]

It was decided to open Megalong School as a House to House School with Cullenbenbong and when, in 1892, it was time to appoint a teacher Inspector Kevin noted that: 'A young man who can ride would suit and he should call at the Public School at Katoomba for directions etc.'[8] In April Kevin wrote that he was unable to nominate a teacher but that the teacher, preferably a male, could travel from Sydney by rail to Katoomba for 14s. 9d., then by horse through Nellie's Glen at a cost of 10s., and that he could board between the two teaching stations at any of the residents' houses.

David Chapman, aged 19 and single, was given his first teaching appointment as teacher of Cullenbenbong and Megalong House to House School on 13 May 1892.[9] A petition signed by parents in October 1892 requested the retention of Chapman at Megalong school when it became (as it was about to) a Public School. The petitioners wrote: 'Since he has been among us he has by his patience & kindliness endeared himself to the children and we all have pleasure in testifying to the progress they have made under him'.[10] The request was unsuccessful as the inspector wrote that 'Mr Chapman is unclassified and has been in the service only a few months'.

In July 1895 Chapman was transferred to Munni School near Dungog. He taught at many schools and retired from the service in September 1932.[11]

Teacher's ulcerated and swollen legs prevent him teaching his Half-Time Schools

Josiah Gettens was appointed to Tallawadja and Bagawa (later Nana Glen) Half-Time Schools near Coffs Harbour in July 1893.[12] In October he was temporarily unable to teach at the Half-Time Schools. He wrote: 'My legs are in an ulcerated and swollen condition thus preventing me from riding or from walking any distance. As I have to ride six miles to the Talawadja School and walk two miles to Bagawa School I am thereby prevented from attending to my duties.' [13]

Francis Griffin's need for a boat at Cabbage Tree Island

Eighteen-year-old Francis Griffin, who had been in temporary charge at Clunes Public School, was appointed as the first teacher of Cabbage Tree Island Aboriginal School near Ballina on 17 October 1893. He was to stay at the school until it closed in January 1895 (although it later re-opened). He remained a teacher at many different schools until his retirement in 1938. [14]

On 9 February 1894 Griffin wrote to Inspector Board requesting

that a boat may be provided for the teacher of the above [Cabbage Tree Island Aboriginal] school. I may state that the only inhabitants of the Island are the Aborigines, upon whom I am dependent for getting to and fro from Wardell each day. Two of these have a boat each but very frequently they have them away from the Island. At such times, I have to wait at the school for their return, and therefore do not get to Wardell until a very late hour in the evening. Should the Department comply with my request, I would undertake to see that the boat is properly cared for, and kept in reasonable repair. [15]

Griffin enclosed two tenders for building a cedar boat, from Stephen Otterbridge and William Hollingworth, both of Wardell. Inspector Board supported this request writing that

As the only habitations on Cabbage Tree Island are the huts of Aboriginals the Teacher is obliged to live at Wardell 2 miles distant. His dependence on the Aboriginals for transit interferes with his punctual arrival at the school and prevents him from returning to Wardell till late in the evening. A punt such as is described in the enclosed tenders can be cheaply obtained and will serve the purpose well. I recommend that the Teacher, Mr Griffin, be authorized to obtain a punt from Mr Otterbridge in accordance with his tender at a cost of £3 10s. [16]

The chief inspector did not agree and the application was declined after he wrote:

The attendance is very small and the experience of the Department in connection with these small aboriginal schools is that they last but a very short time, especially when a school or too many other civilizing agencies are forced upon the aboriginals. [17]

Contrary to the chief inspector's expectations, Cabbage Tree Island School survived to attain its centenary in 1993 and (as at 1996) is probably the only school which began as an Aboriginal School to do so.

West Wyalong teacher delayed by roads being 'a sea of mud'

Thomas Thompson, classified as a 2A teacher, took over as teacher in charge of West Wyalong Public School on 12 September 1894. [18] Thompson had been meant to take charge on 10 September. In explanation of the delay he wrote:

On Wednesday I made an early start towards Bathurst [from Sydney], intending to catch Friday evening's train thence to Temora. But the heavy rain & the dreadful state of the roads, wet and cut up by the teams made this impossible, and hence Saturday's coach was missed. None other, of course, left till Tuesday's, by which I came, but here again, the roads, which were nothing but a sea of mud, axle deep, converted the one-day's journey into two. We arrived on Wednesday afternoon, and I came straight from the coach-box to the school. [19]

Teacher of Half-Time Schools injured in a fall while riding between his schools

Charles Coombs was the teacher at Argyle East and Marian Vale Half-Time Schools near Marulan in November 1896 when he was granted sick leave for some days because of injuries to his back and side which had occurred when he fell from his horse on the way to Marian Vale Half-Time School. On 15 December Coombs applied to be appointed to a Public School. He wrote:

Owing to injuries received through falls from my horse while travelling from one school to the other,

The Horse and sulky used for transport to Cumbalum Public School by the teacher Joseph Mortimer, 1895–1907. The passenger is Mortimer's daughter Olive. The corner of the Cumbalum School building is at the right of the photograph. (Photograph courtesy of Norma Gray)

I am unable to perform the journey without great physical pain, and would therefore beg to be relieved, by appointment to a Public School. Out of 14 years active service, more than 10 years have been employed in Half Time Schools.[20]

Coombs, however, was still at his Half-Time Schools in June 1897 when he applied again for a Public School, noting that 'I am married and am now 37 years of age'.[21] Coombs's request for a Public School was not successful until January 1898, when he was appointed to Burraneer Bay Public School.[22]

Travelling difficulties for the teacher at Wandook Provisional School

In September 1902 Ellen M. Perrin, the recently appointed teacher at Wandook (later Mundiwa North) Provisional School near Deniliquin, wrote to Inspector Drummond successfully seeking forage allowance. She wrote from Deniliquin:

it is compulsory for me to go out every morning to the Wandook School & I have to go into town again every evening as I cannot obtain accommodation closer. The School is 6 miles from Deniliquin and the bush tracks are too rough to ride a bicycle. The first six weeks I rode on a bicycle. Now I have bought a sulky, horse & harness which have cost me more than I have earned since my appointment to the above named school. Of course the horse wants feed & I would like to obtain a small allowance from the Department as fodder is very expensive here now.[23]

In April 1905 Ellen Perrin, now Mrs Daish, wrote to Inspector Murray:

I have the honor to apply for leave of absence for today (11th April). The roads are in a very bad state after the late rains. I tried to get out to the School but got 'bogged'. I had to leave my horse & buggy on the Common & walk into town (through mud & water) to get assistance. Find enclosed certificates showing the state of the roads from Mr Garstang (P.M.) who met me & saw the state I was in & also one from Mr Lloyd Member of the School Board.[24]

Quite apart from her travelling difficulties, Inspector Murray was not pleased with Ellen Daish's work. He wrote in May 1905, that 'It is unfortunate Mrs Daish did not resign when she married as I feel sure she will never do satisfactory work'.[25]

Inspector considers horse's appetite excessive

On 7 May 1903 the teacher at Fernleigh Public School near Ballina, James Mankey, who was travelling 11 miles a day to and from the school because he could not get closer accommodation, applied for forage allowance. He wrote:

According to my estimate, my horse would require two bags of chaff, and two bushels of maize or oats in three weeks, for school work alone.

The price of chaff in the district is 6s/6d per bag, and of maize or oats 4s/6d per bushel.[26]

Mankey was given forage allowance of £10 per annum after Inspector Cornish wrote:

The cost of fodder to satisfy this horse appears to me, considering the beautiful grass in the Fernleigh District, excessive at the rates quoted, (7/4 per week) or £19 1s. 4d. per annum'.[27]

Fatal purchase of a horse by Tiri teacher

Twenty-year-old Thomas A. Jones was appointed to Tiri Provisional School on the Upper Manning River in April 1909.[28] On 21 June 1910 Jones applied for forage allowance as, 'Owing to the inconvenience caused by wet feet and the short winter mornings I have found it necessary to purchase a horse for school use'.[29] Inspector Kennedy wrote of this application on 25 June:

Mr Jones is compelled to reside about two miles from the school to which the track leads across grass paddocks, a part of the road is very rough.

Children from the same house walk to school daily.

There are no rivers or creeks to cross.

I recommend that this application be declined.[30]

A few months later, Inspector Kennedy wrote to the chief inspector on 2 September 1910:

I have to report the death, by accident, of Mr T A Jones, Teacher, Tiri Provisional School on Friday 26th August, 1910.

No definite particulars have yet come to hand but it appears that he was returning from school on the date mentioned, mounted on one horse and leading

Geographical excursion, Old Junee and Woodville Public Schools, 1918 (From the Education Gazette, *1 January 1918, p. 3)*

another. The horses passed on opposite sides of the same tree and Mr Jones was pulled off and his head violently struck the tree. Death was instantaneous.[31]

Travel and other hazards for young James Ready at Willala

James Ready, aged 20, was appointed to Willala Provisional School near Boggabri in August 1915. Willala was Ready's first teaching appointment after a six months' training course. On more than one occasion during Ready's time at Willala the inspector was to note that he was 'a young inexperienced teacher wanting in judgment'.[32]

In October 1915, not long after his arrival, Ready was stung near the eye by a 'poisonous fly' [33] which affected his eyesight for three weeks although he did not have any time off school. In November of that year his father, who had written to the Department about the eye injury, wrote again to say that his son had recovered from the eye injury but that 'now he writes to say that the hot weather has a most distressing effect on him, the most distressing symptom being sleeplessness'.[34] The Department's reaction (a typical one) to the news of these discomforts was to assume that Ready had had time off school, although he hadn't, and to instruct him to apply for leave without delay.

Ready re-opened the school a day late after the 1915-16 Christmas holidays as he thought that the first day, 31 January, was a holiday for Anniversary Day (later called Australia Day). Although he did not conduct school that day, Ready was at school and sent home the two children who came because they had sandy blight and were not meant to be at school anyway. The Department took a very dim view of this unsanctioned holiday and Ready was severely censured. Again when the school was closed on 12 days in 1916 because of impassable roads and heavy floods, the Department notified Ready that 'this frequent closing is unsatisfactory'.[35]

From the time the school opened, Ready lived 3½ miles from it and rode a bicycle over roads and tracks which were later described by the inspector as 'very rough'.[36] In February 1917 he applied for forage allowance and he was asked whether he could not find a place to stay closer to the school. Ready replied: 'There is no place nearer the school where suitable accommadation [sic] can be obtained as most of the residents have big families or have not the time'. [37] His application for forage allowance was then granted and, as requested by the chief inspector, his incorrect spelling, i.e., 'accommadation', was pointed out to him.

Some months later (in September) Ready fell off his bicycle about 6 p.m. when he was returning from school. The fall occurred when one of the pedals of the bicycle struck a stump 'thereby causing me to fall to the ground and as I was wearing pedal straps I was unable to extricate my foot in time to avoid the accident'.[38] He sprained his ankle and needed to have a day off school (two children attended, not knowing he would be away).

Ready was transferred to Llanthony Provisional School at the beginning of 1918. He was later the last teacher at Eton-Harrow Travelling School before it closed in May 1923. He remained a teacher until his retirement in 1960.[39]

George Laverick at Mulwee

George Laverick, who was appointed to Mulwee Public School at Port Stephens in 1914, was the first of many teachers at the school to complain about the marshy ground it was necessary to cross in order to get to the school. On 8 March 1915 he made a successful application for forage allowance to be paid to him from the beginning of the year because he wanted to buy a horse. He wrote:

It is almost impossible to traverse the roads in wet weather, especially winter. Last winter I managed it under great difficulties, sometimes borrowing a horse, of which perhaps one could be had one day in a fortnight.

The ground is swamp and marsh for almost the whole distance. It is necessary during wet weather to carry a pair of boots and socks. A pair of boots will last about six weeks in winter. Such travelling is most detrimental to my health, causing colds & influenza almost all the year around.

George Laverick, c.1916 (From Mulwee School Centenary 1889–1989, *p. 12)*

There is no escape from this difficult and unhealthy way, as it is surrounded by thick scrub. The distance is '2~' two and a quarter miles. Almost the whole distance is knee deep in mud & water after a heavy fall of rain. It is never dry or hard during the whole of the winter.[40]

Laverick, interested in military matters, asked in June 1915 either to be moved closer to his parents or to be given a promotion at Mulwee. He wrote:

It is impossible for me to board here and assist them [his parents] on my present salary. I have been asked by the citizens of Swan Bay and Karuah to conduct the training of a squad of recruits at Karuah. It is impossible for me to give them the answer that they are so eager to have.

By so instructing these recruits I would be doing the state a better service than by going to the front, for which opportunity I am waiting. I could remain and carry out this work if classified, but as I am now situated it is impossible.[41]

Inspector Finney recommended Laverick's transfer, noting:

He is a worthy young fellow and up to [the] time of his father's illness—who is old and unable to work—he housed his father and his mother at Mullwee [note different spelling]. Asking for favourable consideration for an early transfer.[42]

Laverick, however, was not transferred. In November 1915 he married Ann Davis and took two days off 'for a tour after my wedding',[43] even convincing the Department to grant him full pay for both days after it had ruled that he should only be paid for one of them.

Laverick was unable to pass his teacher's examinations for classification. He enlisted in the army in January 1916 and on 22 February 1917 his wife wrote to the chief inspector:

I heard you were calling in the Teacher's [sic] photo's [sic], as my husband 'Lieutenant', G. J. Laverick, [is] now 'fighting in France', who was teaching at 'Mulwee', Swan Bay, would you need his photo, am I intruding by sending his photo along.[44]

Chief Inspector Dawson, per a lower-ranking officer, replied:

I have to acknowledge with thanks the receipt of photo of your husband, formerly teacher of the Public School at Mulwee. Only photos of teachers killed or wounded at the War are reproduced in the Education Gazette. As so many of our teachers have gone to the War space would not permit of reproducing all photos in the Gazette.

I am returning your husband's photo.[45]

Meanwhile on 30 March 1917 Laverick, giving his address as 'Somewhere in France', wrote to the Department asking to be classified. He wrote that before enlisting he had been

on the verge of obtaining my classification, but after careful consideration I came to the conclusion that serving my country over here was far before my own interests in NSW ...

By obtaining my classification now, it will assist me a great deal in obtaining my next grade on returning to Australia. I am a married man with one child.[46]

The Department's classification committee decided to recommend Laverick for 3B classification as a concession. Laverick, however, was killed in action on 7th June 1917, a week and a day before his 25th birthday.[47]

Stanley Bignell and his motor bicycle at Tullamore

Twenty-five-year-old Stanley Bignell was appointed to Tullamore Public School in 1923.[48] In July 1924 Bignell applied for sick leave following an accident. The inspector noted that 'this is the second occasion that Mr Bignell has had a motor accident after a vacation. From reports that reach me he is rather notorious for his speed.' [49] When called upon to explain, Bignell wrote:

I spent the recent vacation in Parkes and district and left Parkes on Saturday July 5 at 5 p.m. for Tullamore. I was riding a motor bicycle and at Gobondeoy Siding about five miles from Tullamore met with an accident about 7 p.m. and was taken from there to Tullamore by Mr L. C. Onley in his car.

The accident was caused by my colliding with a large loose stone on the road which overturned the machine.[50]

Teacher's horse slips on a banana going to Gulargambone Aboriginal School

In March 1932 the teacher at Gulargambone Aboriginal School, Lilian Wilkins, reported:

On Wednesday 2nd March: while on my way to school: my horse: trod on a Banana lying on the. Bridge over the river & slithered & fell: Throwing myself & a little boy out of the sulky. I was thrown right over, flashboard of sulky & landed, on my hip: & back: ... I came to school but by 2 pm I was so ill, a friend drove me to the Dr ... I am going again today— after school—I cannot walk: with out: severe pain. have to, move very carefully: & sit : to [do] things one usually stands to do—... Can I receive Dr's expenses for this accident please?[51]

The Department, however, noted that Lilian Wilkins, a temporary teacher, was not entitled to compensation under the Act.

Gulargambone Aboriginal School, 1931 (NSW Dept of School Education)

Teachers travelling to examinations

Frederick Miller rows 10 miles to be examined

In order to sit for his teachers' examination at Lismore in the 1868 Christmas vacation, Frederick Miller, the teacher at Tucki Tucki (later Wyrallah) Public School rowed a boat 10 miles up the Richmond (later Wilsons) River to the examination centre at Lismore.[52]

Two nights in the scrub for Tumbulgum teacher

In the early 1890s Tumbulgum Public School teacher, George Yansen, encountered difficulties in attempting to ride to Lismore to attend the teachers' examination. He left Tumbulgum after school on Friday and did not reach Lismore until midday on Tuesday. In his account of events, after saying that he had spent Friday night at Byangum, he wrote:

On Saturday I tried to reach Lismore first by the Nightcap road and afterwards by the Nimbin road, but failed owing to the very bad state of the road, and as my horse refused to go any farther at about 6 p.m., I was forced to remain in the scrub that night. On Sunday I attempted to reach Lismore through Jiggi and Blakebrook, but within a distance of 22 miles I was again forced to remain in the forest the whole night. Owing to the remaining part of the road distance to Lismore being almost impassable and my horse worn out I did not reach within five miles of Lismore on Monday night. So that after the most strenuous efforts on my part to be in time for the examination I have been unable to accomplish it.[53]

Inspector McLelland reported that he had offered to let Yansen sit for the remaining papers, on the chance of being allowed a supplementary examination in those papers which he had missed 'but he felt so upset after two nights exposure without food that he decided not to attempt any paper'.[54]

John Fegan and some the school's pupils at Kyogle Public School c.1909 (See p. 22) (Photograph courtesy of Bruce Gulley and Kyogle Public School)

Over-exertion in trying to reach Wagga for examination

Eighteen-year-old pupil-teacher at Ganmain Public School in 1900, Edward Connelly, wrote that he had not attended his pupil-teacher examination because he had been 'unable to reach Wagga [about 35 miles away] in time for examination as I had undertaken the journey on a bicycle and had to give up through over-exertion'.[55]

Claiming removal expenses

John Fegan at Tregeagle does not undercharge the Department for expenses

John Gerald Fegan took over as the teacher at Tregeagle Public School near Lismore in 1901.[56] Fegan, an Irishman who had a colourful turn of phrase, had been employed as a teacher by the NSW Department of Public Instruction in 1884 at the age of 24.[57] For his removal expenses from Clairville Public School, near Glen Innes, to Tregeagle near Lismore he claimed a total of £11 7s. 6d. Fegan had travelled ahead of his wife and children and, when asked to produce receipts, he wrote:

I had to pay accommodation at Glen Innes on Thursday and Friday night. A married man cannot put on his hat and walk straight away. I had breakfast at the Railway Station on Friday morning. I also had meals at Tenterfield, Sandy Hills, Drake, Tabulum, Casino and Lismore enroute. I had to make arrangements at Lismore to get a bed, some cooking utensils, and food out [to Tregeagle] which detained me ...

The 5 shillings cartage on cases Lismore to Tregeagle was paid by Mrs Fegan to some man who brought cases from one of the creameries to which they had been sent from Lismore. She does not know his name. I am endeavouring to ascertain. Goods sent out here come part of the way on the cream vans, then any passer by with a team brings them on. My horse is at Glen Innes and the roads are impassable to foot passengers so I am unable to get about to make inquiries ...

I had to pay for a week's accommodation at Glen Innes for my wife and family while I came forward to prepare a home. A family cannot walk into an empty house in the bush.[58]

When Fegan was exchanged with the teacher of Kyogle Public School in 1905, his explanation of why he needed a week off to make the change from Tregeagle to Kyogle Schools was as follows:

Monday 28th August was occupied by me in hunting up a team to take my furniture. The team was unable to come until Saturday 2nd September. It was the only one I could get. Teams cannot be obtained at a moment's notice in an isolated country locality. On Tuesday, Wednesday and Thursday I was down with influenza ...

I respectfully submit that 4 days is a very short time to allow a married man to move from one school to another. In a country place you cannot get anyone to do business for you. You must do it yourself.[59]

Christopher McCallum is careful to avoid undesirable people

Christopher McCallum was removed to Kurrara (later Banora Point) Public School in 1902. In justifying his removal expenses from Craigburn, near Glen Innes, to Kurrara he wrote: 'why I had first class at the large places was—because one doesn't know who sits at the shilling table.'[60]

4

Eton-Harrow Travelling School

Eton-Harrow Travelling School (the name was 'partly based on the name of a nearby railway siding—Eton—and possibly the name of a nearby property'[1]) was the first of three travelling schools conducted by the Department.[2] It was established in 1908,[3] with Albert Biddle, aged 22, as teacher.[4]

On the subject of the rural families for whom this school was established, whose isolation was such that their needs could not be met either by subsidised schools or by conveyance of children to a central school, the 1908 *Report of the Minister of Public Instruction* (see p.11) noted:

In the Narrabri district, between the Gwydir and Macintyre rivers, are several such families, and early in 1908 it was decided to provide them with some means of instruction by appointing an itinerant teacher to travel from homestead to homestead, and convey necessary school equipment with him.

Eton-Harrow Travelling School, 1909; from 'The Travelling School' in the Public Instruction Gazette, *30 June 1909, pp. 183–5*

Types of pupils of Eton-Harrow Travelling School, 1909; from 'The Travelling School' in the Public Instruction Gazette, *30 June 1909, pp. 183–5*

The children concerned are those of station employees or of men who make a small living at fencing, rabbiting, etc. This proposal involved the provision of a vehicle and suitable equipment. In designing the vehicle, one important requirement was that it should be of the first quality both in material and construction. Specifications were prepared and tenders obtained for a covered van 7 ft. by 3 ft. 6 in., with waterproof canopy 5 ft. high. Provision was made for a bunk (so that the teacher might camp in the van), locker, shelves, &c., and while built to carry a load of 6 cwt., care was taken

that the van was not too heavy for one horse. The cost of the complete outfit including the van, horse, and camp requisites, came to about £80, this amount including a tent 12 ft. by 14 ft. to be carried in the vehicle, and used as a schoolroom when other accommodation was not available.

In appointing a teacher, it was realised that some special qualifications were needed. It was desirable that he should be a single man thoroughly reliable and tactful, well acquainted with the bush, and accustomed to the management of a horse.

The *Public Instruction Gazette* of 30 June 1909 (p. 184–5), quoting from the *Sydney Mail*, 13 January 1909, reported of Eton-Harrow Travelling School teacher Albert Biddle:

The teacher chosen to launch this new experiment on the ocean of the far-stretching plains of the West has been specially selected. He is a classified teacher of the Department, and has been trained as a pupil-teacher. He does not stop at the three 'Rs'. He is the holder of a St. John's Ambulance certificate and departmental certificates in drawing and brushwork; is a good amateur photographer, is skilled in the use of the magic lantern, and in the manufacturing of slides for it, and is also an enthusiast in cricket, tennis, and other sports. Above all, he has had experience in the bush and in the management of horses. He fully understands that he is entering upon a work widely different from the ordinary routine of a school, and the exercise of all his energies will be necessary. To convey the teacher from point to point of the circuit a serviceable horse and van, and the necessary harness, bedding, lamps, and camp requisites have been provided.

Biddle was to spend one week in four at each of the four teaching stations and in the three weeks before his (and the school's) return to that station the children were to work on set exercises and reading material. Biddle was teacher of the school from its opening in August 1908 until he was transferred from there in 1910.[5] He resigned in 1912,[6] and Eton-Harrow Travelling School remained in operation until 1923.[7]

5

Accommodating the Teacher

Myrtleville teacher's residence unfit for accommodation of teacher

When Inspector Thomas Harris visited Myrtleville National School near Goulburn in 1865 he noted that

the Teacher's residence is under the same roof as the schoolroom and consists of four small rooms in an unfinished state. The building is built of slabs, with a shingled roof ...

The teacher [Rosanne Murphy] does not reside on the premises. It is scarcely proper that she should in the present condition of the house, especially by herself.[1]

Henry Garnett at Codrington buys himself a tent

Henry Garnett, who was appointed as teacher of Codrington Public School near Woodburn in 1883, found that the residents, towards him as towards his predecessor, 'acted in a very unfriendly manner'.[2] As a consequence he

purchased a tent so as to live at the school. And as I could not cook my food in the open air when it was raining, there being no fireplace in the school house, I purchased 3 sheets of galvanized iron to make a little kitchen galley to cook in.[3]

Robert Dennis builds himself a bark hut at Herons Creek

In November 1894 the teacher at Herons Creek Public School near Kendall, Robert Dennis, applied unsuccessfully to be transferred from the school. In support of his application he wrote:

Herons Creek Public School, c.1895; Robert Dennis Snr holding horse, teacher Robert Dennis and wife Lizzie Dennis in carriage. Dennis's bark hut residence is in the background. (From Herons Creek Public School Centenary 1893–1993)

for two years past I have been compelled to reside in a bark hut erected at my own expense, owing to the utter impossibility of obtaining accommodation within 6 miles, and as I intend to marry shortly, I wish to arrange for a suitable home and hence this application.[4]

Emily Cunnynghame finds Wedallion a very lonely place

Twenty-one-year-old Emily Cunnynghame was the first teacher at Wedallion House to House School near Young when it opened in January 1894.[5] One of the conditions of the establishment of this House to House School with only one teaching station was that the residents would board the teacher free of charge until the classification of the school was raised.[6] On 26 October 1894 a local resident, James Dwyer, wrote to the local member of parliament, Thomas Slattery, that he had been boarding the teacher free for six months. Dwyer successfully requested that the school be raised to a Provisional School.[7] On 21 February 1895 Emily Cunnynghame wrote from Wedallion School to Inspector Friend:

I beg to inform you that I believe there is to be a new school opened near Marengo [later Murringo], [I] also beg to be considered an applicant for the position of teacher of that school. My reasons for applying for the position are; 1st, Marengo is more convenient to my home and this is a very lonely place; 2nd, I have not comfortable lodgings here.

I desire to state that at the <u>two</u> inspections held at Wedallion School during the thirteen months that I have been in charge of the school, I have obtained very high marks.[8]

Inspector Friend supported this request, writing on the same day that 'the results are exceptionally creditable ... Under present circumstances, this place (Wedallion) is unsuitable for a female teacher. It is 35 miles from the nearest town, & the lodgings are not suitable for a girl.'[9] Emily Cunnynghame was subsequently moved to Hillmont Provisional School.[10]

Sara Cole, the first teacher at Medowie Public School (Photograph courtesy of Sid Finn)

Teacher gains Department's permission to build herself a small residence in the school ground

On 18 April 1895 Sara Cole, the 38-year-old teacher at Medowie Public School, who had been at the school since it opened in November 1894 and who was to remain there until the beginning of 1912,[11] wrote to the district inspector:

The poverty of the people in this neighbourhood, and the small size of their habitations make it impossible to obtain suitable lodgings.

I therefore respectfully request the Minister's permission to erect a small residence for myself upon the land attached to the school—10 acres—and to remove such building when I relinquish the charge of the above school.[12]

While Inspector Waterhouse was not in favour of this proposal, preferring instead to have Sara Cole replaced at the school by a single male teacher, it was approved and the residence was built after Deputy Chief Inspector William McIntyre wrote on 30 April 1895:

Provided Miss Cole is made to distinctly understand that she will have no claim whatever on the Dept. in regard to the proposed building and that it is placed on a portion of the school site to be approved of by the Inspector, I see no objection to consenting to the proposal.[13]

When she left the school in 1912 Sara Cole removed her residence and also offered to buy the school building and outhouses but the Department wished to keep its own buildings although the school was closed at the time. This did not prove wise as they were destroyed by a bushfire in 1915.[14]

Anti-German feeling causes Buxton teacher to move her place of residence

Alice Adams, who was in her thirties, was the teacher at Buxton Public School near Picton during 1916 and 1917.[15] On 22 February 1916 the Minister received his first letter from Buxton's local Member of Parliament, George Fuller, concerning teacher Alice Adams's place of residence. Fuller wrote:

Strong dissatisfaction is expressed by some of my constituents at Buxton in consequence of the Teacher who has just been appointed there having gone to reside with people who are represented to me as being Germans. Will you have enquiries made at once, and have the matter fully considered.[16]

Inspector Thomas reported on this matter on 6 March 1916:

I visited Buxton on Friday, and interviewed the teacher and several of the residents. The facts are as follows:

Miss Adams, the teacher, boards with Mr and Mrs Wendt, 1½ miles from the school. Mr Wendt, who is a German by birth, is an Ex Sea-Captain of a sailing ship—the *Margarita*—his wife is an Australian and sailed with him until about two years ago, when he gave up the sea, and bought a poultry farm at Buxton. Locally, he bears the title of 'Captain' and is well spoken of by the principal

Failford Public School, 1912
(NSW Dept of School Education)

residents. In the recent visitation of bush fires, when a local 'fire-fighting' brigade was organised, he was always one of the first at the fires, and one of the last to leave, and his services were invaluable. He and his wife have supported local functions of 'farewelling' soldiers, and they contribute to the Picton Red Cross Assocn. Miss Adams has never heard him utter a disloyal sentiment, or indulge in adverse criticism of our side in the war.

Miss Adams is particularly well satisfied with her quarters, and would be most unwilling to leave. She is driven to and from School on wet days, or when she is not well. She does not think she could get suitable accommodation elsewhere in Buxton. From enquiries I made, I could hear of only two other places, neither of them desirable. One is close to the Railway Station, and is where the single men, employed on the Railway, board. It is not a suitable place for a single girl. The other is a private boarding house, bearing a somewhat shady reputation, and, by no means, the place for a decent girl.

The previous teacher boarded with a Mrs Watsford under special circumstances. She provided her own tea and breakfast, and slept alone in a detached bungalow. Mrs Watsford informed her that she would not take another teacher, and, for that reason, Miss Stack [the previous teacher] made enquiries, and submitted Mrs Wendt's name on [the] Quarterly Return, as one who would accommodate a teacher. On Miss Adams' appoint-ment to the school, the Department furnished her with the information.

There is nothing in Mr Fuller's letter to show from whom the expressions of dissatisfaction have come, but from what I can gather, they emanate from a Mrs Kennedy, a political organizer with a house (of sorts) at Buxton, and an office in Sydney. She professes to interest herself in Factory girls, and aims at establishing a Home for them at Buxton. She was heard to express her opinion that all Germans should be interned, and her intention of approaching the Minister upon the enormity of Miss Adams' offence.

I do not think that the Department has any right to interfere with a teacher's choice of abode, as long as the moral surroundings of the place are above reproach, that the people are law-abiding residents, and that it is within reasonable distance of her school. If Mrs Wendt is to be debarred from taking the teacher as a boarder, because her husband is a German, the question naturally arises as to where the line is to be drawn between what she may do, or may not do towards earning a living. I recommend that Mr G.W. Fuller M.L.A. be informed that enquiry has been made into the matter with the result that the Department sees no reasonable objection to the arrangements that the teacher has made for her accommodation.[17]

On 1 May 1916 Samuel Emmett of Elphin, Picton Lakes, wrote to the Department:

On Saturday the 29th ult. I was invited to attend a public meeting at Buxton Re the teacher residing with a German. At which meeting I was elected Chairman. Some parents were absent. The most of those attending the meeting have no children attending school. One thing was very apparent viz. that the meeting was purely pro German ... This man's Germanic diplomacy has apparently captivated some of the Buxton Residents who in my opinion are under pecunary [sic] obligations to him. hense [sic] their pro German proclivities I would like to suggest that you send an Inspector to Buxton School and thus hear first hand from parents whoes [sic] children are on the roll why they object. In my opinion the [sic] lacking in patriotism who will submit to share the home of an unnaturalised German.[18]

Having received this letter the Department took no further action on Alice Adams's boarding place at this time but pressure to do so continued. Mrs Kennedy said at a deputation to the Minister on 12 July concerning the Buxton School of Arts Committee, which had become most aggressively divided over the question of Wendt, that 'The Teacher now introduces Captain Wendt's travel to the children. I do not want to know where he has travelled and I do not want my children to learn.'[19] Also at this deputation one Buxton resident, Mr O'Brien, said:

Meetings can be called on one side and when we get there we find the room full of women and children and men under the influence of liquor. On one occasion a challenge was issued almost as soon as we entered the room.[20]

At the same deputation another Buxton resident, Mr J. O'Donohue, said:

Each faction holds meetings in the school on succeeding Saturday nights. I and others went to one of the meetings of the Secretary's side of the house and we barely escaped with our lives. The proceedings threatened to end in a riot.[21]

In December 1916 Mrs Kennedy, giving her address in a street at Mascot, complained to George Fuller, who on this occasion wrote to Peter Board, the director of education, that 'the school teacher at Buxton is boarding and lodging with a German who, on more than one occasion, has exhibited disloyal tendencies'.[22] The Department replied that the matter had been investigated earlier in 1916 and that 'The Police and Military Authorities have dealt with the case. The Military Authorities state that so long as Wendt continues to report and behaves well, no action need be taken.'[23] In January 1917 Board noted on a departmental report that 'In view of all the circumstances, I am reluctant to advise any further action in the matter'.[24] With regard to Alice Adams, he wrote to George Fuller MLA, Chief Secretary, on 31 January 1917:

I am directed by the Minister for Education to inform you that in March last year it was decided by this Department after full and careful investigation that there could be no reasonable objection to the arrangements made by the teacher for her accommodation. She is a single woman, and the Inspector's report shows that no other accommodation in the locality would be equally suitable for her.[25]

Mrs Kennedy had written to George Fuller again when the latter wrote to the Minister on 7 May:

I again have been requested by Mrs Kennedy and others, who, in the circumstances, will not send their children to Buxton School, but are sending them to Picton, to ask if you will kindly alter the state of affairs, and see that the teacher takes up residence somewhere else. I know that there is a difficulty about this matter because a report went in to you that there is no other suitable accommodation available. But it has now been suggested that arrangements might be made with a Mr.

Fludder. I do not know whether this is correct, but if it is, knowing Mr. Fludder personally, I certainly should say that his home would be quite a suitable place for the teacher to reside.[26]

Alice Adams was then apparently asked to report and on 16 May 1917, having tried (it would appear successfully) to have one of her sisters come and live with her so that they could take a small cottage near the school, she wrote concerning Mrs Kennedy's statement that her own and other children had been withdrawn from the school:

I have the honor to state that Mrs Kennedy has two children living in Buxton. They have been attending the Convent in Picton, I understand. These two children, Orrell and Lyla, attended Buxton Public School until, in Lyla's case, October 27th 1917 [sic], and in Orrell's case, November 9th 1917 [sic—both of these dates were 1916 rather than 1917].

These are the only two children who have left this school to attend a school in Picton. Their ages are now, Orrell fourteen years, and Lyla eleven years.

No reason was given to me for their removal from this school. I received no communication from the parents whatever.

On my arrival here, Mrs Kennedy told me that she considered it very wrong that I should be boarding with a German. I told her that I had been sent there by the Department, that Mrs Wendt's name was the only name on the Quarterly Return for December 1915. I do not remember saying anything further to Mrs Kennedy on the subject but I did say to others, when the subject came up, that, of course, if the parents objected, I would endeavour to make a change.

A public meeting was held to consider the matter at which Mrs Kennedy was not present, and at which, with one exception, every parent approved of my place of board.

The dissenting parent was Mr Emmett, who shortly afterwards moved to the Bargo and in regard to him, I would like to say that when Mrs Emmett first brought the children to school, I mentioned the matter to her and she expressed herself as indifferent concerning it.

From 21st ult., I have been endeavouring to find suitable accommodation and have been away from Captain Wendt's since May 5th. Mrs Kennedy has been cognisant of the fact from the day of my entry into the little cottage I took, May 5th.[27]

Alice Adams remained at Buxton Public School only until the end of that year, being moved to Camperdown Superior Public School at the beginning of the following year.[28] She continued teaching, mainly at the Correspondence School, until she retired in 1944. Later she returned as a casual teacher to the Correspondence School.[29]

Accommodation difficulties at Hannam Vale

Teacher Thomas Lynch rented a house at Hannam Vale near Kendall after arrival at Hannam Vale Public School at the end of 1916 or early 1917.[30] In May 1918 the landlord increased the rent sharply and Lynch wrote to the Department:

I find that his [the landlord's] brother-in-law is anxious to get the place if I can be got out, but, as the cottage was built purposely to accommodate a married teacher and has been occupied by such ever since, my landlord would incur the displeasure of parents by putting a teacher out to suit private ends, so he adopts the 'raise the rent' plan. There is no other house to be had and as proof of this I can state that there are at present two families occupying one house.[31]

On 13 December the new tenant began moving his belongings into the house before Lynch had finished moving his out. Lynch bundled the remainder of his belongings into a cart because there was no time to pack them and took them to the school. He and his family prevailed upon a resident to put them up for the holidays and then Lynch, who had been promised a transfer, was told to remain at Hannam Vale. He wrote to the Department that this was impossible as there was nowhere to stay and he didn't think the situation would be any better for a single teacher.[32] Lynch left Hannam Vale in January 1919 after which a temporary teacher ran the school until April of that year when 44-year-old Thomas F. Jones was appointed.[33]

The initial reception received by Jones when he arrived was not promising either. On 30 April he wrote to the inspector:

I arrived at Hannam Vale on 29th April and was compelled to spend the greater part of the day in looking for accommodation. The local storekeeper took compassion on me and gave me breakfast. Nobody was anxious or willing to give me lodgings and made all kind of excuses. Residents with no children said they could not be expected to board the teacher, whilst those with children gave that as excuse for not boarding me. On Wednesday morning (this morning) I came to Chatham intending to see you about the matter but, as I have been suffering from a very bad cold or influenza I went to bed. I am not in a fit state to resume duties for several days and am applying for sick leave for a week.

With regard to lodgings, I let it be known that, if there were no lodgings available, there would be no teacher available. I am quite prepared to go back next week when well enough, possibly some of the residents were of the opinion that I was dangerous [this was the time of the influenza epidemic] on account of having come through Sydney.[34]

The next day, 1 May, Jones wrote again, more promisingly:

Since writing the above I have heard that some of the residents are willing to give me accommodation, taking it in turns. I intend getting back as early as possible next week and no doubt accommodation now will be forthcoming.[35]

By 9 May however, when he was well enough to open the school, he again wrote:

I am having difficulties in procuring lodgings at Hannam Vale. Parents are very anxious to have a teacher, especially a married man, but are very loth to give accommodation to any teacher. Most of the residents are dairying and lodging a teacher comes awkward to them for many reasons. Just at present there is no house available, though there may be one shortly in rather an awkward place on account of flooded creeks in wet weather. From experience here, I may say that the accommodation offering is not what could be called suitable, but I am quite prepared to 'put up' with this and await developments which I hope will be more suitable.[36]

On 14 May, Jones was staying temporarily at Mr W. Redman's and asked, as suggested by the parents, that he be allowed to close off one end of the school verandah to use as a bedroom. He wrote: 'I can secure suitable meals at the local store, but getting a room is the difficulty. By closing in one end of the verandah I would be comfortable and near the School as well as [the] Store'.[37] The inspector replied on 19 May, instructing Jones not to proceed yet with his plan to use the verandah as a bedroom. He wrote: 'Mr E. Buttsworth of Jones Ltd called at my office on Saturday to say that a cottage would in all probability be available for your use at Hannam Vale in about two weeks' time'.[38] The next day Jones replied that this house was unsuitable, mainly because he would not be able to get to school in wet weather, but also because of a difficult neighbour who permitted nobody to cross his paddocks.[39] The inspector then asked E. A. Buttsworth whether the teacher could get to school from the house. Buttsworth replied that his son, Ernest A. Buttsworth, owned the house and that the teacher could get to school from it.[40]

Thomas F. Jones stayed at Hannam Vale School until June 1925 and remained a teacher until his retirement in 1935.[41]

Department supplies tent residence at Newnes

Douglas Macrae, who had a wife and family, was appointed in October 1918 to the school at Newnes,[42] a kerosene shale mining centre near Lithgow. In an article titled 'Newnes Public School: The Teacher's Tent Home', which had an accompanying photograph, he wrote in the *Education Gazette* of 1 October 1919 (p. 241):

When I was appointed to the charge of this school nine months ago, there was not a home to let, nor could we board, so as a last resort we asked the Department for a tent. This they supplied, and built us a kitchen. The picture illustrates these. Thanks to the Department, we have been made very comfortable, in fact, the home we now have is

Teacher's tent residence occupied by Douglas Macrae and his family, Newnes Public School (From the Education Gazette, *1 October 1919, p. 241)*

much preferable to living in a poky cottage such as are existent here.

Tallandoon residents unwilling to board teacher

Mary Dawson, who had been the teacher at Tallandoon Public School near West Wyalong in 1918, and who had arrived ready to go back there for 1919, wrote to Inspector Harvey on 31 January:

I arrived at West Wyalong on Saturday morning at 11.30 and at once rang up the lady with whom I boarded last year and was told by Mrs Pilon that she had no room for me and that the conveyance which had been at my disposal last year had been broken up during the holidays so I would have no way of reaching the school three miles distant. I also rang up Mrs Lemon the wife of the share-farmer who has four children attending school and she says she is not [in] good health and could not make me comfortable and she will soon be leaving for a farm seven miles from the school so that it does not matter to them. The only other family who have children attending school, James Cattle, I did not ask to board me as since last Easter they have been very disagreeable in all matters relating to school & for some time past have not been on speaking terms. As far as I know the cause of the trouble is over returning of the Defaulters [i.e., defaulters on attendance], as the attendance of this family was most unsatisfactory & I sent in the names every four weeks. On Tuesday I hired a sulky & drove out from West Wyalong, eleven miles but as I had nowhere to stay at night I had to return in the evening. When first I went there in the beginning of 1918 I had some trouble to get board but as a satisfactory decision was arrived at & [sic] I remained there till Easter Vacation. Then a report against me was sent in by the person with whom I boarded & after it had been investigated proved to be only the outcome of petty spite regarding a private matter. I then went to Mr Pilon's, three miles from the school & remained there till Dec 14th. I found the drive anything but convenient owing [to] the great heat & wet weather but I would be quite willing to remain there if some satisfactory arrangement could be made for me though ever since I have been there, I have felt I

am in the way. I have been instructed by the Chief Inspector to attend temporarily at West Wyalong and report fully to you.[43]

After her temporary attendance at West Wyalong Public School, Mary Dawson was moved to Calleen Siding a few months later[44] and the school at Tallandoon closed.[45]

Quandary teacher finds too much to fight against

On 9 November 1920 Elizabeth Mitchell, the teacher at Quandary Public School near Temora, who was considered by herself and by her doctor to be suffering from a nervous breakdown, wrote from the school to Inspector Dart:

I do not care for any more small schools and have come to the conclusion that men are best for them as there is too much to fight against. It is not the school part or the teaching but the after school conditions that get on my nerves. I could not endure the life any longer as I have had a hard time at Quandary.

The people I boarded with at first let me clearly see they did not want me and only let me stay for fear the school would be closed. When I could endure it no longer I asked a share farmer here to take me a while or I would stop at the school. These people are now willing to board a teacher but prefer a male teacher although they do not mind me. They think the place would suit a man better.[46]

Fifteen years later, in 1935, Elizabeth Mitchell, then at Miranda Public School, was in the inspectorate of George Cantello who wrote that 'She is, I understand, and has been, a very conscientious teacher'.[47] She retired in 1936 at the age of 58 [48] with crippling arthritis.[49]

Teacher only stays three hours at Five Mile Tree

Teacher Bartholomew Murphy arrived to take up his appointment at Five Mile Tree Provisional School near Crookwell in January 1928.[50] The man with whom the previous teacher had boarded wrote to the inspector on 25 January of that year that

a teacher came on Monday last the 23rd to take charge but only stayed at the school about 3 hours

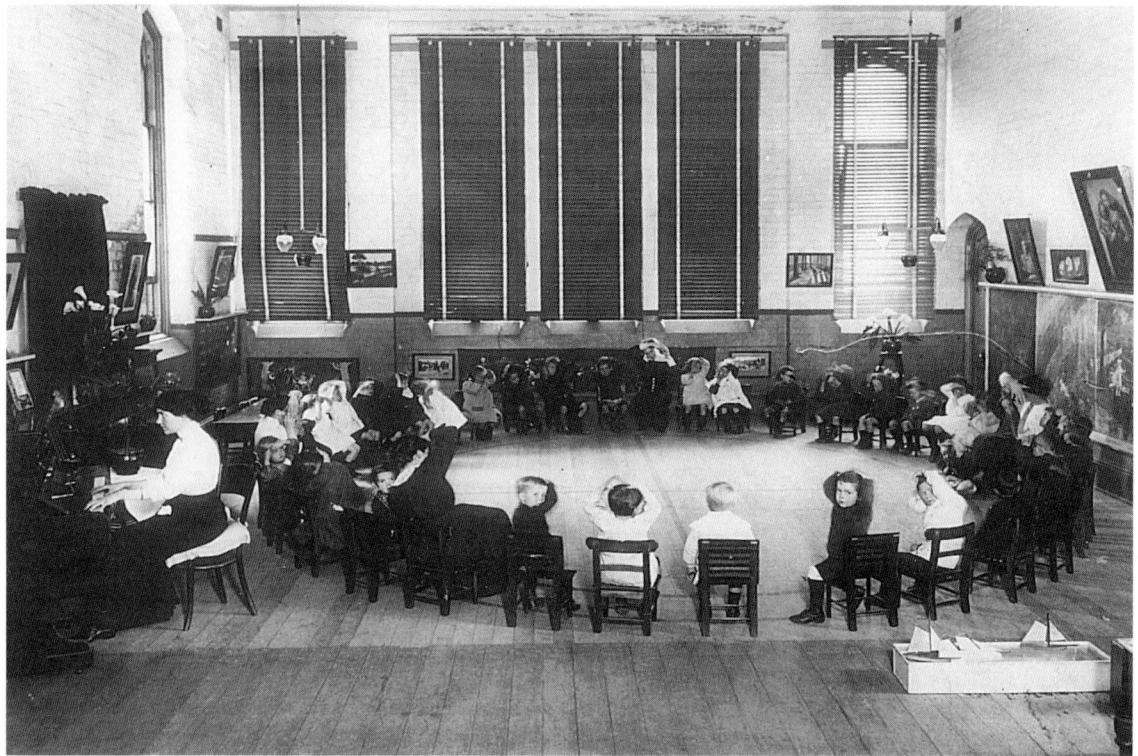

Action song; Blackfriars Superior Public School, 1913 (NSW Dept of School Education)

and went away again. He only interviewed one person viz. Mrs Writer [who lived near the school and who gave him his dinner] and as far as I can learn no one else knew that he had been here until the next day. So whatever his reasons for leaving were I wish it to be clearly understood that we were not approached for board and never saw the man. We would be pleased if a teacher is sent to take charge at an early date.[51]

Willala residents take the matter of a teacher's residence into their own hands

At Willala Provisional School near Boggabri in 1945 difficulty arose in accommodating a single teacher because the residents wanted a residence built and a married teacher appointed. The Department noted in 1945 that 'the parents are said to be comfortably off and it is surprising that none of them is in a position to board a single teacher'.[52] Again in 1947 the inspector noted: 'Though these people are particularly obstinate about providing accommodation for a single teacher, I can see no reason why they should not'.[53]

So determined were the residents to have a teacher's residence at the school in order that a married teacher could be appointed that in 1954 they moved a residence onto the site without the Department's approval.[54]

6

Teachers' Living Conditions

Parents too poor to pay fees, and the high cost of provisions at Tucki Tucki

On 3 August 1868 the teacher at Tucki Tucki (later Wyrallah) Public School near Lismore, Frederick Miller, wrote to the Council of Education that his income was insufficient for him to live on. In the course of explaining why this was so, he wrote:

The people about here are in a state of almost starvation and are quite unable to pay even the low scale of fees, viz. threepence per week so that my income is not materially augmented in that way.

From the high price of provisions and of almost every article necessary for household purposes it is impossible for a teacher to live unless he has private means of his own. Such not being the case with me at present, I have thought it best to bring the matter under your notice.[1]

In January 1869, reporting on the grounds for exemption from fees, Miller wrote of the case of one free scholar: 'The parent though a Free Selector is so poor that it is a rarity to see tea sugar or flour in his hut'.[2] In 1872 on the subject of school fees Miller wrote to the Council of Education that 'there are a few who cannot pay, & who are too proud to allow their children to come free'.[3]

Residence close to a swamp at Bulahdelah

Applying to be moved from Bulahdelah (later Green Gully) Public School at Bulahdelah in 1870, teacher John Green wrote that he wanted to be

where easy access can be had to call in a medical gentleman if required ... In consequence of our nearness to a swamp ... and the floor of our house being quite on the ground [it had earthen floors] ... in damp weather, the atmosphere of the inside of the house has quite an earthy smell. Both Mrs Green and I have been complaining of pains and aches for the last six months.[4]

Henry Havelock Ellis at Sparkes Creek and Junction Creek Half-Time Schools

English-born Henry Havelock Ellis (1859-1939), who was later a psychologist and author,[5] taught at Sparkes Creek and Junction Creek Half-Time Schools in 1878.[6] He lived in the Sparkes Creek school building, 'eighteen miles in the bush' from Scone.[7] In his autobiography he wrote of this experience:

It [the school building] was built of rough-hewn slabs, letting in the air at places, and had a shingled roof, through the chinks of which at night I could see the stars pass across. The house consisted of two rooms ... The room on the right was the schoolroom; it contained the usual large open fireplace with a broad chimney; and it was supplied with a table and rough school forms and desks. The other room was for the teacher's use and contained nothing but a makeshift bed, formed by the framework of four poles supporting two sacks and resting on four legs which were so insecurely attached that occasionally the whole structure would collapse during the night ...

The first night, certainly, was wretched. I was desolate, not happy on my rickety couch, and in the large chimney I heard wild beasts of some kind noisily scampering up and down, while in the morning I found that a bandicoot or some

Sparkes Creek (From Henry Havelock Ellis, My Life, *Heinemann, London, 1940; opposite p. 120)*

such marsupial had evidently made a comfortable nest in my silk hat, leaving some of his hairs behind ...

On the days I went to my other school—two days of one week and three days of the next, for my time had to be divided equally between them—after I had my breakfast of porridge and perhaps placed a saucepan containing meat and rice over the smouldering wood-fire in the hope that it might be done (it was sometimes burnt) when I returned in the evening, and put in my pockets biscuits and a flask of tea for lunch, I started on my walk across the range of hills which separated me from Junction Creek. The aspects of Nature were my only source of interest, beyond my own thoughts, for there was no human dwelling within sight all the way, and I cannot recall ever having met a single person during my year's walks.[8]

An appreciation of the beauty of the locality of Sparkes Creek remained with Havelock Ellis as his autobiography contains a photograph of the creek with the caption 'an enlargement of this photograph always stood by Ellis's bedside during his last years'.[9]

Female teacher can't even get a bed to herself

Kate Anderson, a 19-year-old ex-pupil-teacher who had been at Albury, was appointed to Derry (later Ganmain) Provisional School near Coolamon on 18 February 1892.[10] She had said that she would be most happy to take it if it were situated on the railway line. In April 1892 she was having trouble finding a comfortable boarding place and on 20 April the inspector wrote that she had been to see him that day 'and informed me that she cannot get anything like decent accommodation at Derry: that she can't get even a bed to herself ... Miss Anderson does not wish to go back to Derry and, under all the circumstances, I do not think that she ought to be required to do so.'[11] Kate Anderson was transferred to the House to House School at Upper Yanko on 25 April,[12] and it was decided that her replacement should be a male teacher.[13]

Frederick Long has to sleep in a small room with two boys at Ivanhoe

Frederick Long, the teacher at Ivanhoe Public School in January 1892, made a successful application for a living allowance giving the following reasons:

1. I was paying 25/- a week and washing and candles extra.
2. On account of things being so dear in Ivanhoe.
3. On account of being so far away from home.

I now pay 15/- a week, washing and candles extra. I had to buy the bed cloth &c, and I have to sleep in a small room with two boys.[14]

Teacher living in hut 'as hot as a baker's oven'

In February 1894, in the course of trying to settle on a teacher for Stockinbingal Public School near Cootamundra which was about to open, Inspector Friend wrote of teacher Alexander Elliott (who, as it happened, was not appointed to Stockinbingal):

If it is intended to appoint a male teacher, I desire to press the claims of Mr Elliott of Cocomingla and Mt Collins HT [Half-Time] schools. He holds 3A,

has done good work, & has been living for some years in what is no better than a two roomed hut, as hot as a baker's oven in Summer time.[15]

Falling plaster in Kiama school residence

Kiama Superior Public School teacher, David Richardson, wrote in 1895 that

The residence at this school is so dilapidated as to be scarcely habitable: fresh falls of plaster are constantly taking place, so that it is quite unsafe to live in some of the rooms. It has the reputation of being the oldest house in Kiama.[16]

S. C. R at 'Borough Road'

In the *New South Wales Educational Gazette* 1 September 1898 (pp. 78–9), 'S.C.R.' wrote of his first appointment at a school he called 'Borough Road'. The Department has never had a school called Borough Road and by process of geographic

Accommodation at Box Tank Provisional School, 1926, galvanised iron and hessian lean-to onto the school. Cyril W. E. H. Job, aged almost 22, was appointed to Box Tank Provisional School near Menindee in January 1926 and was at the school until it closed in September 1927. (NSW Dept of School Education)

Ballandean Public School, c.1887 (NSW Dept of School Education)

elimination it seems certain that the school was Ballandean Public School (very close to the Queensland border between Tenterfield and Jennings), of which Samuel C. Rose was instructed to take temporary charge on 19 October 1888 and where he remained until the school closed in November 1889. 'S.C.R.' wrote of his first teaching appointment for an audience of departmental readers in 1898:

The Hawkesbury bridge was not at this time constructed, so all the passengers and their belongings had to cross in a steamer and take another train on the other side; and on a wet and cold night this was by no means a pleasant interruption. Eventually Tenterfield was reached, but I went on to the New South Wales border station and took refuge for the night in the Queensland town of Wallangarra. Next morning I started to explore. The school was about three miles from the station, and proved to be a fair-sized weatherboard structure of the roughest kind. It accommodated about seventy children, and when

the railway was in course of construction the enrolment reached this number. But alas! the navvies had departed, and the enrolment reached twenty. A report spread that the school was to be closed. A day was spent in removing this impression. Then I opened school, and had for the first week an average attendance of sixteen children. The nearest habitation was more than a mile away. This was a small selector's cottage. Here I was able to procure board and lodging at eighteen shillings per week and washing at four shillings the dozen. My bedroom was small. The cracks in the slabs were very large. Sometimes the wind would almost blow the candle out. Thus good ventilation was assured. We dined in a bark-covered shanty called the kitchen. A tablecloth was not always considered necessary; but the food, although plain, was wholesome. The fowls roamed under the table and picked up the crumbs. The dogs waited about the table to secure the spare bones. It was an economical household. There was little table-talk, and mostly in monosyllables. The family met to eat, not to talk. I did try hard to keep up the conversation, and one day made some remark which called forth the reply from the head of the family that 'I would do for a parson.' As it was evident that parsons did not stand high in his estimation, I made no other remarks of a like nature. However, he for the first two or three days blackened my boots. When I expected a continuation of this attention he flew into a towering temper, and wanted to know who was I that *he* should blacken my boots! I meekly rejoined that I did not exactly know who I was just yet, but I expected a continuation of his kind attentions. This seemed to add fuel to his rage, and the swear words began to fly about. Fearing that the old fellow would have an epileptic fit, I held my tongue, though surprised at his eloquence. Afterwards I deemed it advisable to blacken my own boots, and found that I was none the worse for so doing.

My bed was of straw, but as this is possibly healthier than feathers, and certainly more comfortable than a sheet of bark, I had cause for satisfaction on this point.

Socially I was well off. Nine miles away there was a School of Arts library, which contained a very fair selection of books, and I took the opportunity of thus becoming acquainted with many of the most classical writers. The distance was considerable, but the thoughts and conversations of these master minds were well worth a much longer journey.

One rainy morning, after I had been in charge for nearly twelve months, I was in the school at 9 o'clock, and writing some work on the blackboard. Going to the door, in order to look at the weather prospects, I noticed a man on a grey horse making for the school. A stranger in the bush is always an object of interest, and I wondered who he was. He came straight to the school, greeted me with a pleasant smile, and introduced himself as 'the inspector.' I was completely surprised, for I was looking forward to the inspection, and now the day had arrived, but the pupils had not. Only three children put in an appearance. However, as the inspector had occasion to visit the border town of Jennings, which at this time was without a school, I undertook to try to get the children together by 2 o'clock. Two of the children were instructed to remain in or near the school. The other, a fair-sized lad, was requested to go to the nearest family, while I hired a horse and rode to the remaining houses. By 2 o'clock fourteen children had assembled. They acquitted themselves very fairly, and the inspector seemed satisfied that continued and systematic work had been done with the materials available.

Rachel Reid made to feel unwelcome by her landlord at Burraneer Bay

Rachel Reid, aged 21,[17] was the first teacher at Burraneer Bay Provisional School in 1893.[18] On 26 April, after a complaint by her first landlord to the Department that she was no longer boarding at his place, she wrote to Inspector Skillman:

From my arrival at Burraneer Bay till the 30th March I resided at Mr De Leurence's house & would not have left but that I was very uncomfortable. I was suffering from a severe cold & when I asked Mr De Leurence for an inside bedroom (there being three vacant at the time) he refused to give me one even for a time. The meals were very poor and were served up in the kitchen (with all the children running about it) in not the daintiest manner. My washing was never done on time & yet not withstanding all I had to put up with Mr De Leurence seemed to deem that he was bestowing a charity in allowing me to stay at 15/- per week (the terms were his own).[19]

Julien Deleurence (as he wrote his name) had written that

She [Rachel Reid] gave no reason for leaving but as she was in the habit of keeping such late hours at night, I spoke to her about it which annoyed her so much that she made up her mind to go elsewhere and board. She was most irregular in her school hours for some time after she commenced here <u>until</u> I spoke to her about it, which altered her in that <u>respect</u>.[20]

Teacher at Tuckaburra compelled to eat and sleep with navvies

Nineteen-year-old Malcolm Lamb, who had been at the by then closed Nashua Provisional School near Bangalow, was appointed on 4 September 1893 as temporary assistant teacher at Tuckaburra (later Billinudgel) Public School near Brunswick Heads.[21] This school had been set up mainly for the children of workers constructing the north coast railway line. Lamb was not happy at the school and a few weeks later, on 21 September, he made an unsuccessful application for an increase in salary, giving as his reasons:

a) I have to pay £1 per week for my board and even then I have not a room to myself, but am compelled to eat and sleep with navvies.
b) The charges for washing are exorbitant. The charge for washing handkerchiefs and collars, is two shillings per dozen, for washing a white shirt, sixpence.
c) As my actual salary at present is £1 8s, 4d. per week, I have very little left for clothes, books, etc., after paying for board, lodgings and washing.[22]

Lamb became head teacher of the school in 1895 and remained there until the beginning of 1897.[23]

Teacher with no money left cannot leave Eringonia for a holiday

Thomas Clothier, described by Inspector Hunt as 'a Superior Young Teacher',[24] was appointed to Eringonia (later Enngonia) Public School 70 miles north of Bourke at the beginning of 1898. At the end of October of that year he made a successful application for climatic allowance, stating:

I am compelled to board at the hotel, in this place, since I cannot obtain private lodging; which I would very much prefer ... considering the small salary which I receive, and the amount I have to pay away for living, by the time I supply myself with a few clothes, & other necessaries, I have nothing left. Also taking into consideration, that I have been teaching in this remote part, since January last, I should like very much to avail myself of the opportunity afforded during, The Christmas Vacation, to go home & see my parents, but the expense incurred by travelling, by rail, & coach is very great, & I cannot possibly do it, while receiving such a small salary, £72, per year.[25]

Swamp, tannery and flies, etc., at Botany

In 1898 the inspector reported that a tannery was being constructed on land adjoining Botany Public School. He wrote:

The ground immediately below the school playground, and for some distance on either side, is a swamp. Into this the whole of the drainage from the land on which the tannery works are being constructed must flow. Under such circumstances the effluvium from the tannery will be most noisome, and possibly most detrimental to the health of the pupils, of the resident teacher, and of his staff.[26]

The head of the school, George Thornton, needed to make two applications before his request for fly screens on his residence was granted. In his second application in September 1904 he wrote:

Living in this district is almost intolerable on account of the swarms of flies, mosquitoes and other insects that infest it, and that are due to the great number of swamps, tanneries, wool-washes and factories in the neighbourhood.[27]

Teachers dissatisfied with living conditions at Thone Creek

In February 1899, with regard to the next teacher for Thone Creek Provisional School (later Byabarra) near Wauchope, Inspector Wright noted that

The accommodation procurable is only tolerable. I think that Mr C. Hayward's (about 1˘ mls from school) would be the best place to board. Either a male or female teacher would suit.[28]

On 8 March 1899 Kathleen Martyn, who had been at Warneton Provisional School, sent a telegram from Port Macquarie, where she was staying at the Star Hotel, to Inspector Wright at Taree:

Appointed Thone Creek School drove there Monday utterly impossible obtain accommodation people would repair outside room for male teacher may I return to Sydney.[29]

A local female resident wrote to Inspector Wright on 7 March 1899:

I have been infored [sic] to day that there was a Lady Teacher sent to take Charge of Thone Creek School and that the place did not suit her and she went away leaving our school still closed I am very sorry the Teacher did not come up here to our place I could have taken her in and gave her a room for her self I did not blame her not staying where the Lady was taken to So Sir I hope we will not be long till we have a Teacher to open the school there is now 21 children attending and please send the Teacher to me I will Board ever who comes.[30]

With regard to Kathleen Martyn's failing to remain at Thone Creek, Inspector Wright wrote that 'the place is rough but I do not think Mrs Martyn made an effort to obtain a suitable lodging place'.[31]

It was then decided to appoint Annie Mather, who had been at Taree Superior Public School, and Inspector Wright's superior officer noted that he should 'inform Miss Mather as to accommodation when appointing her'.[32] Despite this precaution, however, Annie Mather wrote to the chief inspector on 27 March:

I beg to apply to be removed from this place as I cannot live here.

It is away in the bush, 17 miles from the nearest village (Wauchope). There is no possibility of my being even comfortable. Driving is the only means to get to town and then the roads are so rough and hilly that it is unsafe for a lady to go alone the only alternative being to wait 3 or 4 months and then be driven by some of the men about who are exceedingly coarse and ignorant.

There is no society for a lady   I will be compelled to live comparatively alone

I have gone round with much difficulty and find most of the houses covered with bark not fit to board at.

The place where I have chosen is 1 mile from school over 2 large hills, it is really not fit for habitation on account of its delapidated [sic] condition and its inhabitants are extremely coarse.

On these grounds I beg for removal to Macleay River if possible. I cannot live here.[33]

The matter was referred to Inspector Wright for 'immediate report'[34] and on 17 April (by which time Annie Mather had already been moved to Collombatti Provisional School) he wrote:

1. This place is about 14 miles from Wauchope, & the road, with the exception of about 2 miles, is good. The difficulty of getting to town is not greater than in the case of most bush schools, & cannot possibly have been a serious drawback to a female reared, as Miss Mather was, in the bush.

2. The society is much the same as will be found in any ordinary country place. Miss Mather's complaint that 'there is no society for a lady' is I consider very frivolous indeed.

3. I went to Thone Creek to see for myself the accommodation. My visit was quite unexpected & there was no opportunity given to the people to make special preparations. I was allowed to examine the whole house in which Miss Mather resided & have no hesitation in stating that her complaint that 'the house is really not fit for habitation on account of its dilapidated condition' is quite untrue. The house is built of slabs, with a shingled roof and a sawn timber floor. It is in fair repair and very clean. The room Miss Mather occupied is 13 ft by 8 ft—the walls are papered with Government Gazettes, there is a proper window in it, the bed is provided with spring mattress flock mattress, & a full supply of clean bed clothes, & the necessary adjuncts of bedroom—washstand & ware, toilet table, looking glass etc.—are supplied. I made full inquiries about the meals and I believe they were quite suitable.

I cannot report fully on the statement that 'the inhabitants are extremely coarse', but I can safely say that on the day of my unexpected visit [the landlady] & her daughters were all neat and respectable looking & I am inclined to think Miss Mather's statement on this point is also untrue.

Miss Mather is, I understand, engaged to a teacher on the Macleay River, & I am of opinion that, in her anxiety to get an appointment on that river, she made statements about Thone Creek that are not true.

Before her appointment to Thone Creek, I recommended that Mr Kennedy, now in charge of the H.T. [Half-Time] Schools at Rolland's Plains and Wauchope [Aboriginal School], be appointed to Thone Creek Provisional. I again recommend that this appoint-ment be made.[35]

Annie Mather married George Parker, the teacher of Mungay Creek Provisional School near Kempsey, in November 1899 and herself became the teacher of that school until she resigned in 1901.[36]

Edward Kennedy was appointed to Thone Creek School on 3 May 1899. He was to remain at the school until it closed at the end of January 1903.[37] The school re-opened as Byabarra in 1914,[38] and the school's records show no evidence of teacher dissatisfaction with accommodation until William Swan, aged 30, was appointed to the school on 28 November 1917.[39] On 2 February the following year Swan sent a telegram to Inspector Harvey saying that he could not get accommodation. Swan wrote to Harvey, who had urged him to try harder, that he had left one place because it was

alive with vermin and I could see the children had to suffer hardships by my presence in the house. On Saturday the second of February 12 miles were walked looking for board but none could be procured therefore a wire was sent to you at Kempsey but a reply was received you were not there. The same day temporary board was procured ... near the school. Meals only could be had at this place therefore two forms had to be used to sleep upon at the school. [The landlady] is now attempt-ing to accommodate me temporarily. The residents here seem to be quite unconcerned about the education of their children.[40]

On 8 March Swan wrote again asking

to be removed from this locality owing to the unhygienic conditions prevailing here. It is impossible for a person to put up with food which is dirty. Puddings are boiled in a kerozine [sic] tin in which washing suds have been standing for the best part of a week. The cat is feed [sic] off the plates in use on the meal table. The drinking cups are used for shaving in. The house not being covered around the bottom allows the dogs and fowls to camp underneath night and day also on the verandah where my bed is situated.

The dogs are covered with body <u>lice</u> and scratch

all day long. The Fowls roost on my bed in the day time. It is quite plainly seen my health is going to suffer if I am not removed ... I am sleeping in the blankets while the unfortunate children sleep under bags. Why these conditions can be I do not know. Trusting I will be removed in due course ...

When I take a bath it has to be carried out in the boys' lavatory [i.e., washroom at the school] with a school bucket and school disinfectant.[41]

On 22 February 1918 Swan wrote to Inspector Harvey that 'I think it is a disgrace that a teacher should have to go round and beg to be boarded as this is practically what it means'.[42] When the holidays came at Easter, Swan sought an interview with the chief inspector and was moved as a result of this interview to Kenthurst School as relieving teacher on 8 April.[43]

With regard to the next teacher, Inspector Harvey wrote on 19 June that 'On no account should a female teacher be appointed & the man selected should be at least middle aged'.[44] Despite this, 20-year-old Ethel Dennerley was appointed to the school on 17 September.[45] She entered on duty at the school on 7 October but only stayed two nights as she found the house in which she boarded was 'alive with bugs',[46] which she found first in her bed and then on her clothes as well. On 9 October she left by the mail sulky and went to Wauchope and was then appointed to Moroko (later Pembrooke) School near Telegraph Point.[47]

Lucy Gow asks to be moved from primitive and lonely Martins Creek

Lucy Gow had been the teacher at Martins Creek Public School near Paterson for a year when in January 1901 she successfully applied to be moved, giving as her reasons:

1. The school, of which I am at present in charge, is situated 17 miles from the nearest post office and coach service. There is no mail delivery—Tuesday being the only day I can get mail, and that only by the courtesy of the neighbours.
2. The place at which I board is situated on a lonely mountain 2 miles from the school, being gettable only by a bridle-track.

3. The conditions under which the people live are very primitive and most unhealthy. The water supply—there are no tanks on the premises—is obtained from an open drain, which is also a drinking fount for cattle and dogs etc. The food is the coarsest and most unwholesome.

4. My health has been seriously affected and I suffer continually from inflamed eyes and skin eruptions.

There are homesteads nearer the school, but the people live under conditions even worse than the above-mentioned. In short, the district is most unsuitable for a lady. I boarded in town—Paterson—for the first 6 months and cycled in and out every day.—I cannot manage a horse—but found the distance—14 miles—too great and trying. In wet weather I was obliged to walk.[48]

Lucy Gow was transferred to Manly Superior Public School in March 1901 and resigned from teaching in 1906.[49]

Christopher McCallum at 'horrible' Kurrara

In 1904 Christopher McCallum, the teacher at Kurrara (later Banora Point) Public School made an unsuccessful request to the Department to reconsider the less-than-hoped-for results he had obtained in the teachers' examination because, he wrote:

* I have been teaching in this horrible place for nearly 3 years; & boarding at an Hotel for I cannot get a private place to stay at, & it is an impossibility to study against such a fearful noise. There are no Police, so you can imagine my situation & no one to assist me in my studies.

* I was very sick, under the Doctor for over 3 months prior to examination, and labouring under the New Syllabus as well.[50]

Dust showers in the Berrigan School residence

In 1910, after local publicity on the bad state of the school residence at Berrigan Public School, Inspector Lynch wrote of this building:

The walls in places are not upright. In summer the dust enters through the roof, accumulating on the ceilings and afterwards showers down on beds, and at times on the table where the family is having a meal. In winter a candle can scarcely be kept alight as the wind enters through cracks etc., and a fire cannot be made unless the teacher's family is prepared to live in an atmosphere of smoke. The building is structurally defective and in my opinion cannot be effectively repaired. The teacher has been very long-suffering in this matter though I have myself urged him to make a complete report on the condition of the residence.[51]

7

School Communities

Teacher's reserved temperament makes him unsuited for a school on a goldfield

Of the teacher Henry Blyth, who was at Nerrigundah National School near Nowra in March 1865, Inspector Thomas Harris wrote:

The Teacher desires to be removed. He dislikes the place and does not associate with the people. His reserved temperament is perhaps about as unsuitable for social life upon a goldfield, as the very opposite evidently is. I think a young married man would do well at this school.[1]

Mary Cameron saves a woman from having her head smashed open at Illabo

Mary Cameron (later Gilmore) (1865-1962) was the teacher at Illabo Public School near Cootamundra for about six months in 1887.[2] In his biography of Mary Gilmore, W. H. Wilde writes that she described Illabo as a 'place of drunkenness and immorality'.[3] He quotes her Untitled Prose (1919):

I lived here in a constant state of shock and horror. Once saved a woman from getting her head smashed open when her lunatic husband got his gun to shoot me. I looked him down.[4]

Wild West Wyalong

In 1894 the head teacher at West Wyalong Public School, Thomas Thompson, asked that the pupil-teacher he had requested might be a female as, 'with a very large sewing class, her services are really needed in that particular'.[5] Although Thompson suggested that the female pupil-teacher could stay

Mary Cameron (later Gilmore) (1865–1962) in her early twenties (Ms 1662 / Gollan Lewis Papers, National Library of Australia)

at Mrs Halliday's Central Boarding House, Inspector Thomas could not recommend the appointment of a female 'as the place [a recently established gold-mining settlement] is quite unfit for a female teacher unless her relatives live here'.[6] Other indications of the unsettled state of West Wyalong in its early days are Thomas Thompson's statement, made in September 1895 in the course of defending himself against a complaint by a parent, that 'in all my previous service [17 years] I have not been 'reported', but it would be almost a matter of surprise not to find trouble in West Wyalong'[7]; Inspector Thomas's statement in May 1897 that 'there is a good deal of lawlessness and larrikinism in the town'[8]; and also his statement in May 1898 that 'the general moral tone of West Wyalong children is distinctly low'.[9]

Parent hides behind bushes to find fault with Stockinbingal teacher

Teacher Alfred Kendall was not happy that the new residence built at Stockinbingal near Cootamundra at the end of 1894 had no fence to separate it from the school. He had tried unsuccessfully to get one while the residence was being erected and again on 13 May 1895 he wrote to Inspector Friend requesting a paling fence and stating that

At present the residence and school house are enclosed by a 3 rail fence, and, as there is no division between the two buildings, and, nothing to obstruct the view of the general public and the pupils, there is no privacy whatever in connection with the residence ...

The neighbour's fowls, goats, and pigs are a continual source of annoyance, and without the ground being enclosed with palings it will be utterly impossible to have either a vegetable or a flower garden, as plants in pots on the verandah of the residence have several times been destroyed by goats.[10]

Just over eighteen months later, on 26 December 1896, four parents signed a petition asking that Kendall be removed from the school and giving as their reasons:

1st That he neglects the education of the children attending the school as [sic] much so that thay [sic] appear to make scarcely any progress in learning.

2nd That he has on several occasions unduly beaten the children under his charge and his general treatment of them has been such that many of them are afraid to attend the school.[11]

At Inspector Friend's inquiry into the matter on 5 February 1897 the main complainant, Thomas Friend, a carpenter, stated (as recorded by Inspector Friend):

Practical bee keeping, 1912 (From Report of the Minister of Public Instruction, *1912)*

My reasons for saying that Mr Kendall neglects the education are these:—I have examined the children of my own family, and found them more backward than when they came to the school. Things which I learnt them, they have quite forgotten since they have been here. They are in 3rd class now and they are not fit for the 2nd. He is continually out in the school yard during school hours, attending to his bees and fowls, & shewing visitors about. I have lost a deal of time watching him from behind the bushes close to the school. Sometimes he has been half an hour out of school selling honey etc. to hawkers, & buying vegetables, clothing etc.

I was compelled to take my children from school because of Mr Kendall's illtreatment. He made my son George's hand swell up like a bull's hoof (about 5 months ago). George used to bound up out of bed at night after this punishment: we had to tie [him] in the bed for a fortnight and he used to say sometimes when he would jump up, that the master was beating him. He was afraid to go to school. He was about 6 years old at the time. I never made any complaint to Mr Kendall about his treatment of my children or about the way they were getting on: but my wife went to him when he made George's hand so bad, and he apologised to her.

He has also beaten my children John & Flossie across the hand and body, and marked them. The caning he gave Flossie once, broke the buttons of her dress, & they flew in the other children's faces. This was about 3 months ago. He offered her (Flossie) an orange, & some buttons to replace those he had broken. I had 3 children at the school—none now. I have brought no witnesses to prove that Mr Kendall is frequently out in the school ground during school hours.[12]

Summarising his findings on the matter Inspector Friend wrote on 8 February:

I inquired into the matter on Friday last, 5th inst. The complaints lodged against the teacher are these:
1. That he neglects the children; so much so, that they are not progressing sufficiently.
2. That he is unduly severe in his treatment of them.
Re No 1 Only four (4) of the parents would sign the petition: the other twenty (20) state that they are well pleased with the progress which their children are making. One of the complainants (O'Brien) says that he is fairly satisfied at present. I tested one of Friend's children and found him above standard. Mr Kendall has done decidedly profitable work since he opened the school: his average proficiency at the last two inspections has been about 70 p c—the last in October 1896. There is nothing to shew that he neglects his school in any way.
Re No 2 Mr Friend stands alone with regard to the charge of severity. The other complainants have no fault of find in this particular. The only evidence in support of the charge, comes from members of Friend's family. I questioned the pupils of 3rd class; and their evidence is altogether in the teacher's favor: so also is that of every other parent.

I recommend:—
(a) That the complainants be informed, through Mr Thomas Friend of Stockinbingal, that the evidence produced at the recent inquiry does not confirm the charges made against Mr Kendall; & that the Minister is not prepared to accede to the request for that teacher's removal.
(b) That Mr Kendall be informed that he has been exonerated ...
Note: I have been informed on most reliable authority that some months ago, Mr Kendall found it necessary to ask Mr Friend to keep his goats out of the school ground, as they were destroying some ornamental trees etc. Friend declined to do this, & the teacher told him that he would have to shoot the goats if they trespassed again. I believe this circumstance will, in a great measure, account for Friend's present behaviour towards the teacher.[13]

Berowra teacher is insulted and threatened with a revolver and an axe

Twenty-four-year-old Louis Aubrey (whose full name was Edward Louis Aubrey) was appointed to Berowra School when it opened in 1894.[14] In February 1901 a local resident, Charles Ginn, wrote to the Department complaining that the teacher, Aubrey, had refused his son a drink of water at the school. The son, 16-year-old Alfred

Berowra Public School, c.1915 (NSW Dept of School Education)

Ginn, had been working in an orchard near the school.[15]

On 28 February Aubrey wrote of this matter that Alfred Ginn had never asked him for a drink and

1. <u>That Alfred Ginn</u>, the son referred to is <u>not</u> a School pupil, but is a man employed on a farm adjacent to my school.

2. <u>That this man</u> could get water close to where he has been working if he desired and that it was not necessary to climb a fence to get water (without permission) from the school tank, as there is a Well from which he has been in the habit of getting water within 12 yards of where he has been working— the pretext of coming to the school being only to annoy me and my pupils.

3. <u>That he has been</u> in the habit of trespassing on the school premises during School hours and that, on several occasions, he has sent per medium of my pupils insulting messages to me.

4. <u>That when I asked</u> him not to come on the ground again he told the lads to tell me, that he 'would give me a lively 5 minutes if I spoke to him

again and the boys would have a job picking up the pieces' and further that 'if I spoke to him again he would give me a punch' He also sent word that if I caned any of the boys he would be listening and come over and make me 'sit up'. He also sent word and shouted to me that 'he would come on the ground and do what he liked.'

5. <u>That he has</u> been howling and yelling outside my school and interrupting the lessons frequently, and he stands impudently close to the school and makes noises at me whenever I step outside the door. To this all my pupils can testify. In fact he seldom passes my school without stopping to screech, or call out something insulting.

6. <u>That on Sunday</u> last (17th Feb.) the school verandah was covered with sand—the school tank defaced with drawings and writing—the key of the Tank missing—the water run out of the Tank and portion of a Stone Wall built by my pupils knocked over. Constable Black of Hornsby to whom I showed these things can testify that the footprints found all round the premises correspond with the foot-marks of Alfred Ginn.

7. <u>I have frequently</u> found the school disfigured and on one occasion broken into; and as I have been in the habit of locking up the Key of the tank and then finding the tap had been knocked about, I thought it as well to leave the key and a cup outside so that the tap might not be damaged. On Monday last (18th) however, the Cup was stolen and the footprints (to my idea) correspond with those found on Sunday.

8. <u>That Alfred Ginn</u> admitted to Constable Black that he had been on the premises when I had requested him not to do so.

9. <u>That my wife</u> and I are often called out to insultingly and whistled at by Alfred Ginn and that my visitors are likewise insulted by him.

10. <u>That the tap</u> has been turned on many occasions and the water allowed to run to waste.

11. <u>That the father</u> of this man, C. Ginn, bears me malice.[16]

Following an inquiry by Inspector Drummond, Chief Inspector Frederick Bridges wrote:

I recommend that Mr C. Ginn be informed that his son has no right whatever to take water from the school tanks, which is for the use of the pupils only, and that steps will be taken to punish any person guilty of trespassing on or damaging school property.[17]

Aubrey's troubles with local residents were far from being over. Two months later, in April 1901, two people who worked at the railway platform where the post office also was, Charlotte Pugh and E. J. Greaves, made complaints about Aubrey because he had objected to their early closing of the mail.[18] Again Inspector Drummond conducted inquiries. With regard to the complaint by Pugh, Drummond wrote:

The trouble appears to have arisen from the fact that Mr Aubrey would not submit to being treated insolently whenever he had occasion to visit the station, and when he resented it, the insults of the whole Pugh family were directed at Mrs Aubrey. She endured it for some considerable time, but when Mrs Pugh in a wild delirium of rage, rushed about the railway platform, flourished a revolver and threatened Mr Aubrey's life, she, unknown to

Infants gardening at Blackfriars Superior Public School, c.1913 (NSW Dept of School Education)

Mr Aubrey, drew the railway authorities' attention to her strange behaviour.

Sometime later two of Mr Aubrey's letters were opened in transit, and he referred the matter to the Postal Authorities, but made no reference to any suspicions that he might have had. However the Postal Authorities, after due inquiry, suspected the official at Berowra, and with the concurrence of the Railway Superintendant [sic], Mrs Pugh was suspended. She then reported Mr Aubrey to the Minister of Public Instruction.

As an example to the annoyances to which Mr Aubrey had to submit, I may mention that on one occasion, Mr Pugh, the husband of Mrs Pugh, who is a navvy on the railway, ordered Mr Aubrey, in the presence of a number of people, to leave the platform, and when Mr Aubrey took no notice of him, he said he would report him, and have his billet taken from him in less than a fortnight.

I consider that Mr Aubrey acted with great forbearance, and the actions taken by Mrs Aubrey and himself were forced upon him, by the continued gross treatment to which they were subjected.

I recommend that Mr Aubrey be informed that the charges brought against him by Mrs Pugh are groundless, and that his action under the circumstances was perfectly justifiable.[19]

With regard to the complaint against Aubrey by Greaves, Inspector Drummond wrote that Greaves had not appeared at the inquiry. At the inquiry Aubrey outlined the manner in which Greaves had been uncooperative about the mail. Other ways in which Greaves had annoyed Aubrey were:

By ordering me to cease using a track across the line, the only one leading to my residence, and used by hundreds on every holiday … With reference to my going home for lunch [Greaves had raised this matter], I may state, that I reside within 5 mts walk from the school, and as all except one family go home to lunch, I usually also go home, carefully leaving the school locked, and the one family in charge of their elder brother who is 16 years of age.[20]

Aubrey also had many witnesses to his good running of the school including Patrick Morris, parent of five children, who wrote on 29 April that

'Mr Aubrey. school Teacher has been boarding with me for about two years I. never knew him to go late to school or never heard any complaints.'[21]

In the case of the complaint lodged by Greaves, Inspector Drummond recommended 'that Mr. L Aubrey be informed that the charges lodged against him were groundless and frivolous, and that he is wholly exonerated from them.'[22]

Again in February and March 1904 complaints about Aubrey were made to the Department by Percival Richards and again by Charlotte Pugh. In addition the Progress Association, per its secretary, James Stewart, supported Charlotte Pugh's complaint. On the other hand, 16 parents signed a petition supporting Aubrey and another parent wrote him a letter of support.[23]

In her complaint about Aubrey's rudeness to her, Pugh had written that

Mr Aubrey's manner towards me so unnerved me that as I say I took ill and my illness culminated last Tuesday in a fit and I was carried to the store where I am told it took four people to hold me down, and it was [while I] was lying there Mr Aubrey rushed in to Mr Richards dinning [sic] room and would not go out when ordered'.[24]

In his reply to the complaints Aubrey, with reference to the trouble he had had with Charlotte Pugh in 1901, wrote on 10 February 1904:

At that time [1901] I was cursed, vilely insulted, slandered, and threatened with a revolver by this excitable woman …

On Tuesday 2 Feb [1904] I was told that Mrs Pugh had 'gone mad' and that 'I caused the madness'— I therefore went with my wife to the Store (owned by the Father of the youth [Richards] who is to marry Pugh's daughter I believe) in order to see what I had done, for as the Pughs and I had been for some time on friendly terms I was at a loss to understand what action of mine had caused the upset.—I went to Mrs Pugh and told her quietly I had done nothing, and I quietened the woman. Mr Pugh however, who is a very excitable man, called my wife 'a bad egg' threatened to have us moved out of the district, and said he would 'ram his fist down my b— throat.' I said nothing to him—Mrs

Randwick School, teacher Jane Gardner, 1918 (From the Education Gazette, *1918, p. 2)*

Pugh recovered in a few minutes after [*sic*] and walked home ... The only witnesses of my 'rushing' in to the store were the Richards (mother & daughter)—Some years ago these people (Richards) expected that I was going to marry the daughter. I did not do so, and they have been spiteful to me ever since, although outwardly friendly ... Since the awful outburst of this bad-tempered woman [Charlotte Pugh] in 1901, I have never on any occasion done or said anything that would worry this woman. —

At a bush-fire which since that time raged here, my house (with all their neighbours around them) was the only house in which they sought shelter, and my help was the only assistance they asked.

Upon the death of their baby about 6 months ago Pugh came to my house, asking for my wife to sing over the dead child and also asking me to pray and read a service (having no minister here)—We did all we could.—

Up to about 3 or 4 weeks ago Pugh's son has been attending night school. Free at my home.—In every possible way I have done all I could for the people. Through my endeavours she [Charlotte Pugh] received the position of Attendant etc.[25]

From his inquiry Inspector Blumer concluded on 18 February 1904:

Mr Aubrey is an earnest skilful 2B Teacher. He seems to me to be rather meek than quarrelsome. Acting on my advice, he did not call any witnesses to rebutt [*sic*] Mrs Pugh's unsupported and inconclusive evidence. As a protest against the actions of Mrs Pugh and the Committee, the mother of every pupil, except Mrs Pugh, came to express her admiration of and respect for Mr & Mrs Aubrey and her unqualified disapproval of any attempt to get Mr Aubrey removed. It was with difficulty they were pacified. [Blumer wrote that he attached] an unsolicited testimonial from a clergyman [Rev. M. Kirby] of a different faith from that of Mr Aubrey. Mr Aubrey holds a 2B Certificate and is a more than ordinarily earnest and capable Teacher. He has now had charge of this 9th Class School for over 9 years. His classification renders him eligible for a better position, the quality of his work gives him strong claims for promotion, and the annoyance he has been unjustly subjected to by the Pughs and their friends render his removal desirable. In a separate communication I have submitted a specific recommendation to this effect.

I recommend that Mr Aubrey, Mr Pugh and the Berowra Progress Association be informed (a) that there are no reasonable grounds for the statement made by Mrs Pugh and endorsed by the Progress Association, that Mr Aubrey was in any way accountable for Mrs Pugh's illness on 2nd instant; (b) that the other matters referred to in Mrs Pugh's letter referring to events that occurred in 1901 were fully enquired into and finally dealt with at the time; (c) that the Minister sees no reason why Mr Aubrey should be removed from Berowra at present unless it be to a better position for faithful and efficient service.[26]

Even after this episode Aubrey's trouble with local residents was not over. On Monday 9 May 1904 two members of the Progress Committee, Thomas Richards and Robert Richards (father and son) came to the school with a horse and cart and, both using axes, cut down 21 sapling gum trees and took them away. Reporting the matter to Inspector Blumer, Aubrey wrote:

These trees I had trimmed for shade purposes.— The school ground, 2 acres, is unfenced.— Thomas Richards is the man who recently threatened me with an axe.—[27]

The police took action in the matter but when the case went before a magistrate it was dismissed without any reason being given.[28]

Yet again, in October 1904, a complaint about caning was made against Aubrey by parents Horace Burton and his wife.[29] Acting Inspector McCoy conducted an inquiry into this complaint and reported on 6 October 1904:

There is no doubt that the complaints are vexatious and that the Teacher is the victim of the persecution of a small clique only two of whom (Burton and Pugh) are parents of pupils attending the school. These people have expressed their determination of having Mr Aubrey removed.

Eight parents out of the total number—10— express their unqualified approval of Mr Aubrey as a resident and all are unanimous and loud in their praise of him as a teacher. He holds a 2B certificate, has 16 years of service, and has been in charge of this school for ten years. The records, wall documents, and art specimens on the walls of the school betoken a teacher of more than average merit. The annoyances to which he has been cruelly and unjustly subjected are affecting his wife's health and wearing him out and render his removal desirable.

I recommend (a) that Mr Aubrey be informed that he is completely exonerated from the above named charges (b) that Mr Burton be suitably informed.[30]

On 28 October Aubrey, who had suffered much at the hands of a small number of residents at Berowra, was moved to Blackwall (later Woy Woy) Public School. He remained at this school until 1923 when he was moved to Neath Public School near Cessnock, from where he was moved to Dapto Public School in 1924. He retired from Dapto Public School in 1935.[31]

Janet Houslar and her dog at Buxton Public School

Janet Houslar, aged 39,[32] the teacher at Buxton Public School near Picton, sent a telegram to Inspector Cornish on 12 May 1908: 'Nervously prostrated may I close'.[33] Inspector Cornish was not pleased with this departure from the usual procedure and replied: 'If you are ill, an application for Leave of Absence accompanied by a Medical Certificate should be made'.[34]

A month previously, in April 1908, Janet Houslar had written to the chief inspector about the lack of suitable accommodation for her at Buxton. She wrote:

I am compelled to live over a mile from the school, along a lonely bush road. Failing to get board, I am obliged to get lodging (poor as it is without common decencies) and board myself.

Having worked conscientiously all day I am too tired to and weary to prepare food for myself on my arrival; consequently I am worse off now than I was in town.

I took the position solely on account of my health—now I am weaker far than before as I have an up-hill journey on a rough road after work.

Having been over twenty two-years in the service, if a place with suitable accommodation cannot be found for me in a small place I am willing to go along the Southern line north of Campbelltown, where I have a chance of regaining my health, taking a position again as Assistant.

The accommodation house for male teacher mentioned on Quarterly Return demanded twenty-five shillings a week or one pound a week if I cleaned my own room and did my own washing. This was entirely out of my power with a salary of £96 a year. They have since decided not to take any boarders. I may mention here that I had good board in Sydney for fifteen shillings a week and the lady assistant at Thirlmere pays the same rate.[35]

Inspector Cornish wrote of the matter of Houslar's accommodation on 29 April 1908:

Miss Houslar waited upon me at Campbelltown on 22nd Inst. and explained her case. I am not able to substantiate her statements with respect to the inconvenience of board, at Buxton, as I am ignorant of the conditions; but she certainly has grown dissatisfied with her position as Teacher at Buxton. I told her to put her case on paper. If she is removed, I suggest the appointment of a male, single Teacher.[36]

In May some local residents complained about Janet Houslar's dog, which they described as diseased, being at the school. Houslar wrote on 20 May:

The dog, or rather puppy, has been reared by me and my friends since it was two months old, and is a thorough-bred, winning laurels at the Kennel Show ... My belief is this report is nothing but malice as the man (reporter) has no children at school. I had not been in the district one week, when this man made complaints to me, of the school boys breaking windows and stealing fruit. A man, Parnwell with whom the last teacher stayed, together with this man, tried to force my boys to acknowledge the deeds. I found the windows had been broken years before, and I believed the boys did not take the fruit, for the house is only a stone's throw from the school and I should have heard the noise, or seen it.[37]

The next day, Houslar wrote again:

I omitted from my explanation the reason why my puppy was not now with me. Having had occasion to visit Head Office on Saturday, I was obliged to take the dog with me, for valuable dogs cannot live in Buxton for fear of baits. Knowing this my dog was never out of my sight, coming from the kennel, sheep-dipped every week and straw bedding (sunned), on a strap with me and back in the afternoon. Although against the rules of the Railway Department, I have travelled with her in the brake-van from stations along the line.[38]

Inspector Cornish wrote on 30 May:

I inquired into this matter [i.e., complaints about the dog] on the 19th Inst. in the presence of John Billin [who had complained], the Teacher and the pupils. It would be well to preface my remarks by stating that, just at the present time, there are 3 or 4 men at Buxton (chiefly single men) who are harassing government servants by reporting them to head quarters for most inoffensive actions—the railway fettler has recently been reported for keeping bees and selling the honey, and the local school Teacher twice reported about her dog. None of these men have any interest in the school whatever—John Billin, an ex-miner, occupies a small cottage, alone, next to the school (his wife & family are elsewhere). It is here that the reports are drawn up. On paper, John Billin's complaint about the diseased dog looks serious; 'the dog' is simply used as a go-between the real source of grievance is that the Teacher declined to board where her predecessor did, & pay 25 shillings a week—the complaints are made by others, and John Billin, practically a new resident with no children attending Buxton School, is made use of.

The dog complained of is a beautiful pointer which accompanies Miss Houslar to and from the school, for protection. She lives about 1 mile from the school, and is obliged to travel a road on which a woman was assaulted a few years ago by a tramp who received several years' imprisonment for the offence. It is quite a common practice at Buxton

Montessori Method lesson, Blackfriars Superior Public School, 1910 (NSW Dept of School Education)

for women to be accompanied by a dog as some form of protection—Miss Small, a lady living near Buxton, always takes 2 dogs with her. On arrival at school, the dog is tied up outside, but near the school door a bag is placed on the ground for the dog to lie on. If the weather is cold or wet, Miss Houslar has allowed the animal to lie in the school lobby. There is no evidence to show that the dog enters the school room. I allowed Mr Billin to question the pupils on this point, but all denied the report that the dog was ever tied up in the school. The dog is very clean; but, some months ago, had the distemper which has left an occasional quivering or shake in one of its legs. At present, it is perfectly clean and healthy.[39]

Janet Houslar was removed from Buxton to Fairfield Public School in June 1908.[40] On 18 June the local Congregational Minister at Buxton, Thomas Kench, who apparently was not aware that Houslar had been moved, wrote that 'About a fortnight since the Public School Teacher left her work here very suddenly and disappeared and the children in this District are left without instruction'.[41]

Janet Houslar also had trouble at later schools to which she was appointed. After Buxton she taught at many different schools before her retirement in 1929 and was frequently warned that her failure to work amicably in a school situation would bring serious consequences.[42]

Teacher accused of giving trees away and only teaching the children to dance

On 22 August 1916 an anonymous letter writer complained to the Department that at Burringbar Public School near Murwillumbah the teacher, Edward Hayes, had given away two trees.[43] This person wrote: 'Mr Sargent [*sic*—his name was Sergeant and he had been a previous teacher at the school] made the boys fence and water the trees and look after them and cained [*sic*] the children if they broke a limb off. And this man gives them away to Mr Dan McCormack a farmer ... The children has [*sic*] not learnt to do any thing ... only to dance There is to [*sic*] much alchol [*sic*] about.'[44] Hayes explained that he had taken out the trees he considered useless because of damage by stock on the other side of the fence, and that he was 'in the act of throwing these over the fence when Mr Daniel McCormack [who had given many plants to the school] a most estimable gentleman happened along in a sulky. He said he wouldn't mind sticking these trees in the hilly country at his farm. Mr McCormack is a retired farmer so I gave them to him, very glad to be rid of them, & hope he has luck with them.'[45]

Inspector Dunlop, who was asked to investigate the matter, accepted Hayes's explanation. On 9 September 1916 he wrote:

Re the trees Mr Hayes statement is correct. The trees were planted too close to the fence, and only prickly trees that the stock will not eat, such as Bunya Bunya, can be planted with success, and the removal of the remains of other trees was done so that the new trees could be planted and the row made uniform. Mr Hayes is an enthusiastic gardener and is laying out the grounds with the assistance of surrounding farmers, and I am sure the school grounds will soon be greatly improved. Several patriotic dances have lately been held in town, and Mr Hayes and his family have assisted in making them a success. His daughter taught some fancy dancing to the girls and this is the origin of the complaint re dancing. There are some sectarian firebrands in the locality and Mr McCormack a Tipperary Irishman is friendly with Mr Hayes and is helping him considerably in the planting of the school grounds. This I believe to be the origin of this mean complaint and I recommend that no notice be taken of the communication.[46]

Threat of violence at the Hannam Vale Red Cross school concert

At the Red Cross School Concert at Hannam Vale near Kendall on 26 April 1918, as later reported by teacher Thomas Lynch in explanation to the Department of why he had been subpoenaed to appear in court,

five parties began to quarrel about a seat ... Blows were threatened and I intervened. Order was restored, but summonses were issued by both parties over things that were said and done later. I was subpoenaed by one party to prove that he had not struck anyone in the hall.[47]

Who owns the best dog at Tullamore

In 1918 an outbreak of head lice at Tullamore Public School was blamed by one family on another family. In his explanation of the complaint teacher William Roach, who was highly thought of by the inspector, wrote that the children of the two families had quarrelled at school 'over who owned the best dog' and that this was the basis of the complaint.[48]

A memorable war memorial at Miranda

On 23 May 1918 secretary of the Miranda Public School Parents and Citizens Association, Catherine Tanner, successfully applied for the use of the school to hold a concert to raise funds for an

Dancing lesson, Blackfriars Superior Public School, 1913 (NSW Dept of School Education)

Honour Roll.[49] The next month, the Department agreed to allow the line of the school's fence to be altered so that the names of local soldiers on the Honour Roll at the base of a monument could be read from the road.[50] On 3 August the war memorial at the school was unveiled, with ceremony, by the Minister of Public Instruction, Augustus James.[51]

On 5 January 1920, the secretary of the Miranda Repatriation Divisional Committee applied to hold a 'Welcome Home' for all the returned men of the district in the school grounds on Saturday 17 January at 2.30 p.m. The head of the school, Walter Chiplin, wrote of this application (which was successful):

The majority of the returned men are ex-pupils of the Miranda School. As there is no local park suitable for a ceremony of this kind, and as the fine

Miranda Public School war memorial in 1919, before the statue was removed (From the Local Studies Collection, Sutherland Shire Council)

Honor Roll in our school grounds seems a fitting centre around which the ceremony might be held, I beg respectfully to recommend that the application be granted.[52]

A statue of a soldier had been placed on top of the pedestal with the memorial plaque listing the names of the soldiers. Not everyone liked this statue and on 5 May 1920 the Department of Local Government wrote to the Department of Education:

As you are doubtless aware, a war memorial was recently erected at the Miranda Public School. Such memorial is in the shape of a statue of a soldier mounted on a stone base. Some of the residents of Miranda and district do not consider the statue of the soldier surmounting the memorial in any way artistic or suitable.[53]

A history of Miranda School written by the Department of Education in 1958 includes the information that 'the argument [about the statue] reached a climax when some of the more vehement opponents of the statue surreptitiously removed it one night and deposited it in a local creek. It was recovered and replaced.'[54] Interestingly, in 1994, the archival material from which this piece of Miranda school's history was written was no longer among the school's records. In Miranda School's centenary book a now deceased local resident, Martin Waddington (1899-1990), is quoted on the subject of this unscheduled removal of the statue:

It [the statue] was the work of a local who was a builder not a sculptor and some residents didn't think his attempt was acceptable. One night a number of men took down the statue and buried it. This caused a stir and so it was dug up and restored to its former position.[55]

The outcome of the objections was a decision that the statue was to be removed, leaving only the pedestal. This was done and Martin Waddington recalled that the statue was 'consigned to the backyard of a house near the junction of the Kingsway and Port Hacking Road, facing the other way'.[56]

The memorial, now minus the statue, was a focal point for Anzac Day dawn services and, from 1936, it was floodlit at night.[57] The Department, however, observed on 15 March 1946, when space was critically short at the school, that 'the local memorial from the 1914-18 War takes up quite an amount of space which could be used for playground purposes'.[58] The desirability of relocating the war memorial became a necessity when the school was to move to a new site in the 1960s. In November 1963 the Department reported:

On 21st May 1962 the Minister approved of action proceeding for the consolidation of the primary department on the former girls' department site. It is pointed out that the primary boys, girls and infants departments are housed on three separate sites. It is planned, when the primary accommodation is available, to abandon the primary boys' site situated at the corner of the Kingsway and Kiora Road North.

In front of the boys' school on the Kiora Road frontage, there stands a sandstone brick War Memorial ... it bears the name 'Miranda Central Public School' and lists the names of men who enlisted for service. Regular annual observances are still held in the school grounds, although the assembly area surrounding the Memorial may be somewhat limited.

In view of the impending developments, the Principal has sought permission to seek approval for the removal and re-erection of the War Memorial in the grounds of the Port Hacking High School, Miranda, in a suitable position opposite the Miranda Public School where it could be used by both schools. He indicated that the playing areas of the primary school will be at a premium, particularly having regard to continued enrolments. The Principal of Port Hacking High School indicated verbally to the Principal of the Miranda Public School that he was in agreement with the proposal.[59]

Another departmental officer wrote on 28 November 1963:

It is known that the RSL Club is not satisfied with the proposed location [of the war memorial] within the High School Site. A meeting is to be arranged by the president of the RSL Club and representatives of the Department in the near future. The responsibility for the cost of removing the structure will be discussed at that time.[60]

By mid-1965 the school had moved to its new site and on 27 October 1965 George Carver, secretary of the Miranda sub-branch of the RSL, wrote to the Department of Education:

You will be aware that within the grounds of the now closed school premises at the corner of Kingsway and Kiora Road, Miranda, there is a War Memorial and associated flag pole. From announcements made, it is apparent that your Department proposes to dispose of the site for commercial purposes and if such be the case, it would appear necessary for the memorial to be re-located. If however, the present site on which the memorial stands could remain a dedicated site, the work of the pioneers of this district and the memorial could remain undisturbed.

Should the foregoing not be possible, it will then be necessary to move the memorial and flagpole to a new location. Several suggestions have been made as to appropriate new sites by various parties, some directly interested others with a passing interest. After careful consideration of all aspects of this matter, the members of this Sub-Branch, which will retain an everlasting interest in the memorial and its significance, feel that the memorial should, if it is to be moved, be re-located in the grounds of the Primary School on the Kingsway. The proposed site is in the immediate vicinity of the flag pole now standing in front of the weatherboard buildings facing the Kingsway.

The request for re-location on this site is made bearing in mind the following points:

I) The memorial in its present location was erected with Departmental and War Memorials approval by members of the Miranda Parents and Citizens Association.

II) The inscription on the tablet specifically identifies it with the school and many of the past pupils of the school have paid regular homage to 'their heroes' of earlier school days at the memorial.

III) The history to the memorial and its associated flag pole is legendary among residents of the district serving the school.

IV) The proposed location will not only retain the memorial within the grounds of the school whose associates conceived it, but will enable it to be in an elevated position easily seen by all who pass.

V) It is as much a part of the school as are the buildings and pupils will be forever reminded of the sacrifice and significance which it commemorates.[61]

The Department was against having the monument moved to the new Miranda Public School site because the site was small. A departmental officer commented on 5 January 1966 that 'it is interesting to note that the RSL who state they will retain an everlasting interest in the Memorial have made no offer to contribute towards the cost of removing the Memorial'.[62] On 20 January 1966 it was noted that 'This issue has held up the disposal of the Miranda site already for some time and it does not appear as if the disposal of the war memorial is anywhere near resolved as yet',[63] and on 14 February 1967 the Department of Public Works reported:

An inspection of the War Memorial revealed it to be constructed from large sand stone blocks cemented together. To remove the Memorial would necessitate the careful cutting out of the cement joints, then each block could be removed. The estimated cost of removing the War Memorial would be $998.[64]

By 15 March 1967 the Department of Education had yielded to local pressure from Miranda residents as on that day the Assistant Minister, Wal Fife, wrote to Sutherland Shire Council: 'The Department is prepared to meet the cost of the transfer of the monument to a new position.'[65] George Carver, secretary of the Miranda sub-branch of the RSL wrote to the Minister on 27 April 1967:

At the last general monthly meeting of the Sub-Branch it was resolved 'that the War Memorial be re-located to a position in SEYMOUR SHAW PARK as near as possible to the end of Central Avenue'.[66]

The work of removing the memorial to Seymour Shaw Park had not commenced by 18 August 1967 but was expected to do so soon after that date[67] and Seymour Shaw Park is the location of the Miranda School war memorial as of 1995.

Head of Willoughby Public School strikes offensive anti-British visitor

On 13 June 1940 the head of Willoughby Public School, Frederick Alldis, wrote to Inspector Cane:

Willoughby Public School, c.1940s (see p. 57) (NSW Dept of School Education)

I desire to report that a person who gave his name as Raquet, & whose address is Molong Guest House, Forbes St. Darlinghurst called at this school on the morning of Wednesday, 12th inst; and, representing himself as the Secretary of the Japanese Ju Jitsu Society of N.S.W. asked to be allowed to demonstrate his art (?) to the boys. He was informed that unless he could produce a permit his request must be refused.

This man then became offensive making disparaging remarks about the Allies and particularly Britain. When rebuked he said, 'If I gave my true opinion of the British I would be put in gaol.' It was suggested that apparently gaol would be rather an appropriate place for one of his opinions. He made other disparaging comments and when told to leave the premises he shouted, 'Alldis, You're a crook!' I showed my resentment of his insult by striking him on the jaw and I regret that I did not feel competent to throw him down the steps!

Epithets suggestive of an extensive vocabulary in this type of language followed but eventually he left the premises.' [68]

On 3 July Raquet appeared in the North Sydney Court in connection with this incident.[69]

8

Isolation

Man threatens to blow out teacher's brains

Twenty-five-year-old Nellie Dillon was appointed as the first teacher at Warner (later Warners Bay) Provisional School in 1892.[1] In March 1895 the school was closed for a day because of a disturbance created by a man of unsound mind who, as the local paper reported,

went up to the school and commenced shouting that he wanted to see Miss Dillon about some telegrams from Sir Henry Parkes and the Governor of New South Wales. He threatened to blow her brains out if she did not stop the telegrams, as they were made up of Tommy Walker's speeches, and destroyed his lungs. Miss Dillon locked the school house door, and witnesses for a time kept him from the door, but he eventually got to the door, and kept shouting out. The school has since been closed one day in consequence of Miss Dillon being afraid of the man.[2]

After this incident the inspector wrote to his superior officer:

Ever since my visit to this school last year, I have

Warner (later Warners Bay) Public School, 1911: <u>3rd from left</u> Mary Feighan, <u>4th and 9th</u> Stan and Abe Sidebottom, <u>13th</u> Vince Feighan, <u>15th</u> Alec Odgers, <u>Teacher</u> Jonathon Longworth (From Warners Bay Public School 1892–1992, *compiled by Rose Greenwell)*

been anxious about the safety of the teacher, Miss Dillon. For some reason, she is unable to obtain suitable accommodation nearer than 4 miles distant from the school; the road is very lonely and through the bush and she has to travel it usually by herself. I am of the opinion the appointment is most unsuitable for a female ... I recommend that Miss Dillon be removed to another and more suitable school and that a male teacher be appointed to Warner; this should be done as soon as possible.[3]

In February 1896 Nellie Dillon applied for a transfer to a Sydney school (she preferred to remain at Warner than to go to another small school). She wrote that she found it 'very tiresome to have to ride four miles through a lonely bush road, morning and afternoon, I have also to cross a creek, which in rainy weather cannot be crossed. I am then forced to go around the head of the Creek which is two miles extra. There is no suitable accommodation near the school.'[4] While the inspector recommended the move, the chief inspector wrote that there were many other teachers who had prior claim to a city school. He wrote that if the parents could not provide accommodation closer than four miles from the school, the school would have to be closed when the teacher was removed.

Nellie Dillon withdrew her application for removal in June 1896 writing that she preferred to stay where she was rather than go to another Provisional School in 'some outlandish place', should one become available.[5] Now taking a different view of her circumstances, she wrote: 'I am very comfortable in my lodgings ... I have always had to ride three or four miles to the other schools I have been, and now I do not think I could do without a ride after being in school all day.'[6] She resigned from Warner School in 1898.[7]

Teacher in a wild locality is without congenial society or tutorial advantages

On 16 July 1913, applying to be moved from a pair of Half-Time Schools (Medowie and Irrawang), Clarence Milton Coombs wrote to Inspector Finney of the Half-Time Schools where he (Coombs) had previously taught from May 1910 until October 1912:

The last place I was in Blicks River & Tyringham Half Times my wife and child had to put up with considerable inconveniences. It was a wild locality situated amongst mountains & scrubs twenty miles from Dorrigo (the nearest town). Myself and family were compelled to live in a tent for some considerable time on account of not being able to get a house. Despite these drawbacks (and it was hard to be kept in such an isolated place, without any congenial society or tutorial advantages) I managed to take some of my subjects for classification.[8]

Capable 66-year-old Mary Fearby at Macarthur Public School

Mary Fearby was 66 years old[9] and had been teaching for 33 years 10 months and 3 days when she retired from Macarthur Public School near Gravesend in 1920.[10] She had been at the school since 1914 and did not suffer ill-effects from the isolation. She was a keen gardener at the school and in her own words, she 'laboured to promote & protect those things which tend to uplift the minds and aims of the children, and tend to beautify homes, by gardens, planting trees and flowers'.[11] She wrote in December 1918 that when she left the school she intended to take with her, 'surplus young trees & bushes of Old Man Salt Bush, which I have raised with the greatest care & attention'.[12]

Although Mary Fearby had no complaint about her appointment at Macarthur, the inaccessibility of the place is demonstrated in some of her explanations to the Department concerning her lateness or her closing of the school because she was unable to be there. In July 1915 in explaining why her application and doctor's certificate concerning her absence during her mother's illness at Uralla were late reaching the Department, she wrote that the doctor was meant to send her a certificate about her absence during her mother's illness earlier, but 'No mail arrived on Wednesday on account of mailman's horse falling ill, & on Thursday the mailman had left my letters behind in his overcoat pocket'.[13]

She wrote to Inspector Noble on 10 July 1916:

I was unable to reach my School, after the Midwinter Vacation, until Friday, July 7th. I came to Gravesend on Saturday July 1st, but found the river too high to cross. Although I kept in communication daily, with Gravesend, nothing could cross until Thursday. I returned to Gravesend on Friday & reached my school, the water still being up to [the] bed of [the] Sulky when crossing.[14]

In 1917 Mary Fearby sent a telegram to the Department asking if she could close the school on Friday 21 September so she could catch the train to stay with her sister at Warialda. The river rose during the week ending Friday 21 September, disrupting the mail because the mailman did not attempt to cross the river which had reached its banks. He went home instead, and she had received no reply to her telegram before Thursday 20 September. In later explaining her closing of the school on Friday 21 September she wrote that on Thursday 20 she had accepted a lift towards her destination with a local family as 'There was not much in staying at the school Friday, Sat. & Sun. when the store cart had left our potatoes behind & the mailman had been unable to bring our bread because of the river'.[15]

Teachers experience isolation at Willala

Twenty-four-year-old William Fletcher was appointed to Willala Provisional School near Boggabri in June 1918 and married in May 1919. Fletcher suffered from nervous trouble and required periods of sick leave from the school in 1921. Doctor Dent of Boggabri wrote on 19 September 1921 that 'During the past six weeks he has been unable to attend his duties & has developed into a neurasthenic ... In my opinion he needs prolonged leave of absence & I think he would be much better in a large school, he has too much time

Staggy Creek Provisional School near Inverell, teacher Eric Moeller, 1947 (NSW Dept of School Education)

here for introspection.'[16] After his recovery Fletcher was sent to Erskineville School and continued teaching thereafter at various schools until he retired in 1959.[17]

In 1928 a later teacher at Willala, Richard Ridden, put a case for an extra week's vacation (to which he would be entitled in 1929 because of the school's location although he did not know this). Among his reasons for seeking the extra week were the following:

Position: 14 miles by bush track to Boggabri, from which we are cut off in wet weather by black soil.

Conveniences: No store, post-office, or such. Two mails per week by slow sulky leaving Boggabri at 9.0 a.m., arriving at school at 4.30, &, in bad weather taking two days to reach the nearest post office—Boggabri.

Accessibility: Hired car at 2 shillings per mile, costs 28 shillings to reach the school, and another 8 shillings to get to boarding place as well. As boarding place is off the main track, and is without 'phone, the chances of obtaining a 'lift' are exceptionally small.

Boarding accommodation—In a district with a heat such as we endure—teacher's bedroom, western end of northern verandah, height of roof under 7ft, small windows open at bottom only, no protection from insect pests. Distance of boarding place from school—4 miles, present teacher walking it. One mile of loose sand, the rest black soil ...

Climate: I will leave this matter to the Department. The school site is open. No weather-sheds are provided in the playground on which there is NO SHADE. The school verandah is not as large as some country fireplaces. The through ventilation of the school is poor.[18]

Teacher late because of need to keep himself from growing melancholy at Five Mile Tree

Twenty-five-year-old Clarence Boyd, the teacher at Five Mile Tree Provisional School near Crookwell in mid-1928, was often late for school on Mondays. He had a fiancee who lived on the Abercrombie and he wrote in defence of his Monday lateness that

this place is difficult to reach in time should one be invited to spend a weekend away with friends. On this account I have had to forego many other invitations, but it is very trying to spend all one's time here as there is no company of the class I am used to within many miles of this spot, and I see no one from one week's end to another except the family I'm boarding with unless I go away for a weekend occasionally and keep myself from growing melancholy.[19]

After six months at Five Mile Tree School, Boyd resigned at the end of August 1928.[20]

9

Teachers' Extra Duties

John Middenway pulls pupil out of tank at Clarence Town

John Saunders Middenway (1855-1931)[1] was appointed to Clarence Town Public School in the Hunter Valley in 1875.[2] In his memoirs he wrote of an incident there:

Connected with the old school premises, which were replaced by a new building shortly after my appointment to the School, was an underground tank covered with slabs and provided with a trap-door. One morning while at breakfast a boy rushed into the house to tell us 'Jimmy Murphy was down the tank'. I immediately rushed to the spot about 100 yards from the house to find a number of children in a great state of excitement and a couple of men trying to remove the slabs from the tank. Looking through the trap-door I saw Jimmy some distance below the surface of the water squirming about like a drowning kitten. Relying on my ability to swim, though quite ignorant as to the depth of the tank, I jumped in without hesitation. Fortunately the water was about 5 feet deep so that the rescue was easy. I have often wondered how I would have fared had the water been a foot or two deeper, for the smooth sides of the tank afforded no foothold and the surface of the water was a few feet below the edge of the tank. Jimmy was taken to the house where mother put him to bed. Besides the ducking, my watch, which had been my father's, was spoiled.[3]

Providing a sleeping place for the little children at North Codrington

William McPherson was one of the four-year-olds attending North Codrington (later Ruthven) School

North Codrington (later Ruthven) School teacher Annie Lyle McPherson (right) with her sister Wilhelmina (left) and her cousin Lilyard (centre), c.1880s. All were teachers. (Photograph courtesy of Jessie Witchard [née McPherson])

near Coraki between 1883 and 1885 in order to boost the enrolment. He recalled that the teacher at this time, young local woman Annie Lyle McPherson, used to roll up her riding skirt to make a pillow so that the under-age children could sleep behind the door.[4]

Jane Hackett collects Department's goods from the closed Swan Bay School

At Port Stephens the Swan Bay (later Mulwee) School, which had been worked as a Half-Time School with Aliceton (later Karuah) School, closed for nine years in June 1890.[5] A few months after its closure, teacher Jane Hackett was required to go to the closed school building to get the Department's goods as the building belonged to the residents who had erected it. From her Half-Time School at Aliceton (later Karuah) where the goods were to be used, she wrote:

I was obliged to rent a boat and go with two boys to Swan Bay for the school material on the 19th August. I left early in the morning with the intention of being back in time for school, but the wind blew so strongly that we could not return back across the Bay until sundown when it lulled. I paid five shillings for the boat; gave the boys two shillings and sixpence each and a man two shillings and sixpence for assisting.[6]

John Anstey and the pit toilets at Wyalong

John Anstey, a married man aged 37, was the first teacher at Wyalong Public School, being appointed there in September 1894.[7] Anstey's parents lived in Lismore and he went there for the Christmas vacation at the end of 1895 to attend the wedding of one of his two brothers who were also teachers.[8] While he was there he received a telegram from the Department stating: 'Police report water closets at Public School Wyalong in such a filthy state as to be very offensive to passers by & a menace to the health of the vicinity will you order steps to be taken to abate the nuisance'.[9] On receiving this telegram, Anstey later wrote that he had

wired the Constable in charge to procure the key of the school which was in charge of Mr Moloney's brother-in-law [Ernest Moloney was the pupil-teacher at the school], and to obtain the disinfectant which is in the School Room and thoroughly disinfect the premises, as I had no idea what had occurred in the buildings during my absence. The Constable was unable to obtain the key, and, owing to the offensive odour emitted, he procured some lime, had it used in the pits which remedied the foulness.[10]

Anstey also reported that 'after hot oppressive days an offensive odour arises from the premises adjacent to Slee Street and I have always been most careful to neutralise this as far as possible'.[11]

This problem recurred and on 15 April 1896

'School's Out', Wyalong, 1906 (Copy donated by M. Mackrell and held by NSW Dept of School Education)

Anstey reported that another complaint had been made by the police. He wrote:

Since the complaint made in January the W.Cs [water closets] have been disinfected on alternate days and thoroughly cleaned out daily, but owing to the decomposition of the nightsoil during the Summer a very offensive odour arises at times and is most unpleasant. I am of opinion that this is partly due to the shallowness of the pits. Typhoid fever has broken out in the household of a person living close to the school premises and owing to this complaints have been made to the police by the residents of the neighbourhood.[12]

On this occasion Inspector Thomas advised early action by the Department 'as the police intend to prosecute the Teacher for allowing a nuisance on the premises'.[13] By 13 June 1896 the pits had been emptied and the police had issued a certificate stating that they were satisfied.

On 21 June 1896 Anstey applied for sick leave because of an attack of pleurisy. On 4 July William Wiseman, the assistant teacher reported that Anstey was in a critical condition and on 6 July Wiseman sent a telegram to the chief inspector:

The Head Teacher Mr John Anstey died this morning. I suggest closing the school for four weeks on account of this, of my removal [Wiseman was being transferred to Canterbury Superior Public School] and of building operations [the builder was about to commence additions to the school] but I will stay here till Thursday to know whether you wish me to take charge or go to Canterbury.[14]

On the same day Wiseman wrote that 'Mrs Anstey who has four young children depending on her, would like to put in an application for appointment as sewing mistress'.[15] The records of Wyalong School do not show whether this application was ever made formally and, if so, whether it was successful.

Department rules that teacher and pupils should keep the school ground clear of growth

On 2 May 1901 the teacher at Medowie Public School, 44-year-old Sara Cole,[16] successfully

Pupils planting trees at Dorrigo Public School, 1947 (NSW Dept of School Education)

requested the Department to pay, for the second time, for clearing the school ground of 'the suckers, thorny shrubs, rank undergrowth and dead timber which render it not only unsightly; but a source of discomfort and danger'.[17] The deputy chief inspector noted on this occasion that 'The children, under the teacher's direction, should keep the ground clear in future'.[18]

A few weeks later a parent wrote to the Department complaining that her children were being made to pull out scotch thistles instead of doing school work and that their clothes were getting dirty in the process.[19]

On 8 July 1901 Sara Cole gave her side of the matter:

I have never, at any time, set her children or any of the other pupils to pull out weeds or do any work whatsoever, out of doors during school hours; nor have I at any time set them work or punishment by which they need soil their clothes or be rendered 'unpleasant'.

I devised a new punishment for Talking, Playing, or suchlike misbehaviour in school; together with late attendance without reasonable excuse. This was, to gather a number of young Scotch Thistles, or other noxious weeds with which the playground is infested. The Thistles were very young and innocent of thorns and the 'Tommy Hards', or 'Cobblers Pegs', with their smooth cane-like stems easy, and not unpleasant, to pull up. They are covering the ground in tens of thousands, and, when allowed to grow, form a dense thicket some four or five ft high ...

As for soiling their clothes while doing it, I can remember no instances where a child soiled even a white pinafore over it.

In a communication received by me from the Chief Inspector dated 12th June last, with reference to the clearing of school ground, the following appears as a foot-note 'In future, the children under your direction should keep the ground clear'. How I am to accomplish this except by the means already adopted I know not, as the class of children under my direction are built on the plan of doing as little as possible except for hard cash. Out of my own pocket I have paid them as much as half a crown

for rooting out Scotch Thistles in the school ground during one dinner hour. Then there were no complaints, and things went merrily; but teachers of small schools cannot keep that up ...

Thousands of young plants are now springing up, and will soon need attention. I trust if the Department of Public Instruction disapproves of the means adopted by me; I may; at the same time; have the value of their advice as to the best course to take.[20]

Sara Cole's explanation was accepted by the Department but the records do not indicate any alternative directions the Department had for keeping the ground clear.

Ernest O'Reilly and pupils bury stones in White Cliffs School playground

Ernest O'Reilly was the first teacher at White Cliffs School, 60 miles north of Wilcannia, and was head of the school from 1895 until January 1908.[21] As at 1996 he is the teacher who has been head of White Cliffs School for the longest time.[22] Ernest O'Reilly was, incidentally, the father of famous Australian bowler Bill O'Reilly, who was born on 20 December 1905[23] at White Cliffs,[24] and who was himself a departmental teacher from 1926 until February 1935.[25]

Upon appointment in January 1895 Ernest O'Reilly was granted a special allowance of £24 as Inspector McKenzie wrote that 'The conditions of life are rough and far from agreeable, and the cost of living is high'.[26] Described by Inspector Nolan in 1898 as 'a trustworthy young man',[27] O'Reilly worked under what Inspector Drummond wrote in 1901 were 'rather trying conditions'[28] because of the climate; the remoteness of the locality; the fact that White Cliffs was an opal field; the over-crowding of the school; and difficulties in getting materials to the place during periods when the Darling River, between Bourke and Wilcannia, was not navigable by steamer.

In 1903 O'Reilly applied to purchase two new rakes as the ones which had been purchased four years earlier were broken and useless. He was asked by Inspector Fraser to give a full account of why

White Cliffs township, 1898. The ground is strewn with 'gibbers'—rounded liver-coloured, weather-worn siliceous stones. (From A Guide to White Cliffs, *Copyright c.1986 White Cliffs Parents and Citizens Association; published by Development and Advisory Publications of NSW, Wheelers Lane, Dubbo)*

the rakes were needed. His request was successful after he wrote on 18 November:

The surface of our ground is covered with an alluvial soil scattered through which are numbers of round stones. These go down to a depth of about eighteen (18) inches. Through the playing of the children the soil becomes powdered and on the first windy day is blown away, leaving the stones on the surface. We then rake them into heaps and bury them in holes sunk in various places on the ground, about five (5) feet deep. We use the dirt from such holes to blind the surface in other parts of the ground.

By keeping continually at them, we keep the ground in a fair condition, but if left for any time, the surface presents the appearance of a stony desert.[29]

Female teacher, aged 57, and pupils make posts from bush trees to mend school fence

On 5 November 1913 Mary Gillespie, the 57-year-old teacher at Thornford (formerly Kirkdale) Public School near Goulburn,[30] wrote of her school:

The present school [building] was finished and opened in August 1890. The enrolment was 36. The first and last Teacher up to the present time is Mary A. E. Gillespie ... The School fence nearly all fell down. The posts are rotted off. The boys and I got stud posts out of the bush, and dug holes 2 ft deep beside the old post [sic]; we stood the old posts up and wired them to the stud posts. The fence will now last for two or three years. It was very hard work building up the fence; and it is not woman's work, but we did it to save the trees that we have planted, and to teach the boys to fix up their own fences.[31]

Seven passenger children ruin upholstery of Willala teacher's coupe car

In February 1945 the residents of Willala near Boggabri proposed that a teacher might drive to school by a roundabout 10½ mile route picking up

15 children on the way. The Department found this teacher/driver proposal entirely unacceptable. By November 1946, however, when Harold Smith (who had been appointed as teacher to the school in September 1945) applied for a transfer (although he stayed at the school until 1948), he wrote that he was 'travelling 7 miles each way, carrying myself and 7 children to school'.[32]

On the inspector's suggestion, the parents then offered Smith £1 a week for conveyance and he wrote in November 1946:

The offer is a very generous one but my car is in very bad order and it would cost more that I can afford to get it ready for 1947 ... My car was laid up for 4$\frac{1}{2}$ years while I was away [Smith had enlisted in the RAN in 1941 and been discharged in 1945] and its general condition is poor. Being a coupe, it gets severe treatment from the children who have to clamber into the dicky seat over the rear mudguards. The rear seat has been absolutely ruined and I estimate that after another 12 months' work, I won't have much of a car left at all.[33]

The Department then wrote that Smith 'should be regarded as a person without a motor vehicle and removed from this school. In any case the advisability of requiring him to take children in the car in its present state is questionable.'[34]

10
Deficiencies in School Buildings

School at Hinton a damp hut

In July 1877, George Sanders, then the head of North Richmond Public School, wrote to William Wilkins, secretary of the Council of Education:

About twenty five years since, the Board of National Education appointed me to the Hinton school [in the Hunter Valley]. I then found myself surrounded with seventy children in a damp hut of two rooms and an underground cellar.[1]

Walls of insecure Long Reach National School twenty degrees from the perpendicular

Inspector Thomas Harris found on his inspection of Long Reach National School near Marulan on Thursday 26 October 1865 that

the buildings comprise a school room, class-room and a hut with three rooms and a kitchen. They are of slabs with bark roofs and are much out of repair, all the windows have been destroyed and the sashes broken. From the effects of flood, the schoolhouse is very insecure, the walls incline about twenty degrees from the perpendicular.[2]

Pyree National School building so wretched that inspector is surprised that pupils attend

On 26 May 1865 Inspector Thomas Harris visited Pyree National School near Kiama and reported:

Both the schoolhouse and the Teacher's residence are wretched places. They are built of cabbage trees and in wet weather are scarcely habitable, in windy weather the work of the school is greatly inter-rupted. This want of proper accommodation seems already to have affected the Teacher's health and

it is surprising that under the circumstances so many children attend the school regularly.[3]

Poor buildings at Tucki Tucki

When Inspector Jones visited the Public School at Tucki Tucki (later Wyrallah) near Lismore in November 1868 he wrote that the school was 'conducted in a small dilapidated ill-furnished

Buildings at Long Reach National School, 1859 (Archives Office of NSW 1.403 p. 394)

building, with bark roof pervious to rain, and wooden shutters instead of glazed windows'.[4]

A new school building was erected in 1872. By 1890 this building had developed dry rot to such an extent that it was beyond repair and there was also a move to have the school on a more elevated site. Prominent local resident James Breckenridge wrote to the Department:

The site is not only objectionably close to a large public work [the saw mill], but also in a most unhealthy position—a public burying place on one side and a swamp full of decaying vegetable matter on the other.[5]

The inspector made the observation that the site could not be too unhealthy 'as Mr Breckenridge's private house at Wyrallah is across the street from it'.[6]

Bourke School moves from ballroom to stable to kitchen to timber store and back to the ballroom

Henry Rienits, the teacher at Bourke Public School from late in 1874 until May 1877,[7] wrote to the Council of Education giving an account of the buildings in which he had been obliged to conduct the school:

The Bourke Public School, after having been closed for several months, was opened by me on the 7th Sept. 1874, in a brick building, an old ball room, rented by the Council of Education ... After school had been kept in this building for about 11 months, the structure gave several signs of giving way. I may mention here that it has been built without foundation, and that the bricks are laid in mud, not in lime. [Rienits had investigated under the building and had also found hundreds of rabbits burrowing under it.] Large cracks appeared in the walls, one end wall bulged out, the chimney stood out of the perpendicular, etc. etc. Parents became uneasy and removed their children, others threatened to do so, if other accommodation were not found ... No other room being obtainable, I was obliged to carry on school in an old deserted stable, without doors and windows, the floor full of blocks and holes, the roof partly uncovered. In this disgraceful place was held our annual public

examination and exhibition ... We remained in the stable for about a month though twice driven out by rain. We were next put in what had been a kitchen, which I enlarged by building against one side of a lignum shed. Here Mr Inspector O'Byrne found us when visiting the school for annual examination and inspection ... Shortly after the inspector's visit the Local Board rented a portion of an old timber store, in which I kept school for about a year, until Mr O'Byrne's next visit in Nov. last. The building is covered with a low iron roof almost flat, which made it cold in winter and unbearably hot in summer. During the hot weather all the children had to wear their hats, as the heat from the iron made their heads painfully hot ... The floor was earthen and no amount of sweeping and watering could keep down the dust. Mr O'Byrne at a Local Board meeting pronounced the place 'an abomination' ... At the above mentioned Local Board meeting, it was determined to go back to the first schoolroom, the condemned brick building, which is still standing, and may stand for years, or fall during the first rain or gale. As soon as we went back the old feeling of fear as to its safety began to manifest itself; several Protestant parents removed their children, and sent them to the Catholic school, thus further reducing our attendances.[8]

Lack of outhouses at Codrington no excuse for teacher to leave

In 1883 Michael Nihill, who had been appointed to Codrington Public School near Woodburn, left almost as soon as he arrived. With regard to this behaviour District Inspector McCredie wrote: 'The fact that it is unprovided with a chimney and outhouses is I think no justifiable excuse for Mr Nihill's conduct in refusing to take charge of the school'.[9]

Stench of rotting cattle carcases pervades Wooram Public School

On 5 June 1886 the teacher at Wooram (later Tatham) Public School near Casino, Henry Garnett, successfully applied to be moved from the school. He wrote:

Because the locality is unhealthy, the school house being situated on the margin of a swamp, the miasma

Moredun Half-Time School near Glencoe, 1903. Sidney Staines was the teacher of the school from 1902 to 1905. (NSW Dept of School Education)

and exhalations arising from the decaying vegetable matter laying there are injurious to the health. Cattle get bogged die and are left to rot in the swamp. As many as six animals, at a time, have been left there in this manner and in proximity to the school.

I had to call the attention of the police at Casino to this matter. A constable was sent here on the 27th November ultimo; but nothing could be done in the matter as the cattle had either been skinned, or [were too] much decayed to know the brand. The carcasses were left in this state; the stench could be smelt by all in the school. When I spoke to those whom I thought were the owners to have the carcasses burnt; from the answers I received I would not do so again.

There is no thoroughfare to the school, the roads by which there were access, being through private property and for private convenience, have been completely blocked up since the commencement of the year by the land [holders]: so that the place is isolated.

The windows of the school room and the two small rooms [adjoining] are broken [having] been completely shattered in a very heavy storm that passed over here some time since, the whole of the building was very much damaged. From the broken windows, the opening between the slabs, the holes in the floor caused by the white ants, there are continual currents of air and the wet comes through, by which there is a liability to catch cold and contract a disease. The school is so begrimed with smoke and soot that it [is] gloomy and depressing.

The school buildings are on a water reserve. Cattle and horses are there, some of these cattle and horses are driven away at times by others not their owners.

It is not agreeable to live alone in an isolated place and these people about at night as I have seen them. For this and the above reasons I would not live at the school house since the commencement of the year. I had improved the place and made a garden which has been completely destroyed.[10]

The hot Nurung Public School building

In November 1887 Mary Johns, the teacher at Nurung Public School near Boorowa, wrote to Inspector Lawford: 'I most respectfully inform you that, unless the Nurung Public School is ceiled, the children cannot bear the heat of the iron during summer several are complaining already'. Inspector Lawford, however, was of the opinion that 'It has been built some two summers without any complaint being made ... I really think they might do without the ceiling.' [11]

Fierce sun on pupils at Wyalong Public School

On 1 December 1894 Harry Woods, then secretary of the Wyalong Progress Association, wrote to the Minister requesting the reconsideration of an earlier unsuccessful request for weathersheds at the Public School. He wrote: 'The children are exposed during play hours to a heat averaging over one hundred and thirty degrees without any protection whatever and it will not surprise this committee if cases of sun stroke occur as a consequence of no protection from the sun's rays having been provided for the children'.[12] The Department, however, decided that 'they can use the school to protect them from heat'.[13]

Smoke causes pupils and teacher to vacate Kirkdale School and endure the cold for the winter

On 5 November 1913, Mary Gillespie, the teacher at Thornford (previously Kirkdale) Public School near Goulburn, wrote:

In March 1889 I took charge of the Kirkdale Public. Miss Lake had resigned ... The Kirkdale School was held in the Church of England. The only means of warming the room was by means of [a] stove, and when it was alight it filled the room with smoke and we had to go outside. So we had to go without warmth during the bleak cold winter.[14]

New Vale Public School next door to a brewery

After the inspection of New Vale (later Zig Zag) Public School on Friday 20 March 1896, the inspector reported, among other things, that the 'room was unswept and undusted; that the fireplace was a receptacle for bits of rag; that the top of the press was untidy; and that the windows were not clear'.[15] Teacher Herbert Bayliss wrote in explanation:

Thursday was a very wet day and the mud which was carried in on the children's feet had been turned to dirt and dust by the warmth of the room. Mrs Bayliss was very ill on Thursday and was not able to tidy the room and as I had to go to town for medicine I could not do it. The rags in the fireplace were put there on Friday morning by myself, I had taken them from two little girls who were making rag dolls.

The girls' sewing and my own books were on top of the press.

I have the bottom sash of the windows painted and I had not cleaned the top of the windows for some time as it is of little use on account of the myriads of flies that swarm on them directly they are closed ...

I would respectfully call your attention to the fact that on account of the above named drawbacks this is a very unsatisfactory school to teach. Being so close to a large school [Eskbank—later called Lithgow] the parents do not care whether they send their children here or not as it is not much farther to go to Eskbank. The school is held in a rented building and is situated on a piece of Brewery property about 40 yds from the cellar door of the Brewery. There is always a crowd of drunk men about the place and on the play ground (which is not fenced) and as a consequence many mothers have removed their daughters from the school.[16]

Two years later, after the school was inspected on 24 October 1898, Bayliss again wrote in explanation of the lack of cleanliness of the school:

The owner of the brewery allows the children to play on any part of the land but denies that we have exclusive right to any part of it. The consequence is that I cannot prevent them [the brewery] from drawing logs and timber past the very door and the yard from being littered with refuse—straw, palings and other things. During my absence also the places at the back are made the resort of those who come to the brewery for 'free beer'. I have therefore to clean up every day to keep the premises in a clean state.[17]

Imminent collapse of Bagawa Public School building

In March 1903 the inspector of Bagawa (later Nana Glen) Public School near Coffs Harbour wrote of the old rough slab school building, which had then recently been replaced, that while it had been still in use 'a recent storm had moved the wall plate from the posts and the whole of one side was in imminent danger of collapsing at any moment'.[18]

Local member of parliament at Miranda is threatened that his vote will be nil

On 4 December 1905 Miranda resident, W. R. Carr, wrote to local member of parliament, Frederick W. A. Downes, about Miranda Public School in what the latter referred to as 'a very strongly worded letter'[19]:

I have sent you several letters & have seen you twice at the House in reference to the enlargement of the State school at Miranda, the enlargement has been promised for the last 6 months and the calling of tender [sic] have [sic] been promised for some time, now what is the cause of this disgraceful delay, the matter has been marked urgent but still the same scandalous state of affairs continue [sic], over 90 children on the roll average attendance 70 packed into a space 30 [feet] x 16 [feet], I do not know, what you are thinking about, to allow this disgraceful state of affairs to continue, and if it's not altered at once, we shall have to get the Labor members to show the matter up from the floor of the House, we are not going to rest until we get our rights in this matter, the people here are so disgusted that your vote will be nil if this is not altered at once.

last week the children received pamphlets, entitled how to prevent Consumption, this was from the Department, overcrowding is one of the causes, its a cruel thing to insult us like that, we shall hold the Department guilty if any of the children suffer from its brutal indifference, this will be a case for the Board of Health to enquire into, so you will see we have come to the last straw, [sic]

we shall appeal through the press other school [sic]

are being enlarged etc why is Miranda left in the cold? is it red tape or other influence at work against Miranda? we are going to know the reason why, and you will remember us when our last card is out. remember you are the reform party.[20]

Downes, the recipient of this letter, wrote to the Minister that 'the local warmth at the delay is, under the circumstances, not surprising'.[21] Downes notified the Minister that he would be asking questions in Parliament the next day about Miranda School where the extension of the building was then quite quickly attended to, being completed early in the following year.[22]

Steamer stuck in Darling River delays White Cliffs Public School verandah

In 1905 the Department agreed to extend the verandah of White Cliffs Public School, 60 miles north of Wilcannia, to reduce what Inspector Fraser described as 'the often almost unbearable temperature of the school (a wood and iron structure)'.[23] After a long delay before the building material for the verandah was available, the contractor for the work, A. P. Robbins, wrote on 11 November 1907 that 'the Steamer [carrying the material], is now on the river stuck, there not being surfisicant [sic] warter [sic] in the 'Darling' for any Boats to travel, to Wilcannia'.[24] The Department could offer no solution for the stuck steamer except waiting for more water in the river. It noted, however, that 'it is now two years since the verandah was promised'.[25]

The 'Ark'—Ganmain Public School building

In May 1909 the Parents and Citizens Association of Ganmain Public School near Coolamon complained that the school building 'somewhat resembled the Ark in wet weather, being surrounded by large pools of water & it is certain that it is not a fit condition for a school to be in'.[26]

Unhealthy conditions at Billinudgel Public School

Mr J. W. Banner, JP, of 'Kiveton' Billinudgel, near Brunswick Heads, wrote to the Minister on 6 July

1911 that he (Banner) had inspected the Public School and surroundings. One of Banner's criticisms of the hygiene of the school building was that 'the whole position is I claim adjacent to very unhealthy surroundings, to wit, a slaughtering yard about 3 chains away which very often is anything but Attar of Roses'.[27]

A month earlier, in June, the teacher at Billinudgel, Thomas Chawner, had renewed a previous request for a residence at the school. He wrote of the house he was living in, that

the verandah is unsafe as the railing has rotted away. The verandah is seven feet above the ground. The stove is sometimes useless and at such times we have to get our meals cooked at a neighbour's house.

At present we are without water owing to a leaky tank and we have to use the water from a creek that has flowed through more than one pig sty.

The house is not enclosed and in wet weather calves, horses, cows and occasionally pigs 'camp'

under it. Within 50 yards of the front door is a butcher's slaughter yard and boiling down establishment.[28]

On 15 July 1912 Chawner wrote to the inspector to draw attention, as he had previously done, to the fact that 'a slaughter yard is within 100 yards of the school premises. The smell of boiling fat and refuse is most objectionable.'[29]

Unsuitable accommodation was again an issue at Billinudgel in 1936. This time attention was drawn to the plight of the younger pupils whose classes were held in the weathershed. In July 1936 William Moffat, secretary of the Parents and Citizens Association, wrote to local member of parliament, Arthur Budd, enclosing photographs of the weathershed which was being used

to house the small children. You can see for yourself under what sort of trying conditions the children are suffering. On cold bleak days they are perishing—it is detrimental to their health.[30]

Weathershed used as a classroom at Billinudgel Public School, 1936 (Billinudgel School File [Archives Office of NSW ref: 5/14924])

The photographs must have made an impact. Prior to this letter, in March 1936, the Department had noted that 'as no financial provision has been made for the work [i.e., additions to Billinudgel School building], it is recommended that it stand over for review when opportunity occurs'.[31] Following the receipt of the photographs, tenders for additions and alterations were called in August.[32]

Wind beneath the pupils at Dungay Creek Public School

When Inspector Henry visited Dungay Creek (later Dungay) Public School near Murwillumbah in 1912 he wrote that

at present the boards do not fit closely together and as the building is raised about 2' 6" from the ground, it is most uncomfortable both for the children and teacher. When I visited the school a fairly cold westerly wind was blowing, and the discomfort to the pupils was very evident.[33]

Teacher and pupils rush out of creaking Collins Creek Provisional School in a storm

Twenty-year-old Leanor Lean was two years out of training school when she was appointed to Collins Creek Provisional School, near Kyogle, in September 1918.[34] In the Christmas holidays she sought an interview with the chief inspector in Sydney who noted: '[She] says school is an old shake down of a place—built by people 9 or 10 years ago—no tank—no closets—in a storm building creaked & all had to rush out—likely to fall over any day'.[35] Leanor Lean, who had been most unwilling to go Collins Creek in the first place, was probably pleased to be appointed to Laurieton Public School at the beginning of the next year.[36]

Children getting roasted and falling through the floor at Tullamore

Tullamore local resident, J. L. Wenzel, wrote many letters to the local member of parliament, E. A. Buttenshaw, concerning the unsatisfactory Tullamore Public School building. In September 1918 he asked Buttenshaw to 'place the matter before the Minister

again and shake him up a bit'. In November 1919 he wrote to Buttenshaw that 'there are between 40 and 50 children getting roasted at Tullamore'.[37] Buttenshaw agreed with Wenzel about the school. He wrote to the Minister that 'the parents ought to burn it'.[38]

Tullamore's problems had not been solved by the end of 1923 when Wenzel wrote to Buttenshaw to 'urge that a new building be gone on with as this one is becoming dangerous to the children There has been three children fallen through the boards and skinned their legs.'[39]

School in a woolshed at Lower Duncans Creek is a disgrace

When Lower Duncans Creek School near Woolomin re-opened as a Provisional School in June 1924 it did so in a screened off section of a woolshed. On 5 March 1925 R. Boyce, secretary of the Lower Duncans Creek Progress Association, wrote to local member of parliament, F. A. Chaffey, that all interested in the school were 'very anxious to see the school building started as soon as possible as the winter is coming on, & the old wool-shed where the school is held is realy [sic] a disgrace'.[40] In 1926 a beehive school building from Upper Dungowan was moved to Lower Duncans Creek for use as the school building.

Five Mile Tree Provisional School ceiling bumping up and down in the wind

In 1927 Edwin Robertson of Garraroo, Binda, wrote to the inspector about the Five Mile Tree Provisional School building near Crookwell:

the old school is very much out of repair and in my opinion unsafe as the ceiling bumps up and down with the wind and in the case of a heavy storm there is the danger of it falling in.[41]

Ceiling collapse at Gladesville

In 1937 a fanlight and portion of the ceiling fell in during lessons in one of the girls' rooms at Gladesville Public School causing a female teacher and an eight-year-old pupil to require medical treatment.[42]

Lower Duncans Creek Provisional School (see p. 74), 1948 (NSW Dept of School Education)

Too close for comfort at Austral

On 24 March 1938 the Shire Clerk of Nepean Shire, C. Cameron who had visited Austral Public School near Liverpool, wrote to the Department about the 'woeful conditions' at the school.[43] Of one classroom he wrote:

There were crowded together 42 pupils, and the Council was informed that 8 were absent. They were tiny children, aged probably up to 7 years old. They were of necessity jammed together with no space between them and it required no imagination to realize what discomfort the poor little people suffered during the recent hot weather. When asked to carry out their writing lesson, it was apparent how uncomfortable it must have been for them—the elbow of one across the chest of the next, or the arm held in an unnatural position. The children could not possibly learn the correct manner of writing. It can also be left to your imagination to realize how difficult it must be for the teacher under these conditions.

Although all doors and windows were open, the odour from all these hot little bodies was offensive, and if one child had an ailment that was in any way infectious, the conditions were such that it could not possibly help sweeping through the whole class.[44]

Cabbage Tree Island Aboriginal School building leaning whichever way the wind blows

On 29 October 1941 the school medical service had reported of Cabbage Tree Island Aboriginal School that the 'School building is very old and dilapidated—50 years old. Foundations very insecure; most of the woodwork has rotted away. The building is in a semi-dangerous condition.'[45] The teacher, Ernest Howard, was asked to report and on 18 November 1941 he wrote:

The school leans whichever way the wind blows, and, when wind is easterly, it is difficult to open the door, though same has been cut and adjusted several times. The floor springs, as children walk about, so much that the movement shakes desks and interferes with writing. It was originally a very small room, then extended, and, later a lean-to store room attached. All done about 40 years ago.

Mr Harkness was here in June last, and his attention was drawn to above. He then stated that endeavour was being made to transfer a school building from Mororo to replace the one here. Later I wrote to the Chief Inspector stating that, I could, if required, hire a lorry and take over sufficient aborigines to dismantle the building, bring same here, and re-erect. (I have done a considerable amount of building for the A W [Aborigines Welfare] Board.)

In addition to foregoing remarks re condition of building, I may add that weather boards are so perished and porous, that water has penetrated to lining boards and warped same out of position. When raining heavily water runs down <u>inside</u> wall on southern side. Several windows are broken, but sashes are too rotten to attempt repairs.[46]

Pit toilets

A serious accident at Erskineville pits

In April 1894 the concrete floor of the girls' and infants' toilet at Erskineville Superior Public School gave way during 11 o'clock recess and 27 pupils fell into the cesspit. Only one 11-year-old girl suffered serious harm. When she had been pulled out of the pit by a teacher she was found to have stopped breathing but was quickly revived although she was still receiving medical treatment weeks later.[47]

Dangerous pits at Brunswick Heads

In 1906 Tyagarah parent, Harry Everitt, complained of conditions at Brunswick Heads Public School which his children attended. Among other complaints he wrote that 'the closets are pits dug in the ground and the floor is rotting away so you might hear of some of the children being smothered in the pit if not repaired'.[48]

11

Resignation Following Inspection

Intoxicated teacher found playing billiards by inspector

On 8 March 1865 Inspector Thomas Harris paid a special visit to Kiandra National School. On 13 March he wrote:

I have the honor to report for the information of the Board of National Education, that I visited Kiandra on Wednesday, the 8th instant, for the purpose of inspecting the National School at that place ...

As I had heard at Queanbeyan and Cooma that the Teacher was addicted to drink, I gave no notice of my intended visit. Upon going to the school at 10 o'clock, A.M. I found it closed, and learned from a child in the neighbourhood that the pupils had been sent home by the Teacher, who was said to be sick. I found Mr Johnson partially intoxicated, playing billiards at an adjoining inn. I declined to have any intercourse with him upon that day. I had an interview with the Local Patrons who stated that the school had been closed without their consent being either asked for or obtained. They were aware that Mr Johnson was a drunkard, but represented that that was his only fault. I pointed out that it was a fault that neutralized every

Kiandra Public School, 1912 (From Report of the Minister of Public Instruction, *1912)*

qualification he might possess as a Teacher. On the following morning, I visited the school at nine o'clock and waited until eleven. As only three children attended, and the Teacher was drunk, I packed up all the books etc. granted by the Board, and gave them into the charge of F. Mant Esq. one of the Local Patrons. Mr Johnson told me that he did not care to retain his situation, and admitted that drinking to excess was his habit. I consider him to be totally unfit to have the charge of children, and therefore unworthy to receive public money for teaching them ...

The Local Patrons are of opinion that if a competent teacher be engaged about thirty children will attend ... I would suggest that the person nominated be told that he should be prepared to forgo most of the conveniences of life, and to resist the immoral tendencies of the place, especially that of drinking.[1]

Henry Rienits resigns from Mount Victoria Public School

Henry Rienits, the teacher at Mount Victoria Public School in the Blue Mountains in 1885, had enterprisingly taken in boarding pupils to increase the school's numbers. Some local residents objected to this but the Department had decided that there was no reason why it could not be done. When the school was visited by Inspector Lobban in April of that year, however, things did not go well. Lobban arrived unannounced on 14 April 1885 and found Rienits building a wash house at the residence after he had been warned that there should be no more additions without official approval. From then on Lobban was displeased with everything he saw during the inspection. Very late in the afternoon, after the classwork inspection, examples of sewing work were shown to Lobban by Rienits's wife. Lobban objected that there was not enough work by the younger girls and Rienits felt that Lobban spoke insultingly to his wife about this matter. That night Rienits wrote his letter of resignation, stating that 'My self respect would not allow me to retain my post after the occurrence of this evening'.[2] He later opened a successful private school of his own at Mount Victoria.[3]

Mount Victoria Public School, 1880s (NSW Dept of School Education)

Empire Day celebrations at Hornsby Public School, 1912 (NSW Dept of School Education)

Melancholy Joshua Ford resigns because of bad inspection reports

Joshua Ford was appointed to Dungay Creek (later Dungay) Public School near Murwillumbah in 1895.[4] On 14 August 1895 the school was inspected by Peter Board who wrote that the 'results of examination together with the absence of recorded lessons in Lesson Register show that instruction in some subjects has been neglected to a serious extent'.[5] In explanation of these defects, Ford wrote on 31 October 1895:

The subjects were not neglected as they may appear to have been but ... the children displayed very slight mental effort in answering questions and made mistakes where I expected them to be correct.

The entries in the Registers were incomplete and some lessons were not recorded, for, since being here, until the Inspector's visit and even now, I have been so despondently melancholy when alone, that when the children had left the school in the evening, I found it an almost impossible task to do the slightest amount of writing, for I then became so depressed with melancholy that five or ten minutes writing has frequently taken two hours, and two hours and a half and even then been incomplete.

After my School Registers had fallen in arrears, many times I have tried to devote Saturday to completing them, I also tried to devote part of the Easter and Midwinter holidays to completing them; but, after spending four of five days at the school I had to take my horse and ramble to save myself from utter collapse.

Within the last fortnight, however I have felt in better spirits, and hope to be able to show far better results in the next inspection, for the children appear to be acquiring a better liking for their lessons as they advance.

I did not reply to your letter before, because whenever I attempted to do so, I felt so horribly miserable that I could not write the words.[6]

Ford's explanation was not considered satisfactory. His classification was reduced from 3A to

3B and the classification of the school was reduced from an 8th Class to a 9th Class from 1 December 1895.

Ford was away from school and the school was presumably closed from 20-31 January 1896. He wrote: 'on Saturday 18th inst, I accidentally fractured my collar-bone, whilst playing with the Dungay Creek Cricket Club in a Cricket match on Murwillumbah Park, and in consequence I am unable to conduct School. I have the honor to enclose a certificate from Dr R. Macdonald.'[7]

Peter Board again inspected the school on 19 August 1896 and noted, among other defects, that the 'interior of the room is untidy; lesson guides— bad ... Organization for which the Teacher is responsible—indifferent. Demeanour of pupils— mentally inactive.[8] In resigning his position as a result of this inspection, Ford wrote:

I can give no satisfactory explanation for the defects noted by **Mr Inspector Board.** I have suffered so severely from melancholy and despondency which have of late been intensified by anxiety caused by private troubles, that when alone I have been almost utterly unable to concentrate my attention upon things which it was my duty to do, thus the Lesson Register, Guides and Time Table have been neglected. Many difficulties have been thrown in my way by the apparent wish of some of the parents to get all the work about home out of the children that they possibly could, and the children are mostly not an ordinarily intelligent lot, under the most favourable circumstances.

However, the most bitter part to me is that I have failed to achieve that which I thought I could accomplish—enliven the children, and gain a satisfactory report from the Inspector by meritor- ious work. Feeling I have failed this time, and seeing no chance to succeed as a teacher while under the influence of melancholy, I beg to be allowed to resign my position as Teacher, at the end to the ensuing quarter.[9]

The Department accepted Ford's resignation from 31 October 1896. On 4 November he wrote to the Department from Leichhardt, his letter being to accompany his repayment to the Depart- ment of £1 of the £2 he had been paid as travelling expenses when he had come to Dungay Creek.[10] This repayment was necessary because he had not been at the school long enough to justify the Department's full payment of his expenses.

12

Difficulties in Supporting Dependants

Wife and six children destitute after Port Macquarie teacher drowns

In May 1874 Port Macquarie Public School teacher, John Hume, drowned in the sea. The chairman of the local school board reported Hume's drowning to the Council of Education:

He [Hume] and some children of the school went for a picnic to a place called 'Nobbies' where there is a large cave in which the water of the ocean pours over a narrow natural bridge covered at each influx of the waves. The day was rather stormy and the sea remarkably rough and so bad that no man in his senses would have attempted to cross and yet he did, lost his balance and fell into the boiling surge. My friend Mr Gardner [the teacher at Huntingdon and Beechwood Half-Time Schools] regardless of his own peril endeavoured to save him and lost his own life. Both were swept away in about two minutes and not a trace left behind. All that has since been found is a portion of the shirt and a part of the vest of Mr Gardner.[1]

Hume left a widow and six children destitute. A notice in the *Sydney Morning Herald* of 12 June 1874 stated that William Wilkins, secretary of the Council of Education, would take donations for a fund to assist the family. The notice also mentioned Henry Gardner 'who lost his own life in a desperate attempt to save Mr Hume'.[2]

Young Elizabeth O'Keefe supporting a family of seven

In 1890 Elizabeth O'Keefe, then in her second year of teaching since leaving the training school, applied for removal from Maclean Public School and for permanent appointment to a school accessible from Sydney by rail. Her reason was that she wished to be able to render more assistance to her family as her father was suffering from an 'apparently incurable illness'.[3] With reference to her obligation to support the family of seven, Elizabeth O'Keefe wrote that 'with my present salary I find it impossible to supply their wants'. Not being granted a move at this time, O'Keefe was appointed to Ballina Public School as infants mistress in January 1892. She married Thomas Russell in 1898 and continued as infants mistress at Ballina until the end of 1919.[4]

Infants mistress unable to afford daily trip from Paddington to Kogarah

On 28 March 1893 Florence Edwards wrote to Inspector Johnson from Kogarah Superior Public School:

I have the honor to apply for removal from my present position as Mistress of the above-mentioned school to a similar position in the Infants' Dept of some school nearer to my home at 19 Liverpool St Paddington.

My reason for making this application is, that at present I am the sole support of my family & the daily journey to & from Kogarah, or the necessity for living there, makes a serious reduction in my salary.[5]

Ellen Kenny of Stockton School is killed by a coal train, leaving dependent mother

Forty-year-old Ellen Kenny, an assistant teacher at Stockton Public School, whose then deceased father had also been a teacher, was killed by a coal train as

Pruning lesson at Carlingford Public School, early 1900s (NSW Dept of School Education)

she walked across the railway line at Hamilton Railway Station in August 1894.[6] Inspector Flashman presided at a meeting called to discuss plans for rendering 'tangible assistance' to Ellen Kenny's mother who had been entirely dependent on her.[7] It was noted that 'The Railway Commissioners have repudiated any claims for compensation, and though the deceased lady has been a contributor to the Superannuation Fund from its institution, her mother is not entitled to receive a single penny'.[8]

Inspector Flashman made special reference to Ellen Kenny's 'kind and lovable nature, which impressed everyone who came into contact with her'.[9]

Teacher's mother asks for special treatment for her daughter who supports her

In January 1899, Judith Aria, who had previously taught at Martins Creek Public School near Paterson from April 1897 until September 1898, and who was then at St Ives Public School, was just reaching the end of six months' leave on account

of illness. On 19 January her mother asked that she be given another six months' leave

in consequence of the weakness of her mind rendering her unfit to resume duty at present, As I believe that this has arisen in consequence of the devotion to her work, combined with the lonely surroundings and unsuitable food in her country appointment at Martins Creek. I trust that the Minister may see fit to regard this as a 'Special Case' and grant such pay as he deems the case deserves, especially as I am a Widow and entirely dependent on my daughter's salary.[10]

The request was successful and six months later, on 16 June, Aria's mother wrote again:

My daughter's leave of absence is up tomorrow she is still ill. Will you kindly give her another week's leave. Martins Creek was so unsuited for a female ... [she] could not get board close to the school and had to go to Paterson five miles distant it was too far to walk, so she had to get a bicycle then she could not afford to pay for it and her board and send me my allowance she is my main support.[11]

After St Ives, Judith Aria taught at several more schools on Sydney's north shore and resigned in 1906 on account of ill health.[12]

Teacher dies of influenza leaving a wife and five children and no superannuation

When William Hall, who had a wife and five children, was appointed head of Wyalong Public School in March 1919 there was no school residence although the townspeople had been agitating for one for many years and it was soon to be erected. He was forced to stay at Wyalong Hotel, a very expensive undertaking for him. On 5 July that year, applying for a living allowance he wrote that he was

paying now £5/10/- and £1.2.6, total £6/12/6. This does not include washing.

Contributions to the Superannuation Fund will lessen my resources. My salary is £348 p.a. plus £36 p.a. sewing allowance for my wife. After paying for Board, there is not much left for clothing and the other necessaries for a family of 2 adults and 5 children.[13]

On 16 September 1919 Hall wrote to Chief Inspector Dawson:

I have been impelled to write to you a personal letter because although in May last the Minister promised me an allowance in aid of board and my receipts of expenditure were sent in over two months since I have no intimation of the decision.

I have been here now six months, have paid my way all the time: but am now at the end of my resources, that is to say I cannot provide clothing etc now needed.

I simply place this matter in your hands quite unofficially.

I believe I am right in saying that you will find the papers in the District Works Office Cootamundra. It is really to state this latter fact that I have written.

ps. Mr Sontar architect has been carrying the papers round with him for the past 6 or 7 weeks.[14]

As he could no longer afford to pay super-annuation, Hall withdrew from the fund. He died of

pneumonia on 16 October 1919 and four days later G. Bland, who was secretary of the Wyalong Parents and Citizens Association, wrote to the director of education:

Mr Hall contracted influenza about 3 weeks ago [the municipality of Wyalong had been declared an infected influenza area in June 1919] but fought against it—trying to attend to his school duties as he considered it obligatory upon him to keep going to prepare his scholars for the forthcoming Qualifying Certificate examination. The school had been allowed to remain understaffed ever since he came to Wyalong about 8 months ago, and he has had an uphill fight all that time to keep the school at the high mark to which it has attained, which strain severely undermined his health, and left him an easier prey to pneumonia.

And the ravages of the recent influenza epidemic, which necessitated the closing of the schools for some time, threw the scholars back in their studies, to overcome which he attended his school during the Michaelmas holidays until he was too ill to continue. He became seriously ill last Tuesday and was removed to the local hospital, at which institution he died on the following Thursday.

Mr Hall was a teacher of exceptional ability, in addition to his sterling qualities as a townsman, and by his strict attention to his duties, the interest he took in the welfare of his school, and in the care and education of the children he gained the deep respect of all with whom he came in contact in connection with his profession. Mrs Hall has, by her husband's death, been left with five children dependent upon her.[15]

Hall's widow, aged 30,[16] appealed to the Department and then to her local member of parliament for financial provision because of the circumstances whereby, since coming to Wyalong, the family had been forced to live in a hotel because there was no residence. Because of this expense, and because of the fact that he had not received a living allowance from the Department, her husband had been forced to withdraw from the Superannuation Fund. Finally the Minister directed in March 1920 that £200 be placed on the next estimates for Mrs Hall's benefit.[17]

13

Teachers' Unusual Behaviours

Teacher far from sober during inspection

When Gunning National School, where Arthur Burton was the teacher, was inspected by Thomas Harris on 11 April 1865 he found:

The discipline of this school is extremely lax. When I entered it, the Teacher was reading a newspaper, and seemed to be very far from sober. He acknowledged to me that he was addicted to drink, and stated that he should resign his situation at the end of the current quarter. During the day, he made some faint attempts to conduct the school, but there was the absence of anything like effort on his part. His hands were rarely out of his pockets. From his intemperate habits, I consider him to be totally unfit to occupy the position of Teacher of a School.[1]

Hot-tempered teacher attacks pupils and adults

John Thomas Green was the first teacher at Bulahdelah (later Green Gully) Public School at Bulahdelah when it opened in 1868. In applying earlier for a temporary teaching job Green had stated that 'I must earn my bread'.[2]

By March 1869 the attendance, despite Green's organised and effective running of the school, was falling partly because of Green's bad temper. He reportedly dragged one little boy across the floor of the school room by his ears. He did not endear himself to a member of the local school board by telling him to sign the quarterly attendance return or Green would give him 'a lick on the chops' and by then throwing 'two missiles of wood' at him.[3]

After this the Council of Education decided to dismiss Green from the service from the end of June 1869. Inspector Allpass wrote that he would

not have recommended this dismissal except for the 'absurd and insolent manifesto to the people of Myall'[4] that Green had written. Green, however, was not dismissed. A local parent, Mr Gooch, wrote that Green, 'in comparison with his [denominational school] predecessor [is] a very respectable and temperate man, quite suitable for the position he is in'.[5] Gooch also sought

to call the attention of the Council to the trouble Mr Green has had in establishing his school. The children on the Myall are wild and unruly, and some of them were never in a school before. Those who were, under our ex-teacher were in the habit of seeing him intoxicated and disorderly, almost every week, and used to be well trounced by him, while they were in school.[6]

Green stayed on and in August 1870 applied to be moved 'nearer to Sydney where one may be able to attend the House of God'.[7] He was not moved and after another series of complaints about his behaviour he was to be dismissed on 31 December 1870 because of a letter with twelve signatures complaining of Green's conduct at a public meeting. He had lost his temper and fired abuse at many of the people present, saying that one was 'an old dotard and in his second childhood' and that others were 'numbskulls and emptyheaded'.[8] To another he said that 'he would like to be his tutor and he would give it to him over the backside'.[9] The letter of complaint said that 'through his misconduct the people got so excited that serious consequences might have ensued if the Police had not been there'.[10] The policeman subsequently denied that Green had been disorderly at the meeting and then one group of school board members, who still supported Green, demanded the dismissal of members who had opposed Green for their 'uncouth and cowardly behaviour towards the teacher'.[11] Again the Council changed its mind about dismissing Green and he was given another chance and sent to Llandillo Public School near Penrith from where he resigned in 1872.[12]

He was re-employed in 1874 and remained teaching until retirement, but not without incident. In 1889, at Bungwall Flat (later Bungwahl) Public School near Forster he was informed of the necessity for 'conciliating the goodwill of the parents and ... raising the efficiency of the school by the next inspection'.[13] In the following year he was 'suspended and called upon to shew cause against dismissal for insubordination'.[14]

In 1896, then at Arakoon Public School near South West Rocks, where he had received several warnings about the need for better results, he was 'called upon to shew cause against dismissal for inefficiency & misconduct (excessive corporal punishment)'.[15]

Moonan Brook teacher so drunk he couldn't remember writing his resignation

John Field was appointed as teacher of Moonan Brook Provisional School in the Upper Hunter valley when it opened in 1869.[16] In December 1870 he wrote his first resignation which he later withdrew, and in May 1872 he wrote the second which he also withdrew. The second withdrawal of resignation was the cause of some suspicion on the part of the inspector who wrote: 'with my knowledge of Mr Field, I am constrained to believe that he was not sober at the time of penning his resignation.'[17]

After an inquiry into the matter the inspector wrote:

Mr Field admits the he wrote his resignation while under the influence of drink—that he was so drunk as to have no recollection of having written it, and only became aware of the fact when in receipt of a communication from the Council requiring him to state from what date his resignation was to take effect.[18]

Popular teacher, Mark Lee, and pupils at Moonan Brook Public School, Upper Hunter Valley, 1895 (NSW Dept of School Education)

The inspector was sympathetic, however, and wrote: 'He is ... far from being an habitual drunkard, and, from what I hear, becomes very easily intoxicated—two or three glasses of liquor being sufficient to overcome him'.[19] The local residents also supported him and he remained as teacher until 1878 when his final resignation was accepted.[20]

Billiard-playing infidel Joseph O'Brien at Bourke

Joseph O'Brien had been appointed teacher of Bourke Public School in January 1873. He resigned without official notice in May 1874 and Inspector O'Byrne reported:

The failure of the late teacher was accounted for by
a) His general want of attention to business.
b) His propensity to billiard playing and other games at which he often remained up all night and was unfit to attend to his school duties the following days.

c) That he openly declared himself an infidel thereby causing a number of the most respectable inhabitants to lose confidence in him. The attendance dwindled down to six or eight pupils before the school was closed.[21]

Trouble-stirring Susanne Bardwell

Susanne Mary Bardwell is well documented in the *Votes and Proceedings of the New South Wales Legislative Assembly*. She appears throughout her time in the New South Wales state education system to have been first selected, and then favoured and protected by William Wilkins, secretary of the Council of Education and later under-secretary of the Department, with whom she was on friendly terms,[22] and upon whom she called when power was needed to advantageously solve the difficulties she created. When in 1882 the chief examiner gave as one of his reasons for discouraging older recruits to teaching the fact that they were 'difficult to

Redfern Public School, c.1880s (NSW Dept of School Education)

manage'[23] he may very well have had Susanne Bardwell in mind. Wherever she went trouble was stirred. Such trouble invariably involved her insubordination to her superior officers and her bad treatment of those who were subordinate to her.

Susanne Bardwell had received her education mainly in Paris and Bonn.[24] She had studied 'French, German, Italian, vocal and instrumental music, some of the physical sciences and general literature'.[25] She had had experience as a governess and also in teaching at a ladies' school and in a private school.[26]

She had come to train at the Fort Street Training School in the late 1870s, but after four months there she was obliged to leave because of illness.[27] She had, however, favourably impressed the training school and the Council of Education who were then on the look-out for a person who had had 'the education and training of a lady',[28] to act as assistant and girls' supervisor at the training school. In April 1878 she commenced duties as the female assistant to the training master.[29] Trouble developed with the training master, John Wright, who had been unhappy about Bardwell's appointment. In December 1878 she wrote to William Wilkins, secretary of the Council of Education:

It is scarcely necessary for me to say that in the present position of affairs it is almost impossible for me to do my duty effectively. A defenceless woman open to the insult of every ill-bred, vulgar, malcontent student, who tries to crush her and everything which interferes with his animal propensities, and who knows that his efforts to carry out Mr Wright's threat to drive me from my position will win him favour.[30]

Susanne Bardwell complained in particular about the behaviour of the female students-in-training. Their examiner, however, wrote: 'I may say that the gaiety and discretion shown by the female candidates, considering their youth, have been to me a matter of gratification'.[31] After considerable trouble, Bardwell was moved from the training school.

She was awarded a 1B teacher classification by examination in September 1879 and appointed to Redfern Public School as mistress of the girls' department in November of that year.[32] After six months she was instructed to take charge of the girls' department at Crown Street Public School in May 1880.[33] She was gazetted as mistress of Crown Street (Girls) in July and a note was made on her teacher record: 'Formal appt sent & urged to qualify herself for the position'.[34] On 1 October she was 'Placed in Class 1A (Revision of 1B exam papers)'.[35]

Hostilities ensued at Crown Street Public School with the head of the school, John Rooney, and an inspectorial hearing was held at which each teacher preferred charges against the other. Each side sought witnesses and statements. One of the statements obtained by Rooney was from Mary Booth of Wallsend Superior Public School who had been at Crown Street School in 1880. On 24 May 1881 Mary Booth wrote to him:

Notwithstanding the unpleasant duty of making charges against any person, I feel bound to answer your request as truthfully as memory will allow me.

I have while in attendance at Crown-street Girls School, seen Mrs Bardwell manifest great violence of temper in the presence of the children towards the subordinate teachers, especially towards Miss Holmes and Miss Chaffer.

As for myself, for some little time Mrs Bardwell's manner towards me was both harsh and unkind; but, other than that short period, I received no ill-treatment.

I have known her scold teachers before the girls, and accuse them of not doing their duty.

I have known her stamp her feet in temper in school.

Repeatedly I have noticed the teachers crying and fretting on account of her harshness, and I have been convinced that the school girls noticed and were aware of the reason of it.

They have even ventured to speak to me of her unlady-like behaviour, but I of course forbade them ever speaking of such a thing again.

I received your letter while very busy, and have had to answer it in the station office very hurriedly.[36]

At the inquiry 19-year-old assistant teacher, Mary McLimont stated:

I received a letter from the Chief Inspector instructing me to go to Redfern ... I then asked Mrs Bardwell if I might go to the Office; she refused to let me go; she displayed bad temper towards me in the presence of the girls assembled on the playground; she closed her fist in my face, and said that Mr Rooney had denied telling me to go to Redfern.[37]

Susanne Bardwell wrote to the Minister on 11 June 1881:

It is now eleven days since the inquiry began, and my health has been seriously affected by its unnecessary protraction, by the strain on my nerves and by seeing my witnesses overawed by the great number of teachers whom Mr Rooney has had summoned from various schools in Sydney and suburbs and even from the Newcastle district.

These teachers, while waiting on Mr Rooney, play at rounders and skipping ropes; and when the question was asked in the Court how they could be spared from their duties, and what might be the expense to the State of keeping them so long in idleness, Mr Rooney's reply was, as near as possible, as follows: 'The expense is nothing to the State, and it matters not what it may be to Mrs Bardwell'.[38]

While Inspectors Johnson and Morris, who had conducted the inquiry, considered that both teachers were at fault and recommended that both Rooney and Bardwell should be 'admonished as to their future behaviour' and removed to separate schools,[39] the Minister, Sir John Robertson, who was apparently influenced by Wilkins, ruled that Bardwell be exonerated from blame.[40] Reporting the way in which Bardwell had announced this outcome at the school, Rooney wrote on 13 August 1881 to Chief Inspector Edwin Johnson:

I do myself the honour to report, for the information of the Honourable Minister for Public Instruction, the following occurrence which took place in the Girls' Department of this school:—

Mrs Bardwell left the school at 10 o'clock a.m. on Thursday 12th instant, and on her return two hours afterwards [she sometimes went to see Wilkins during school hours], waved a letter she held in her hand, and thus addressed the pupils in the main room:—'I have gained a glorious victory—Sir John Robertson has completely exonerated me. Show your approbation by clapping. All Mr Rooney's accomplices will be punished—he has been turned away from this school.' Mrs Bardwell then visited each class-room, repeating what she said in the main room. To one class she said, 'I dare say you are afraid of Mr Rooney's friends who are by, but he has to leave this school; all who are glad, clap hands.' She led off the clapping herself.

Trusting you will lay this letter before Sir John Robertson at your earliest convenience.[41]

Having been appointed back to Redfern Public School in 1882 Bardwell clashed with, and verbally attacked, Inspector Jones while he was conducting

First page of letter from Bernard Baron Von Sandon to the Council of Education, 1879 (Wandook School File [Archives Office of NSW ref: 5/18014])

an inspection of the school. In his report Inspector Jones noted of Bardwell that 'the teacher is elderly, respectable and intelligent ... but she is somewhat self-willed, over-bearing and indiscreet and is not satisfactorily punctual'.[42]

In January 1883 Susanne Bardwell was 'under suspension for her conduct in connection with a certain pamphlet'.[43] She was appointed to the position of First Assistant at Newtown Public (girls') School in September 1883 and resigned in 1884,[44] having made quite an impact on those with whom she had come in contact in the New South Wales public education system.

Extravagant Prussian aristocrat Bernard Baron Von Sandon at Wandook School

Bernard Baron Von Sandon (he later spelt his name 'Von Sanden'), a Lutheran, had been born at Tussainen castle in East Prussia and was 28 years of age when, in 1879, he applied to the Council of Education to be employed as the teacher of Wandook Provisional School near Deniliquin.[45] His predecessor at the school, Augustin Chauffourier, who was employed there by the parents rather than by the Council of Education, had resigned by 27 March 1879. Chauffourier, who had had previous unsatisfactory service with the Council of Education, was described by Charles Brown, secretary of the Wandook school board, as 'a very able man but unfortunately intemperate'.[46] Inspector O'Byrne went further, describing Chauffourier as 'an irreclaimable drunkard'.[47]

In November 1878 a local resident, John Hanlon, who had great interest in the school and provided

Pages 2–3 of letter from Bernard Baron Von Sandon to the Council of Education, 1879
(Wandook School File [Archives Office of NSW ref: 5/18014])

the building in which it operated, wrote to Inspector O'Byrne asking him 'to be kind enough to use your influence in procuring us a good Male Teacher & if he was acustomed [sic] to Music I Would Pay him extra to teach my Children Music, that is on the piano'.[48] In March 1879 Charles Brown, secretary of the local school board wrote that 'A number of the Scholars are from 12 to 16 years of age and should the council entertain our application I would respectfully suggest that a male Teacher be appointed'.[49]

In answer to questions about his background asked of him by the Council of Education, Bernard Baron Von Sandon wrote:

I received my early education under the guidance of a private tutor. When fourteen years old I entered the Military College in Berlin where I completed my earlier studies. Received a commission in the Prussian Guards in 1868 ... I held a commission in the 4th Uhlan Guards for 6 years 6 months. Left my regiment in 74 and came to Australia.[50]

During his time in the Prussian Military he had, he wrote, been a 'Teacher of Mathematics at the School of War for uncommissioned officers in Nuisse, Prussia—18 months'.[51] He wrote that he spoke 'English, French, Italian, Spanish, and German, am a good Latin and Greek scholar and a fair Mathematician, and am also a Musician, the ordinary branches of elementary education are naturally not neglected'.[52] He wrote in November 1879 that his current means of subsistence were by 'Teaching and private means, forwarded from my mother to her agents'.[53]

After living in Victoria he had, in his own words, been 'Charged in a Criminal Court of Law in Victoria with false pretences. Sentenced to three years imprisonment. Released after a short time under a free pardon. Such proviso made by judge. Paying of debt.'[54] Inspector Hookins later wrote of this episode:

His crime for, which he suffered, seems to have been this:—Pushed by his creditors, and at the same time, advised of a large remittance coming from his mother in Germany; he altered a word in the telegram; and by these means, induced certain money-lenders to advance him money, wherewith to satisfy his creditors. The remittance did actually come: and the money lenders were paid: but he was charged with obtaining the money by falsifying a telegram.[55]

He had then gone for help to the Victoria Discharged Prisoners Aid Society, the agent for which, George Wilmot, wrote of him that 'previous to his getting into trouble, I knew very little of him; but I believe he was rather erratic, but never vicious really'.[56] He then worked as a private live-in tutor to the children of Richard Holmes of Brassi Farm, Deniliquin, leaving there in March 1879. Holmes wrote of him that

he has lived with my family as tutor for nine months ending March 1st of the present year; during which time the progress made by the children under his tuition was highly satisfactory, while his own conduct and bearing were such as became a gentleman.[57]

On 28 April 1879 Von Sandon mentioned, in writing to William Wilkins, the secretary of the Council of Education, to seek employment:

I am a gentleman by birth and education—having some considerable abilities,—who for some reason or other is compelled to earn his living—and begs to offer his services to the Council as a teacher ... I am a thoroughly sober man—but perhaps adicted [sic] to extravagances—only too common in the class of Society to which I belong.[58]

Von Sandon began teaching at the school at Wandook on 13 April 1879 although the Council of Education had not given approval for this. On 6 May the secretary of the local school board, Charles Brown, wrote that Von Sandon 'continues to give satisfaction both as to sobriety and ability ... I don't think we are likely to improve on him.'[59] As the only other likely candidate the Council of Education had under consideration for teaching at Wandook School, Mr Beddy of Wanganella, was, Inspector Hookins wrote, 'said not be sober in his habits',[60] Von Sandon was given a trial appointment to the school.

Having received notice of his trial appointment Von Sandon wrote to the Council of Education on 19 May 1879 :

Under all circumstances I shall most minutely observe all the rules, which are provided by the Council and being fully aware of the responsibility placed in me by the Council, do my duties consciencousely [sic].[61]

In November Von Sandon, still enthusiastic in carrying out his charge, wrote:

When Mr. f. Bridges inspected the school at Deniliquin I made it my business to drive this gentleman to my school and draw his attention to the fact, that there were not sufficient registers.[62]

Von Sandon, who preferred to deal with only the most powerful people in the organisation, wrote to Wilkins, secretary of the Council of Education, on 22 January 1880 :

I am compelled to draw your attention to the fact, that parents are withdrawing their children on account of the health of their children failing.

There were 46 applicants at the commencement of this quarter, of which I admitted 30. Twenty six children have attended regularly, but the room is not sufficiently large for them even. The children in the first class can not be kept awake during the hours after dinner.[63]

On 22 July 1880 Von Sandon, foreshadowing his future difficulties, wrote to Wilkins: 'I find it hard to keep myself and two horses on the very small salary'.[64] He was away from school for one day in September. Reporting this on 14 September he wrote to District Inspector Hicks (no doubt in the unfulfilled hope of bypassing the lower ranking Inspector Hookins to whom he was directly responsible):

I have come into possession of the family Estates in Prussia, which rendered it necessary for me to go to town, for the purpose of settling affairs with my attorney and forwarding documents by the mail leaving Melbourne on the 15th.[65]

Inspector Hookins, to whose attention this explanation of absence inevitably came, was not impressed by it. On 30 July he wrote: 'According to general opinion, he [Von Sandon] really does not seem to know truth from falsehood; and is so given to romancing, that he really believes in the creations of his own erratic brain'.[66] On 1 October 1880 Hookins reported that

though in receipt of a sufficient income to maintain him in comfort and respectability, since his probationary engagement at Wandook he has been constantly, and is now in debt ... he has made himself so obnoxious to the residents, that he cannot obtain Board and Lodging with them; so that he had some time ago, to live in the tents of a road party; and now lodges at a roadside inn, four miles from his school. His Landlord, to whom he is in debt, only keeps him, I believe, until he has paid off his liabilities to him ... he has been known to make monetary engagements of the most absurd character (he has recently purchased a buggy and pair of ponies). His frequently repeated statements of 'money coming out to him' as frequently turning out to be fables, and his haphazard, reckless manner of talking, have given him a reputation for untruthfulness, hard to live down ... Upon my last visit, I counselled him to avoid the faults imputed and pointed out to him the conduct and demeanour required from a teacher, to make him a useful member of the community: but my advice has had little effect; he is no better liked than ever; and the people of Wandook earnestly desire to get rid of him.[67]

Von Sandon was informed that if the conduct complained of by Inspector Hookins continued, his employment with the Department would cease. In response Von Sandon answered Hookins's allegations one by one. On 13 November 1880 he wrote:

With regard to obnoxious conduct etc.: I beg to state that I consider myself sorely agrieved [sic] by this expression in the Inspector's report—and there again it is quite evident, that Mr. Inspector Hookins has formed his opinion by the slanderous represent-ations of one, perhaps two individuals in the locality ... No residence has ever been offered me and there is no residence and board to be obtained, since only one settler lives closer than three [illegible word] four miles to the School. For a long time I was compeled [sic] to sleep in the wretched building, which is used for schooling purposes, the character of which was condemned by Mr Hookins twelve months ago and he promised me <u>then</u> to report to the Council of Education the difficulties under which I was labouring here.—I now live at the Royal Mail Hotel Conargo Road, because it is the <u>only</u> suitable place. My life at the Public House close to the school, which is kept by Mr John Hanlon proved a series of miseries. Mr Hanlon's conduct from the very first has been so ungentlemanly towards me, and his system of drawing money from my pocket so barefaced, that I could not bear it any longer;— taking at all times a mean advantage of my somewhat extravagant tendencies ...

I have been conscious of the great loyalty which the late Council of Education and its Secretary have shown, when they afforded me a generous opportunity of reconciling the past in my blotted life—and I feel the severity of the reproaches in the Inspector's report keenly on that account ... Under all circumstances I beg to say, that my stay in the Colony can only be a very short one—but I shall perform my duties conscientiously to the last moment—adhering litterally [sic] to the Regulations in all points.[68]

A man named Burrell of Deniliquin, who was described by Inspector Hookins as a man who lent money at usurious interest, wrote to Hookins on 14 October 1880 that Von Sandon had begged him to pay a debt for him as his creditor had threatened to report him to the Education Department.[69] Burrell wrote that in order to pay this debt for Von Sandon he 'rode over 20 miles to do it on a very wet day 10 miles in and 10 out'.[70] He had also lent other money to Von Sandon and now wished to be paid back.[71]

On 27 October nine residents signed a petition in support of Von Sandon. John Hanlon wrote to Inspector Hookins on 3 December 1880 to tell him that Von Sandon left the school to go to Deniliquin on Friday afternoon and did not return on Monday. He added:

I have ... heard that he has been getting a requisition signed by Several people Saying that he was a fit & proper person to teach a school among whom are people who know nothing whatever about him and allso [sic] some that he owes money too [sic] [and who therefore wanted him to stay until it was paid

back] and one of the members of the Late Local Board Mr Nisbet who has been considered out of his mind for sometime ... the school is utterly disorganised as the parent [sic] refuse to send thare [sic] children any longer.[72]

Inspector Hookins reported on 6 December 1880:

From information received, I visited the locality on the 2nd instant, and went to the school after dark. I found the door open, the desks outside: and the floor occupied by a rough bed: an aspect of careless untidiness pervaded the whole.

I examined the books, and found them some days behind in the entries.

Mr Von Sandon had not been seen by the pupils since the Friday night previous; when he was seen going in to Deniliquin; and school has not opened since, up to Friday last the 3rd inst on which morning I passed the school at 9.45, and saw no scholars assembled.

I afterwards saw Mr Von Sandon in Deniliquin. He states that he was sick in town, on Monday: that on Tuesday he returned to Wandook, but did not teach, as neither on that day, nor the following, have the scholars reassembled ...

I have on previous occasions reported on Mr Von Sandon's conduct; and the prejudice he has excited against him; and I again beg to remark, that the school is languishing, and will dwindle utterly away, unless he be removed, as soon as a vacancy occurs.[73]

After his visit from Hookins in Deniliquin, Von Sandon wrote with indignation:

I was absent on Monday the 29th of November on account of being too ill to attend to my duties ... Mr Inspector Hookins has informed me, that he has been told that this sickness was caused by indulging in intemperance.—Such I beg to deny. It is totally false, since I am not subject to this ungentlemanly habit.[74]

Hookins commented on this explanation:

I do not think, Mr von Sandon a vulgar drunkard, but, I say that he has wasted his money, foolishly treating his friends, indulging in champagne etc.

as a young nobleman would. Every one knows 'the Baron' in Deniliquin, as an eccentric and very few would rely upon his word, I fear.[75]

In a later explanation of what Hookins had found when he visited the school after dark on 2 December, Von Sandon wrote:

The school building has at all times been the resort of travellers and drovers, sent there by the owner of the building John Hanlon, a publican, who receives no rent from the Government for the use of his building ... The desks had been removed on the Friday previous for ... Divine Services ... If Mr Hookins states that an aspect of untidiness pervaded the whole, I certainly corroborate that statement—but the question is—<u>who is to blame?</u>—Is the Department aware of the fact that there have been <u>no windows</u> in the building used for school purposes—that the dust from the road has a free access—that the people interested in the school have <u>declined to find material for cleaning</u> the premises.[76]

Back at school on 7 December Von Sandon reported that he had no attendance of pupils at the school that day. He blamed the poor school building and John Hanlon's hostility towards him for this occurrence. He wrote that 'My task has been rendered, at times, so arduous and my situation is so uncomfortable, that I should be glad to be released from further responsibilities in connection with this school'.[77]

On 14 December John Hanlon wrote to Hookins that 'Wandook School have [sic] been deserted by the Teacher. he is now in Jerilderie & the Swag men of the roads are sleping [sic] & stopping in the School room'.[78] Later, on 4 October 1881, Inspector Hookins wrote of this time that

no earnest effort seems to have been made after 7th Dec [1880] to collect his pupils: if there were, it failed; and we find, that Mr von Sandon removed to his present residence Jerilderie, abandoning the school to the winds.[79]

In December 1880 Hookins, giving his opinion that Von Sandon should not again be employed in a departmental school, referred to the 'mercurial unsteadiness of his character'.[80] He also wrote:

He has quarrelled with his landlord, McKenzie, about money matters: McKenzie assaulted him; and turned him out of doors ...

There is no doubt that Mr von Sandon is a high-spirited and a generous young man; most probably, as he says of noble birth; and doubtless, some portion of the illfeeling displayed against him, arises from envy of his superior rank, in the minds of the lowly born farmers around him.[81]

The district inspector, writing of the case on 4 April 1881, noted that

much of the personal discomfort which he [Von Sandon] alleges he has suffered at Wandook has resulted from his own want of tact, judgment, and adaptability to the circumstances in which he was placed.[82]

On 14 February 1881 Hookins wrote of Von Sandon and his running of the school:

There is no doubt, as Mr von Sandon states, that to the discomfort of the schoolroom, is attributable the absence of several pupils during the recent summer heats; but not the complete desertion during the summer month of December last: Hot and close, as the room undoubtedly is, the pupils have had no better for years; and until now, have attended all the summer through with fair regularity ...

Giving out that he is a Prussian noble, expatriated for fighting a duel, he has on two occasions, shewn letters purporting to announce the remittance of large sums to his credit here; which seems have not yet arrived, nor are likely to arrive. His mother has sent him the race horse 'Shah of Persia', to run on the turf! He owns a section of land at Brassi where he was once a tutor! and he lately buys of MacKenzie, a pair of buggy ponies to be paid for out of the remittance. These eccentricities of conduct, are the talk of the district: in Deniliquin, the name of the 'Baron', invariably creates a smile.

He has forwarded a petition in his favor, signed by several names; many of them are strange to me, as well as to Mr Hanlon ... Is it credible, however, that these parties, holding Mr von Sandon in great esteem and respect, would have allowed him to camp for some days in the tents of a road party, without some effort to accommodate him; or forced him to take quarters at a bush inn, 4 miles away from their school, without some attempt to mitigate the hardship of his position!

As to the charge of drinking made by Mr Hanlon, I cannot find upon enquiry that Mr von Sandon is open to it. Of an open, generous, social, disposition, I can only hear, that when in Deniliquin, he is fond of meeting his friends, and treating them liberally to the detriment of his pocket ...

Personally, Mr von Sandon is a man of agreeable address, and gentlemanly demeanour: he is, apparently, well educated. His habits away from the foolish habits of romancing, he possesses are <u>moral</u>: and there are many, who while they laugh at his peculiarities, like him for his sociable affable manners.[83]

Von Sandon, who did not re-open the school after the summer vacation ended in 1881,[84] resigned from 28 February 1881.[85] John Hanlon, the local resident who owned the building where the school was held, wrote to William Wilkins, under-secretary of the Department of Public Instruction, on 31 March 1881 that Von Sandon had 'closed the school hear [sic] Some (4) months ago & left this district & he is now living at Jerilderie some 50 miles from hear [sic]'.[86] In Jerilderie Von Sanden (he was by this time spelling his name 'Von Sanden' rather than 'Von Sandon' as he had earlier spelt it) advertised himself as 'Br. Von Sanden, Land, Financial, Commercial, and Stock and Station Agent, Jerilderie'.[87]

After Jerilderie, Von Sanden went to Melbourne where his calling card stated: 'Herr Von Sanden, Professor of Music and Singing, Teaches Foreign Languages, and Prepares Students for Matriculation, At 2 Pulteney Street, or their Private Residences. Terms according to Agreement'.[88] In March 1882 Von Sandon, writing from the Star and Garter Hotel, Robert Street, St Kilda, Melbourne applied to be re-employed as a teacher in New South Wales. The Department noted on 3rd April 1882:

Mr Sandon had charge of Wandook Public School and was thoroughly unsuccessful. His career there was sufficiently troublesome to the Department

and injurious to the school to make it clear that he ought not to be re-admitted into the service.[89]

Having been informed of the decision not to re-employ him, Von Sandon wrote to the under-secretary (William Wilkins) on 14 May 1882, this time from Adelaide, stating: 'I fail to understand how the Chief Inspectors Report on my late Career as teacher under the Department can contain anything calculated to injure my reputation as a teacher'.[90] In this letter to Wilkins, Von Sandon went on to appeal (in vain) to 'the loyalty you have, personally, shown to me always'.[91]

On 20 June 1881 Hanlon, who had had much to do with Von Sandon, wrote to Inspector Hookins requesting that a teacher be sent and adding this time, probably with his experience of Von Sandon in mind, that 'for my own part I would rather, have a female Teacher.'[92] Hanlon's wish was granted as Maria Crowe was appointed to the school in June 1881 and was there until December of that year.[93]

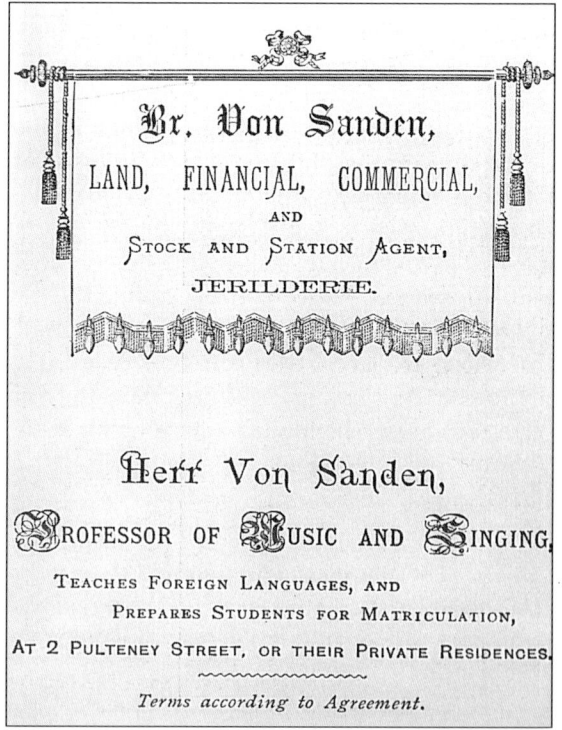

Business cards of Bernard Baron Von Sanden, c.*1881–1882 (From the* Education Gazette, *1 September 1969, p. 443)*

Scandal of female teacher living by herself 'in the wild Orara'

Local school board representative, Eugene Rudder, wrote to Inspector Lobban in September 1892 concerning the teacher of Dunvegan (later Upper Orara) Provisional School near Coffs Harbour:

Miss Edwards who is in charge of the West Branch School [i.e., Dunvegan School] Camps in the School building at night entirely by herself. You know the building, and it is isolated from any protection. I spoke to Miss Edwards kindly on the matter but she thought she was the best judge of what is the proper thing, so I told her I would report the matter, and leave the Dept to deal with it.

I made enquiries, and find her action is prompted by a desire to economise, as she can get board and residence at three respectable places, at from 8/- to 10/- per week.

Will the Department countenance a Lady Teacher (?) using a School as a residence? or acting in a manner to create a scandal?[94]

Inspector Lobban commented that 'Miss Edwards is a strong-minded young woman, and has more than once given Inspectors trouble. I agree with Mr Rudder that living by herself in the wild Orara is a scandal that should not be allowed under any circumstances.'[95]

Sarah Edwards, who was 24 years old at this time, moved out of the school and into lodgings.[96] She remained at the school until April 1895.[97]

Alfred Langlands—unsound or incapable?

Alfred Langlands became a pupil-teacher at Cambewarra Public School near Nowra in 1891.[98] He was the son of teacher Thomas Langlands[99] who was at Tomerong Public School near Nowra from 1884 to 1903.[100] In December 1891 young Langlands absconded, his father not knowing his whereabouts.[101] He then resigned without his father's consent.[102] He was allowed another trial with the Department and became a pupil-teacher at Milton Public School in September 1892.[103] In July 1893 he was moved to Burrawang Public School near Bowral where the head of the school, John

Lyons, wrote after Langlands's failure at the examination of 1895 that 'Alfred Langlands is, now, 21 years of age, and was only fairly obedient to me, during the year (1895)'.[104]

In 1896 he was at Nowra Superior Public School and in May 1896 Inspector McLelland wrote: 'Mr Langlands is not a good disciplinarian, and does not therefore manage a fairly large class of lively town boys with sufficient firmness.'[105] He was then moved to Yalwal Public School near Nowra in 1898, where the head of the school, Lenod Johnson, wrote in April 1898 that Langlands's work was 'most unreliable'.[106] In May 1898 the chief inspector, Frederick Bridges, wrote that 'In view of Mr Langlands' unsatisfactory record, I recommend that he be transferred to the position of Teacher of a second class Provisional School in a remote district'.[107]

Consequently Langlands was appointed to Warge Rock House to House School near Tullamore in June 1898.[108] In September, having inspected the school, Inspector Thomas wrote that 'Mr Langlands, the present teacher, exhibits certain eccentricities in his habits, and is doing unsatisfactory work as a teacher'.[109] Thomas did not specify these eccentricities. Having obtained Langlands's service record, Inspector Thomas wrote on 23 September:

A perusal of the outlines of Mr Langlands' past career in the Service, taken in conjunction with the opinion I formed of him when inspecting the School, convinces me that he is mentally unsound, and that there are strong grounds for the residents' dissatisfaction with him.

I beg to suggest that his case be submitted to the Public Service Board in order that arrangements may be made to test his mental fitness to remain in the Service.[110]

Chief Inspector Frederick Bridges did not agree. On 4 October, giving Langlands another chance, he wrote:

Mr Langlands does not evidently possess the mental equipment requisite in a Teacher. Between mental incapacity and mental unsoundness however there is a marked distinction. It may be that Inspector Thomas' opinion, based principally on Mr Langlands' demeanour on the occasion of his recent visit to the school, and the light in which he is regarded by the residents, is correct. [Papers connected with his career however] show no evidence of mental unsoundness on his part ... I therefore recommend ... that he be warned that unless satisfactory results be shown at the next Inspection of his work he will be removed from the Service without further caution.[111]

Langlands, however, resigned from the end of January 1899.[112]

Amusing William Lewington acts in a manner 'unbecoming of a teacher'

William Lewington had been a pupil-teacher at Young Superior Public School from 1895,[113] resigning from there early in 1897 because a doctor had told him his health was not good enough to be a teacher.[114] He had then joined the NSW Permanent Artillery. He applied for re-employment as a teacher on 16 July 1898, writing from Middle Head Barracks at Mosmans Bay. Chief Inspector Frederick Bridges wrote of this application on 22 July:

In view of the pressing necessity for male teachers for small schools, I recommend that Mr Lewington be accepted as eligible for re-employment as Teacher of a school carrying a salary not higher than £72 a year.[115]

Lewington was appointed to Ivanhoe Public School at the age of 21 in August 1898. On 20 March 1899 a young woman named Bessie Young wrote to Inspector Nolan:

It is with great reluctance that I have to bring under your notice the conduct of Mr Lewington the teacher of the local Public School. I engaged with Mrs Gallagher as Governess in August last, since when I have been continually annoyed by the vulgar behaviour of Mr Lewington, and often in the presence of <u>his</u> and also <u>my</u> pupils. When I had only been in Ivanhoe a week Mr Lewington proposed marriage to me in a very vulgar manner (although I had not given him the slightest encouragement) this proposal I promptly but politely rejected; which evidently has annoyed Mr Lewington, as since then his behaviour to me has been more rude and vulgar. He adopts all possible means of insulting me and is continually sending me insulting notes by the school children during school hours. He has circulated a report all over the district, and in Hay (Much to

Young School, c.1900 (NSW Dept of School Education)

my annoyance and embarrassment) that he is going to marry me and declared to myself that he is going to do so whether I like it or not. Since Xmas, his conduct and vulgar behaviour has been gradually getting worse and now unless I can prevent his annoyances I shall be obliged to leave my situation, and the town. I do not wish to injure Mr Lewington but I am obliged to take this step to preserve my character and to keep my position. I will feel extremely grateful to you if you will kindly ask Mr Lewington to desist in his persecution and annoyances to me.[116]

Lewington did not believe that Bessie Young intended no harm to him. He wrote: 'I proposed to marry Miss Young and I don't see why Miss Young has reason to complain of this trifling and frivolous offence.'[117]

Other residents also complained of different aspects of Lewington's behaviour. In response to these other complaints Inspector Nolan obtained from Lewington the following admissions:

(1) that on a few occasions after ringing the 9 o'clock bell I have returned to Gallagher's hotel but I always returned to school before 9.30 a.m.
(2) That I have on several occasions played billiards at Gallaghers Hotel, during dinner recess, with two of my pupils,—Terrence Gallagher 14 years of age, and Walter Gallagher 12 years.
(3) That on a few occasions I have left the school premises during 11 o'clock recess ...
(4) That I have permitted the school girls to dance on the school verandah.
(5) That on several occasions I have had drinks at the Hotel bar with residents of the town, and that on several occasions I have taken part in singing and piano playing in the hotel parlour.
(6) That on three or four occasions I sent notes to Miss Young by two of my pupils when they were going to her for music lessons at 11 a.m.
(7) That during hot weather I, on a few occasions, went to school without wearing a coat.
(8) That I may have visited Gallagher's Hotel (where I used to lodge) on one or two occasions at 11 o'clock recess, and during such visits I may have had a drink.[118]

Inspector Nolan reported on 28 April that 'Mr

Lewington has failed to realize the dignity and the responsibility of his office ... I find on inquiry that Mr Lewington does not drink to excess, but his frequent visits to the local hotels and billiard rooms have considerably detracted from his usefulness as a teacher; his ordinary conversation is interlaced with larrikin vulgarisms.'[119]

It was decided to remove Lewington to another small school with a warning as to his future conduct. A majority of the parents then signed a petition asking for his retention at Ivanhoe but a resident named Gallagher wrote to Inspector Nolan on 27 May 1899 saying that people had only signed the petition because they believed that the school would close if Lewington were removed and that 'he has not improved one bit since you were here'.[120]

In July 1899 Lewington was appointed to Overton Provisional School near Urana.[121] In July 1900 he applied to sit for the third class teacher's certificate with his application being refused because his last inspection report rated his 'skill and usefulness' as 'Moderate to Tolerable'.[122] Inspector Board also commented that 'Mr Lewington's speech was frequently ungrammatical'.[123]

An Overton parent, Mrs W. Holland, wrote to Inspector Board concerning Lewington on 16 April 1901:

After inspection last year when 5 attended 3 of whom were mine he said now we will take things easy & the children did just what they pleased He would come to school at 10—10.30 & 11 o'clock then throw out the Football they would have a reading lesson all out of the one book or something easy then out for a couple of hours—in again for 1 lesson then home, this went on all the time until Xmas ... In an object lesson 'last week before Easter' on the bones of human body he pointed out the different bones on his own person when he came to Pelvis he turned his seat to the class and smacked it saying this is the pelvis, He keeps his hat on his head the <u>whole</u> of the day while <u>in</u> the school last Oct—several children were punished because they did not put on their slate pumpkin as it was written on the Board 'Pumpquin' I sent the lesson the next day, & he said oh well! some people

Overton Public School, 1916 (see p. 97) (NSW Dept of School Education)

call it pumpquin he says he likes to put his own haccent on a song. Since january the children have had to teach each other ... he said Lord Almighty Hedith Mackinnon you will never learn—[I was going to] complain last year but as he said he intended to try & get into the Mounted Police I thought there would be no need to complain he said he intended to try at Easter but he did not go away ... When he came to the District first he boarded at Mrs Lanes, without giving warning he left & went to Mrs Pateys 4 miles further he seldom used the door of his room there, going in & out through the window—then it was 11 o'clock when he got to school after 2 months there he asked to be taken back at Lanes they did allow him—& one Sunday he came from the Public [house] 2 miles off with a cart & told Mrs Lane he was moving he stayed from July until March there & left the same way asking Mrs L. again to take him bk which she has, the excuse to the Publican was he liked change he says he hates teaching & told me some months ago he intended trying to get into the Force. I said you will find the Officers are very strict: Yes he says I suppose they will be & I am my own master here.[124]

Again several residents wrote to the Department in support of Lewington but, after an inquiry by

Inspector Board, he was severely censured and warned of dismissal if his poor performance continued.[125] He was moved to Glenellen Provisional School near Culcairn in July 1901.[126]

At Glenellen he was again inspected by Peter Board who wrote on 29 October 1901:

On three occasions I have informed Mr Lewington of his inaccurate speech ... Such expressions as 'them two front feet', 'he hasn't wrote in it', 'the first thing Henry I [Henry the First] done', were heard from him at my last visit. I recommend ... that should he fail to remedy the defect, his services will be dispensed with.[127]

Following another unsatisfactory inspection report by Peter Board in 1902, and a recommendation that he be given one further trial, Chief Inspector Frederick Bridges wrote that 'Mr Lewington has proved a most undesirable addition to the ranks of the teaching profession, and this should be his final trial'.[128]

In March 1903 Lewington was moved to Burrumbuttock East and Walla Walla West Half-Time Schools near Culcairn.[129] On 19 May a parent, Mrs J. H. Linder of Burrumbuttock, Spring Vale, wrote to Inspector Drummond:

We regret having to complain of our school teacher <u>Mr Lewington</u>, as we really think that he is not in his right state of mind, especially to teach children, they are terrified the way that he carries on, trusting you will see into the matter.[130]

On 3 June, a letter replying to Inspector Drummond and signed by J. H. Linder, J. Bremer, I. M. Gresanke and B. Farrell, stated:

Yours to hand stating to let you know how the Teacher acts and these are some of the Following things. He makes the children believe there is someone out side he goes out runs twice around the school, then tells the children he hunted him a way one day he took one of my little boys from the play ground in to school laid him on the floor pulled out his Pocket Knife & said he was going to cut his throth [sic] he said he has to die some day he make [sic] fire in the school worms [sic] himself & puts it out opens the windows & door & makes the poor children sit in the cold. he make [sic] the older children teach the little ones while he sits at the table & says he is sick then calls out doctor doctor come quick he some times leaves the children out of school when these are gone a little way calls them back into school gives them the cane & says now they can go home

I think the teacher is not to be trusted with the children when he carryes [sic] on in such a manner hoping you will see into the matter.[131]

Inspector Drummond visited the school on 23 June 1903 and further similar complaints were made. In answer to these complaints Lewington declared that he was only trying to amuse the children and Drummond accepted that this was so. With regard to an accusation that he had sung an unbecoming song in the hearing of the children, he stated: 'I may have sung it at school when lighting the fire, but this is the same song as I sang at a concert at Walla, and no objection was made to it'.[132]

Inspector Drummond wrote of a complaint which had been made about caning the children: 'I do not think there is much truth in this charge, as I am convinced he would rather play with the children than punish them'.[133] Drummond concluded on 26 June:

I think the Teacher has acted on the whole, in the most silly, eccentric, and childish manner, and most unbecoming of a teacher, and although his object appears to have been the children's amusement, I consider his actions of such a reprehensible a nature, that I recommend he be severely censured, and informed that a repetition of the offence will lead to his dismissal. I also recommend that he be transferred to another locality, as he has forfeited the respect both of the parents and children of the settlement.[134]

Lewington resigned from 7 July 1903.[135] In an undated letter of about this time he asked to have payment of his last salary settled as 'I am going up country very likely tomorrow'.[136]

Defiant William Small at Bondi Public School

William Small was to be suspended from Bondi Public School in August 1900 after a visit from Inspector Skillman at which Skillman had found

no programmes for 4th and upper 3rd were on the walls ... I asked him to show them to me and he refused to do so. He also refused to produce his Lesson Register ... He was defiant and threatened if I reported him he would make matters very disagreeable for me; that I should find that he had heaps of friends while I had very few.[137]

In 1902 at Bondi, Small was severely reprimanded for the dirty condition of his school and other defects pointed out in the report of inspection.[138] He was moved to St Ives Public School where he was promoted for good service.[139] He retired from Coogee Public School in 1912 and was re-employed in 1918, from when he taught again until the end of September 1919 when his services were dispensed with.[140] At that time he was at Meroo (later Meroo Meadow) Public School near Kiama.[141]

John O'Brien has too much to drink at the Crookwell bicycle sports

The inspector noted that the teacher at Crookwell River Half-Time School near Crookwell in 1904, 26-year-old John O'Brien, had a fondness for liquor and could not drink in moderation.[142] On 15 November 1904 a Crookwell resident, C. S. Webster, sent a telegram to the inspector: 'John O'Brien not teaching today, in Crookwell worse of liquor'. O'Brien's explanation was:

I went to Crookwell on the 14th inst to see the bicycle sports, and met a number of friends there, and unfortunately took too much liquor and was under the influence of it that night. Nevertheless, I left Crookwell at 11 p.m. that evening to return to my work, but took the wrong road and went to Grabben Gullen instead: I returned to Crookwell, reaching there about 5 a.m. on Tuesday morning (15th inst.). My horse was very tired, and I was worn out, so I went to bed in Crookwell, and stayed there that day. I returned to Binda that evening and resumed duty at Crookwell River at the proper time on 16th inst. (Wed.) but no scholars attended.[143]

O'Brien was penalised by losing two days' pay, although he had only missed one day's school, and the inspector arranged for his transfer at the end of the year.[144]

Wollun Public School, 1911 (Copy held by NSW Dept of School Education)

Frederick Capp, head of Kurrara (later Banora Point) Public School, and older pupils at the school, 1926 (see p. 101).
<u>Right hand row—furthest row from window—(rear forward)</u>: Cassie Gilliat, Peggy Wilson, Ester Soorley,
Heather Abernethy, Jean McIntyre, Mena Bonning, Mary Garbett, Hazel Ahrens, Dorrie Waugh, Ron Abernethy
<u>3rd row from window</u>: Bill Soorley, Charlie Madden, Eileen Brown, Adelaide Smith, Marjorie Gray, Lora
Madden, Sid Herman, Ivy Herman, Iris Phillips <u>2nd row from window</u>: Milton Madden, Ted Bell, Eric Fraser,
Arthur Vercoe, Ron Gray, Eric Abernethy, Marwood Luxton <u>Near window</u>: Don McIntyre, Jim Abernethy,
Gladys Tierney, Violet Ahrens (From Kurrara-Banora Point Primary School Centenary 1883–1993)

Children in danger of being crushed by falling hysterical teacher

Elsie Ponton was appointed to Kurrara (later Banora Point) Public School on May 1918.[145] She required frequent short periods of sick leave and in August 1919 local doctor, James Aiken, was of the opinion that Elsie Ponton, who was 31, was suffering from anaemia and nervous debility.[146] Inspector Dunlop wrote on 21 June 1919:

Miss E. M. Ponton, Asst. at Kurrara has had frequent leave of absence for half and single days on account of illness.

The Teacher Mr Capp, called on me to-day and reported that Miss Ponton is often unfit for duty for shorter periods. These attacks take a mental form at times, and she does not know anyone nor understand what is said to her while they last. She also takes sudden fainting fits and has fallen in the school on several occasions, and on recovering is highly hysterical. There is no female near at hand, and Miss Ponton has taken an insensate dislike to the one called from a neighbouring farm when she has been ill.

Mr Capp [the head of the school] is a single man and he finds these attacks embarrassing, and the parents are now remarking on Miss Ponton's mental condition. I recommend that Miss Ponton be removed to some position near her own people who live in Manly, Sydney.[147]

On 8 August 1919 the head of the school, Frederick Capp, wrote:

Miss Ponton has never been well since her appointment to this school in May 1918. She is often ill and unable to attend to her duties. Several times she has without warning fallen heavily to the floor amongst the children during school operations. She then becomes hysterical & laughs & cries alternately. During the time I am rendering first aid the school work becomes disorganised. On two other occasions she became delirious at school & said & did foolish things. I then had to send for neighbours (females) & get her removed from the premises to neighbours' houses. During these times school work was delayed. There is danger that she may fall heavily on small children in her classes & crush them against the desks or seats & permanently injure them.[148]

Elsie Ponton was then appointed to Manly Public School in October 1919 and spent the rest of her teaching career around Manly, resigning in 1946.[149]

'Mentally deranged' assistant jumps over hotel balcony

Forty-nine-year-old Jane Barry was appointed as assistant teacher at Cumnock Public School in January 1922.[150] On 24 October the head of the school, Edward Rohan, sent a telegram to head office: 'Assistant mentally deranged. Beg apply for assistance.'[151] In further explanation Rohan wrote to Inspector Price:

Miss Barry has not looked well since she returned from her Michaelmas holidays and although I several times suggested she should apply for leave, she always refused to do so. She went out of her mind on Friday night and on Saturday morning clad in her night dress, jumped over the balcony of the Royal Hotel, but escaped practically unhurt ... After what has happened I do not think it would be wise for her to return here when she is well enough to resume.[152]

Jane Barry was taken to Sydney by a member of her family and after some time in the mental hospital at Gladesville resumed her teaching career in Sydney, retiring in 1928.[153]

Teacher hangs upside down in tree 'like a chook'

Ron Collins recalls that when he was about nine years old and a pupil at Dunbars Creek Subsidised School near Muswellbrook in about 1924, the young female teacher aged about 20 (Ethel Moffatt was the teacher at Dunbars Creek Subsidised School for at least part of 1924[154]) was 'not much more than a kid herself'[155] and that she used to play hide and seek with the pupils, about ten in number. One day she hid up a tree and, when she went to jump down to run to the whippy post, she caught her ankle and was 'hanging upside down in the tree like a chook'.[156] Her pupils, politely averting their eyes, lifted her up from beneath so that she could free her ankle and then, as she was unable to walk, wheeled her home in a wheelbarrow to local resident Budden's place where she was staying.[157]

Teacher with nervous trouble murders adult daughter in school residence

Alfred Watson, aged 50, took over as head of Kingswood Public School in July 1920.[158] From August 1925 to 17 March 1926 his son, George Watson, relieved at the school in place of his father who was on long-service leave followed by further leave without pay.[159] The elder Watson's wife had died on 13 February 1926 and Alfred Watson was suffering from nervous trouble, the seriousness of which was revealed when, on 17 March 1926, he murdered his adult daughter in the school residence while school was in progress.[160] Police Sergeant John Walsh of Parramatta Police Station reported on 19 March:

Ada Muriel Watson, aged 22 years was murdered at the Public School Residence Kingswood at about 10.15 a.m. on the 17th instant. Her head was battered in with a claw hammer, and whilst doing so her assailant broke the handle of the hammer, she was then struck on the side of the head with the blade of an American axe, which penetrated the skull and brain. The walls of the room and floor were splashed with blood, which has adhered to same.

Alfred Thomas Watson aged 56 years father of the victim, late Public School Teacher at Kingswood and at present on extended leave of absence admitted that he committed the offence and made a signed statement to that effect. He was later charged with feloniously and maliciously murdering Ada Muriel Watson. On that charge he appeared at Penrith Police Court on the 17th instant, when he was remanded to appear at Penrith Police Court on the 23rd instant when an inquest will be held. Watson is at present confined in Parramatta Gaol.[161]

Watson's 26-year-old son George, the relieving teacher at the school during his father's leave, wrote to the Department on 18 March:

Owing to a tragedy that happened in my home yesterday I dismissed the school at approximately 10.15 a.m. and closed for the remainder of the week. The case was shown in Daily Telegraph (18.3.26).

I feel that under the conditions I cannot do further duty in the Kingswood school and desire to apply for leave for 1 month; or as the Department sees fit. I am trying to call personally on the Department as early as possible.[162]

George Watson visited the Department two days later on 20 March. It was noted that he was suffering from shock and he was granted a few weeks' leave. The residence was to be available for another teacher and it was thoroughly cleaned and renovated before being occupied.[163]

Alfred Watson was later placed in Long Bay Gaol. He later spent some time at the mental hospital at Parramatta, and died on 28 March 1927.[164] George Watson was appointed to Belmore South Public School on 9 April 1926 and stayed in the Department (at various locations) until 1948 when he resigned.[165]

Crowds collect around teacher Maude Welch

The appointment of 49-year-old English-born Maude Welch as a teacher with the Department was annulled on 31 August 1929.[166] She had entered the service on 29 May 1913 and as the Department noted on 23 October 1929, from the time of her first appointment until her appointment was annulled

she was a continual source of annoyance to the Department. She disturbed the staff at each of the sixteen schools to which she was appointed in her sixteen years of service. These constant removals (8 in the last 4 years) were necessitated by her misconduct. She has been warned and censured repeatedly. She did not leave the service on account of ill health, as implied [by her], but because of continued misconduct (impertinence, insubordination, and the like).[167]

The mistress of Woonona Infants School, where Maude Welsh had been in 1921, reported that 'when I asked her to go in the playground she refused and

Outdoor drawing lesson, Blackfriars Superior Public School, 1913 (NSW Dept of School Education)

told me that I had better be careful how I treated her because she had influential friends among them Mr Peter Board'.[168]

At Manly West Public School where she had been in 1928 it had been noted by Percy R. Price, JP, that 'her actions outside the school have on several occasions excited a good deal of comment and caused crowds to collect around her. Her teaching seems to run to giving the children long accounts of murders, inciting disloyalty, silent reading & tables etc. for classes of much younger children.'[169] Inspector Henry wrote in October 1928 that 'some of Miss Welch's actions and her general mien at Chatswood, Willoughby and at Hornsby are such as to raise doubts as to her sanity'.[170] Early in 1928 Inspector Riley, who wrote that he had much sympathy with Maude Welch, had unsuccessfully suggested that she be employed at the Correspondence School as 'she has fair teaching ability, writes a good hand, and is fairly systematic.

I believe she is suffering from a neurosis and this is the cause of her temperamental clashes in an ordinary school.'[171]

Maude Welch underwent a medical examination and on 4 January 1929 Dr Harvey Sutton, the Department's Principal Medical Office, who wrote that 'Miss Welch appears to be a difficult subject to deal with',[172] reported: 'The various symptoms were considered to be due to endocrine disturbances so commonly seen with the change of life in teachers 40 to 45 years old, the result being considerable mental and nervous instability'.[173] In a letter on 21 January 1929 the chief inspector wrote to Welch a list of points against her, the first of which was: 'You are reminded that you were convicted in 1917 of travelling in a railway carriage without having paid your fare'.[174]

With Welch having been appointed to St Ives Public School at the beginning of 1929, Inspector Price reported on 23 April: 'Miss Welch has been either absent or late on every school-day since her entry on duty (January 1929) ... Her latest explanation is that she has a private letter signed by the Director intimating that there is no objection to her continuing to arrive at school after 9 a.m. Under no circumstances, however, would she be prepared to show that letter to anybody.' [175]

Having had her appointment annulled on 31 August 1929, Maude Welch made an unsuccessful appeal against wrongful dismissal. On 4 October 1931 she wrote to the Governor:

I am out in Australia alone and in confidence I wish to tell you that it is not safe for me to be out here alone. My mother, brothers and sisters are in England. I come from a good family. My mother is related to the Plowdens of Shrewsbury and you will no doubt have heard of Sir William Plowden, one of London's Judges ... I am thoroughly dependent on your protection and sympathy.[176]

Teacher admits to laziness being a family failing

Twenty-two-year-old Ronald Burns was the teacher at Calleen Siding Provisional School near Wyalong[177] on 25 February 1931 when an unexpected inspection of the school took place.[178] Inspector Ravenscroft reported:

I reached the school at 10.25; I was compelled to enter, as a key had been broken, through a window. The room was disgracefully untidy and dirty; it had not been swept for four days at least; paper and nibs were littered about. The teacher was seated at his table typing last quarter's Quarterly Return...

My honest opinion is that Mr Burns should never have become a teacher. He told me this afternoon that laziness was a family failing; I believe him to be physically incapable of continuous effort and his teaching ability to be practically nil. I have no means of judging his usual teaching manner; his voice is poor and marked by a distinct nasality. His body

Teachers' staffroom, 1930s—school not named (Photograph by S. J. Hood, courtesy of NSW Teachers Federation)

movements are heavy and labored. Yet I cannot recommend his dismissal, for he would have nothing to recommend him in another pursuit. I am not certain whether he can be believed, but he informs me that he has family troubles, a brother has failed in the Leaving, his father is in Kenmore Asylum.

But I do certainly recommend that he should be transferred without delay to an assistantship and that he should not for many years be trusted again as teacher in charge of a school.[179]

Burns was then sent to Wyalong Public School where he was away from school from 31 August 1931 until 4 September 1931. For this absence he had a local doctor's certificate stating that he had been suffering from chronic nasal catarrh for some years and that 'he has been unable to leave the house from August 31st to September 4th last'.[180] The head of Wyalong Public School at this time, Charles Bensley, wrote on 4 September:

On Monday last I received a wire from Mr Burns stating that he was unable to be on duty owing to illness. I visited his boarding house on Monday afternoon; the lady there told me he had just got up for a little tea, as he had had nothing to eat all day and had been vomiting all the night before.

I heard from reliable authority that he was in the street that night. He did not put in an appearance on Tuesday. On Wednesday I met him at the West Wyalong show where he informed me he was well and would be at school on Thursday, but he did not resume duty and I have had no message from him. On Wednesday night he was at a dance in the West Wyalong Masonic Hall. My own girl was there and saw him, in fact, danced with him.

I am quite ignorant of what plausible story he will have when I do see him ...

He **must** be stopped. I have advised him fatherly, I have censured him, I have assisted him and finally I am convinced he will never make a success as a teacher.[181]

Burns was transferred to Junee North Public School in October 1931 and at the beginning of 1933 to Toongabbie Public School from where he resigned in April of that year.[182]

Teacher alters pupils' examination papers while in 'hysterical twilight state'

Fifty-five-year-old Alfred Lane had been in the teaching service for 39 years when, in November

Narara Public School (see p. 106), photograph undated—building erected 1889 (From Narara Public School Centenary 1889–1989*)*

1936, without knowing that he had done so, he got up in the middle of the night, walked from the school residence to the school and changed his Narara Public School pupils' answers on their Primary Final examination papers.[183]

Lane had intended to take these examination papers to Gosford on the afternoon of the examination but had been delayed. Realising that he didn't have time to take them to Gosford that day, he put them in his table drawer at the school. The next morning, to his horror, Lane found the papers scattered on the table with answers added where there had been omissions and with corrections to existing answers. The alterations were in Lane's handwriting and the inspector later commented that 'the alterations were done very ingenuously and no attempt was made to disguise handwriting'.[184]

In explanation of his behaviour on this occasion Lane wrote that, very soon after he had begun to teach almost four decades earlier, he had had sunstroke. This had been followed by brain fever during the course of which he had almost died and for some time he had had periods where he could not remember what he had done, but these had ceased decades before this incident. He had also had chronic meningitis and recurring bouts of neurasthenia.[185]

The Department noted that Lane 'had been the subject of excellent reports by a number of different inspectors'.[186] His current inspector had reported 'that the general condition of Wyong Creek Public School, where Mr Lane was stationed last year, improved under his management to a marked degree as did also that of Narara this year'.[187] The Primary Final examination papers which Lane had altered were, as the Department reported, 'even after drastic remarking ... the best all round set from any school in the Gosford section'.[188] It was also noted that the keynote of inspectors' reports on Lane 'for the past three years had been the high moral tone set by him in his schools and its reflection in the bearing and conduct of his pupils'.[189]

As Lane's case went up through the ranks of the Department, and to the Public Service Board, a note was added to the papers on the case in January 1937: 'It now transpires that two of the candidates for bursaries from this school [Lane had not altered the bursary papers] occupied a very high place among the competitors, although they were not successful in gaining bursaries'.[190]

In February 1937 Lane wrote that since coming to Narara about a year earlier:

I have devoted all my spare time and holidays to improving what seemed to me to be a badly neglected state of affairs.

Teachers had got no help from the P&C Association. I tried, but did not succeed so I did the work myself cutting rock to edge flower beds, erecting a large trellis for wisteria etc ...

In the school there was a shortage of class books, and parents were too poor to buy them. The P&C gave no help, so I decided, although the Primary Final Examination was only 6 weeks ahead, with the assistance of my wife, to stage a school concert which proved a great success.

Then followed all the family sickness and my own up to and right past the Primary Final Examination. I believe and am sure everything would have been well with me had I given in and taken a period of sick leave before the examination, but I thought my pupils needed training right up to date of examination and remained on duty.[191]

The Department's medical officer concluded, in February 1937, 'that the tampering with the examination papers occurred during an hysterical twilight state, in which Mr Lane was not responsible for his actions'.[192] The Department decided not to charge Lane with misconduct as it had intended to do.[193] Instead he was transferred to Coopernook where the school and the residence were in a poor state similar to that of Wyong Creek and Narara Schools when Lane had taken them over. He remained at Coopernook for the next nine years until he retired in 1945 at the age of 64.[194]

14

Removals

Teacher to be removed from Tinonee to a school not near a public house

In 1869 an allegation (which was later withdrawn) was made that the teacher at Tinonee Public School near Taree, James Birch, had been found drunk.[1] Inspector Allpass noted of Birch, who was to be removed, that 'the fact is that the habit assumes the form of a disease in Mr. Birch and if appointed to another school it should be as remote as possible from a public house'.[2] In fact Birch's services were dispensed with because of intemperance in December 1869 but he was appointed three months later as teacher at Sugarloaf (later Mulbring) Public School near Kurri Kurri. After other appointments he resigned in 1885.[3]

Annie T. M. Jones's frequent requests for removal

Annie T. M. Jones taught for 41 years with the Department from 1886 until 1927.[4] She came from Sydney and her first appointment at the age of 20 was to Bevendale Provisional School near Gunning. She was the first teacher at this school which opened in January 1886 and a year later, in January 1887, a local resident named Armatage wrote to the Department

to apply to you for a male teacher and also a protestant as we are all protestants and the children also & the last teacher we had here was very insolent to most of the Parents and in fact behaved herself very badly the last quarter, taking the children in as late as 11 o'clock sometimes & on several occasions sending six or seven of the children home and not going to the school at all herself.[5]

Annie Jones was appointed to three different schools in 1887 and then to Nurung Provisional School near Boorowa in June 1888.[6] In December 1888 she applied to be moved from Nurung to the district of Parramatta as 'I have for the past six months been getting very bad health and would like to get nearer my parents'.[7] No move was forthcoming, however, and when school resumed in January 1889 she sent a doctor's certificate and applied for an extra week before resuming school. Inspector Lawford wrote to District Inspector O'Byrne: 'I think this is a try on. The Dr's certificate does not state any particular ailment & the application should have been sent in sooner.'[8] Inspector O'Byrne wrote:

It is greatly to be regretted that holidays make so many of our young lady teachers ill. Before granting leave, in this case, the applicant should be required to produce a certificate from the Department's Dr. There can be no hardship in this as Miss Jones is in Sydney. If she does not do this I recommend that her week's pay be stopped.[9]

She then forwarded a medical certificate on 18 January 1889 which specified her ailment as nervous prostration. The certificate was from Dr Clune, who was not the Department's medical officer, and who recommended leave for a further fortnight (three weeks in all).[10] On 28 January 1889 the Department's medical officer, Dr Knaggs, wrote to Edwin Johnson, the under-secretary of the Department:

I received a message from that young lady [Annie Jones] requesting me to call upon her at her residence in Olive Street Paddington. Upon enquiry of the Messenger I found that she was not confined to her bed and was not unable to go out walking. Under these circumstances I did not consider it my duty to wait upon her at her residence as requested—nor is it my intention to do so unless expressly requested by you.[11]

The next day Dr Knaggs wrote again to Edwin Johnson at the Department:

I beg to state that she [Annie Jones] called upon me today and I made a careful examination of her. I also saw Dr Clune under whose treatment she has been for the last six weeks. I have no reason to doubt Dr Clune's statement that she has been suffering from nervous prostration; but have formed the opinion that she will be able to resume her duties early in February.

From my examination of Miss Jones and from what I have gleaned from Dr Clune concerning her, I have no doubt but her removal to a colder climate than where she is now residing and teaching would materially benefit her health.[12]

Annie Jones returned to Nurung and the school was inspected early in 1889. The inspection did not go well and Inspector Lawford did not accept Jones's explanation of her poor performance. He wrote on 23 March 1889:

I have spoken to Miss Jones before for keeping records in a slovenly way ... She certainly seemed very languid & weak at the inspection & I consider her not physically strong enough to teach. I recommend that she be requested to resign on account of her weak state of health.[13]

On 29 March she applied again to be moved from Nurung 'as the climate does not agree with my health'.[14] Inspector Lawford wrote of this application: 'Nurung is one of the healthiest spots in probably the whole world. Miss Jones' statement that it does not suit her health only accentuates my recommendation that she should be requested to resign on account of her ill health.'[15] It was noted on her teacher career record in April of that year that she had been warned that 'unless the school was found to be in a reasonably efficient state by the next inspection, her services will be dispensed with'.[16] On 1 May she requested removal to a school

in the Port Macquarie district.[17] On 6 June a note was made on the file that 'Mr McMillan wishes to ascertain certain facts as by his friends letter now returned'.[18] It seems likely that the Mr McMillan referred to was William McMillan, MLA, the local member of parliament for East Sydney. In any event two other entries were made on the file on the same day, the first reading: 'From the papers dealing with this case, and appended hereto, it would appear that Miss Jones' application for removal was declined on the ground of her inefficiency as a Teacher, and on that ground alone. There is nothing to shew she has received other than fair treatment from the local inspector, Mr Lawford.'[19] This entry was followed by another indicating a substantial change by the Department, and which strongly suggests that Annie Jones was to be given special treatment. It was now considered that 'this teacher is in a very bad state of health & she should have the chance of a removal nearer the coast if possible'.[20]

As a result of this change in approach by the Department, for a few weeks in July 1889 Annie Jones was at Fern Glen Public School near Grafton.[21] Applying to be moved from there very soon after she had arrived, she wrote: 'I am unable to get lodgings near the school. Where I am now boarding, there is a creek between [there and the school], which in wet weather is uncrossable even on horseback. I am also obliged to wade through water on my way to school.'[22]

Her next appointment was to Bungay Public School near Wingham from where, in December 1891, she applied for an appointment 'more convenient to Sydney as I have been ill for some time past, and the sea voyage renders me still weaker'.[23] After Bungay, Annie Jones was appointed to Crookwell River Public School in 1892.[24] When this school was changing from a school which operated full-time to a Half-Time School in 1898 because one family, as the inspector wrote, 'forsook Miss Jones their teacher and went to Yarranoo',[25] she wrote to the Department asking

if you would be kind enough not to send me too far up the Southern Railway Line: viz Wagga Wagga, Hay or Junee, I am sure I could never endure the heat of those climates. I should prefer remaining in this district as the climate agrees with me better than any of those I have been in, but I am afraid inspect. Smith has no vacancy.[26]

Annie Jones then went to Lake Plain (later Cootralantra) Provisional School near Cooma and to Pipers Flat near Wallerawang before being appointed, at her own request, to Megalong in January 1900.[27] Soon after her arrival at Megalong Provisional School she wrote to the Department requesting removal to Woollahra Superior Public School. The next week, on 2 February, she made another application, this time writing to Inspector McKenzie:

When I applied for Megalong I was quite ignorant of the unsuitableness of the place. Previous to applying I wrote to Mrs England [the postmistress] re the place and the reply was not unfavourable, so I thought being near home I would apply. I had no idea that such a terrible mountain was between Megalong and Katoomba. Neither was I aware that my predecessor died here. [Lucy McHarg, aged in her early twenties, had died of pneumonia and influenza on 11 November 1899.] I am not very strong and the gloom of the place seems to add to my nervous condition. Please remove me if possible.[28]

Although she had been appointed to Megalong at her own request, Annie Jones was then moved to Hurstville West (later Beverly Hills) Public School in Sydney and did not again teach outside Sydney during the remainder of her career from 1902 until 1927.[29] From Hurstville West she successfully applied to be moved to Woollahra Superior Public School.[30]

In November 1914 while she was teaching at Gladesville Public School Annie Jones married Walter Swain, taking six months' long-service leave at this time. She retired in September 1927, taking six months' long-service leave from 1 April 1927.[31]

Napoleon Poidevin is removed 'to a school distant from the railway'

Napoleon Poidevin was the teacher at Wilberforce Public School from August 1894 until the end of 1897.[32] In June 1897 a complaint had been made against Poidevin for slanderous remarks against a Wilberforce woman whom he had called a liar.[33] It was also hinted that his general conduct in the district was not all that a teacher's conduct should be.[34] Inspector Dettmann held an inquiry and felt that the charge was not proved.[35] During December 1897, however, Poidevin was fined for travelling on the train to Parramatta without a ticket. Chief Inspector Frederick Bridges commented: 'I believe that it is not the first time he has been guilty of similar dishonourable conduct. I recommend that

Wilberforce Public School, c.1895. The teacher at the left of the photograph is probably Napoleon Poidevin as he was at the school from August 1894 to December 1897. (NSW Dept of School Education)

he be severely censured and removed to a school distant from the railway.' [36] Poidevin was accordingly removed to Moruya Public School at the end of 1897.[37] After several more reprimands by the Department, one of which was for selling a stove without the Department's approval, he retired from Araluen Public School near Braidwood in 1913.[38]

Unpopular Eliza Clark is removed from Badgerys Creek

Eliza Clark, aged 46, was appointed to Badgerys Creek Public School in January 1902.[39] She was not popular with the parents, eight of whom signed a petition dated 5 June 1902 to have her removed. The petition stated:

Several children have already left and should Miss Clark return after the Hollidays [sic] six (6) familaes [sic] will remove thier [sic] children prefering [sic] thiere [sic] walking six miles daily across the Bush than have them any longer under her influence.[40]

In his report on 25 August, Inspector Henderson wrote of the petition:

The parents evidently resented the removal of the preceding teachers. They were persons who did good work, were pleasing in appearance, and made themselves agreeable to the residents. Miss Clarke [sic] was appointed. She was elderly, somewhat unprepossessing in appearance, has a harsh and discordant voice, and her demeanour savours more of acidity than cheerfulness. I think too she is uncompromising in attitude and wanting in tact. She, of course, soon came into conflict with Mesdames Williams and Wye, who evidently were outmatched. Failing to humble Miss Clarke [sic], they drew up this petition and led into it others who evidently were ashamed of it afterwards for two point blank denied the charges, while the others absented themselves, leaving the two principals Mrs Williams and Wye to see the matter through.[41]

Mrs A. Wye also wrote a letter to the Department against Eliza Clark on 25 July 1902. On the same day as he wrote the above, Inspector Henderson wrote of his inquiry into the matters raised in this letter:

As this person, Mrs Wye, may trouble the Department again, I think it desirable to point out that her conduct during the inquiry was most unseemly. She announced her intention to make it hot for Miss Clarke [sic] called her a thing and after failing to prove anything said it was the Dept's fault for sending a foolish old woman to take charge of the school. I had to ask her to retire. She apologised no less than three times and said she could not control herself which I readily believe.[42]

Inspector Henderson found no fault with Eliza Clark's teaching. He noted that at the regular inspection he 'could award nothing less than Good for both Organisation and Discipline'.[43] Yet Eliza Clark remained unpopular and, following requests for her removal from local residents to local member of parliament, T. R. Smith, Inspector Beavis reported on 24 November 1903:

I visited Badgery's Creek on 11th Sept. last. The attendance at the school was small, and the attainments of the pupils were not high. The Teacher is earnest, and has I believe done her duty faithfully but her capabilities are not great ... She is not popular; I gathered during my visit that the residents wished her removed: she herself, being uncomfortable under such circumstances, is desirous of removal. I believe that the attitude of the parents towards Miss Clarke [sic] is largely the result of prejudice arising out of the contrast between herself and her predecessor [Maude Rhodes] who was young and apparently well liked.[44]

Thirteen residents signed another petition for Eliza Clark's removal which was dated 29 April 1904. On 18 October 1904 the acting chief inspector wrote:

Miss Clark is unpopular and becomes so wherever she is teaching. It is owing to her unpopularity that the attendance at Badgery's Creek is below that for an eighth class school. on reduction of the school to the ninth class I propose to transfer the teacher to Winburndale.[45]

Eliza Clark's transfer to Winburndale Public School near Bathurst took place in October 1904, with the teacher from Winburndale, Lauristina Carver, being appointed to Badgerys Creek

School.[46] Eliza Clark retired because of ill health from West Maitland (later Maitland) District School in June 1907.[47]

Lauristina Carver, aged about 30, was presumably more to the liking of the residents of Badgerys Creek as she married a local man named Longley and resigned from the school in February 1907.[48]

Kathleen Coatsworth so tired of cows and rural life in general

Kathleen Coatsworth, aged 29, was appointed to Burringbar Public School near Murwillumbah as assistant teacher on 31 August 1915.[49] Before her previous appointment to Tweed Heads Public School in 1914 she had been living for two years in the Women's College at the University of Sydney where she was a second year student.[50] She was not happy at Burringbar.[51] The head of the school, Edward Hayes, wrote on 9 June 1916 that 'she is attentive to her work, but seems to lack sympathy with young children'.[52] She had trouble finding accommodation in a private home and she declined to live at the hotel because of the bad language and rowdy behaviour she had observed there.[53] On 5 June 1916 she wrote to Inspector Henry:

Mrs Hockey (my sick landlady) is going away & will not be able to take me again for nearly 2 months she says. At present a woman with 7 children has turned 2 of her sons out of their room that I may have it & is waiting for me to move myself. At the same time I am paying storage for my luggage. I would like to stay at Burringbar till Xmas, but not under the existing conditions of housing. I find the children delightful & Mr Hayes as headmaster is exceedingly kind.[54]

On 9 June 1916 the head of the school, Edward Hayes, wrote to Inspector Dunlop that

Miss Coatsworth ... has been staying with Mr. A. Gray a highly respectable, successful dairy farmer living some few hundred yards from Burringbar Public School. Mr. & Mrs. Gray & family are people of unblemished characters & have a lovely home, a lovely residence. Miss Coatsworth's room contains a fine double bed & other requisites such as one would expect at a first class hotel. The floor

is covered with linoleum, very neat & clean; hot water is served to her in the mornings & she has 3 meals per day with refreshments at other hours such as 4 or 4.30 p.m. if she is inclined to indulge ... Most assistant teachers would welcome such a home. There is a very nice Broadwood piano there where Miss Coatsworth may enjoy herself if she so desires.[55]

Forwarding her resignation on 10 June 1916 Kathleen Coatsworth wrote to Inspector Dunlop who, knowing that she was unhappy, had written to her encouraging her to do her bit. Coatsworth wrote:

I had imagined that I was doing 'my bit' by remaining in this abominable place so long & by being willing to return later. I thought I was killed by being sent to Tweed Heads & when [I was sent] to Burringbar buried alive wasn't in it.

I think there may be many women who could have quite a pleasant time at Burringbar, but me, I loathe it most heartily. Besides my class I have one pleasure & that is to get out of it for the week ends. The friendly advances of the grocer & butcher boys etc. serve to add to my wrath ... I would rather resign than remain on here under the given conditions, this I must do at once in order to get other work. A Mr Gray is going to build a room for the teacher, but not me I am so tired of cows.[56]

Teacher's 'cold and unsympathetic nature' causes trouble at different schools

Katherine Hogan taught at a larger than average number of schools—25 schools in her 31 years of teaching (1914-45).[57] Her fifth appointment was to Wyrallah Public School near Lismore. On 30 April 1918 Inspector Dunlop wrote:

A crisis has been reached with regard to accommodation for Miss Hogan. The centre [Wyrallah] is ultra Protestant and practically every eligible male has enlisted. Miss Hogan is a Roman Catholic, and, it is rumoured, is not demonstrative enough in regard to the War as the residents would like. She does not like her appointment at Wyrallah and does not trouble to make herself agreeable. Further she is of such a cold and unsympathetic nature that

Wyrallah Public School, 1927
Teachers: Vivian Skippen, Ivy Sommerlad <u>Back row (left to right)</u>: Clive Rutledge, Tom Short, Vic Moss, Cec Webber, Ken McPherson, Peter Burley, Cyril Small, Alan Kenwood, (unknown), George Tulk, Lester Childs, Gordon Robson, Ted Cafe <u>3rd row (left to right)</u>: Beryl Childs, Mary Edwards, Marie Kenwood, Thea Skippen, Marie Essery, Doris Smith, Eunice Webber, Myra Andrews, Hazel Robson, Aub Walsh, — Childs, Beryl Essery, Iris Paisley, Annie Robson, Keith Walker <u>2nd row (left to right)</u>: Elsie McPherson, Delva Webber, Phyllis Edwards, Alice Smith, Bertha Smith, Bernice Walker, Dot Webber, Cliff Gilbert, Heather Summers, Alma Andrews, Edie Moss, Ethel Cafe, Reta Small, Gordon McDonald <u>Front row (left to right)</u>: Roland Small, George Smith, Stuart Small, Bill Kenwood, (unknown), Frank Essery, (unknown), Vic Webber, Kevin Partridge (Photograph courtesy of the late Cyril Small)

every house at Wyrallah is closed to her. I recommend that Miss Hogan be removed.[58]

Removed Katherine Hogan accordingly was, to a number of schools in rapid succession. In 1923, while at Camdenville Superior Public School, she was informed that 'your action in refusing to perform playground duty ... shows an insubordinate spirit on your part, and such action is viewed very gravely by the Dept.' [59] In 1931 she was 'Warned against any further misconduct. Repetition will lead to serious action: Hitting pupils.' [60] In 1939, while she was at Stanmore Public School it was noted: 'Appln for removal: Infd not proposed to remove her at present & that it was expected that she would

carry out more efficiently the duties entrusted to her'.[61] During 1940 the Department noted:

Infd that the recent inquiry revealed that she had acted offensively towards the Headmistress the First Asst and an Asst on the staff, 1) that she failed to carry out official instructions 2) that her undignified conduct at the inquiry was most reprehensible.

(a) reminded of the previous warnings given by the Dept.

(b) severely censured for her offensive conduct & warned that should she give any further cause for complaint in regard to the carrying out of her official duties, her case will be submitted to P.S.B.

[Public Service Board] with a view to her dismissal from the service.
To be removed to a country school.[62]

Katherine Hogan was then removed to Waratah Public School and then to Cardiff Public School from where she retired in 1945, aged 63.[63]

Daphne Lindsay, a popular teacher, 'goes too often to Coopernook'

Daphne Lindsay was a reluctant appointee to Herons Creek Public School near Kendall in July 1921 as she had wanted to stay at Coopernook School.[64] She was not happy at Herons Creek and in April 1922 the head of the school, Charles Kable, wrote to the inspector:

I think Miss Lindsay had been doing good work during the last six months, and your inspection of her work bore this out, she received an efficiency mark of 30. Since inspection I am sorry to say she has been not quite so satisfactory. She has the habit of going to Coopernook each week end, where there is apparently a congenial atmosphere.

She has come back twice in the Goods train 1½ hours late. I courteously but pointedly spoke to her pointing out the unfairness of this to her class, to me, and to your estimate of her worth as a teacher ...

Lately relations have been somewhat strained between her and the people (Noones) that she has been boarding with, and I think they have treated her very well. She goes too often to Coopernook, and comes back too tired to work her best, and more discontented with Heron's Creek. It is as you know, a rather dull sort of place, but with the very comfortable home, board and lodging that the Noones gave her, the comfortable work she has in the school, the help I know I have given her, the total absence of any friction whatever between her and myself, the satisfaction she expressed at having gained an advance of 6 in her mark from your inspection, these should be comforting things to her, and I am disappointed at her attitude to her work lately.

The children here like her, and I wish her well, but I venture the suggestion to you that an exchange with another assistant may be a good thing for her, and for my school.[65]

Daphne Lindsay was appointed to Heddon Greta Public School near Maitland on 6 January 1923. She married in 1924 and resigned in 1925. Later she resumed teaching and died in 1961.[66]

Teacher in a hurry to leave Willala

Vincent Wall was appointed to Willala Provisional School near Boggabri in September 1926 and was transferred to Tempe School in May 1927.[67] He was in such a hurry to tidy up the school for his successor and to get to the train at Boggabri—14 miles away with no regular transport—that he forgot to tell the inspector that he was going, and was reprimanded for this oversight as the inspector, on hearing a fortnight after Wall had left and that the school was closed, had driven 50 miles from Narrabri to Willala before 9.30 a.m. one day to investigate.[68]

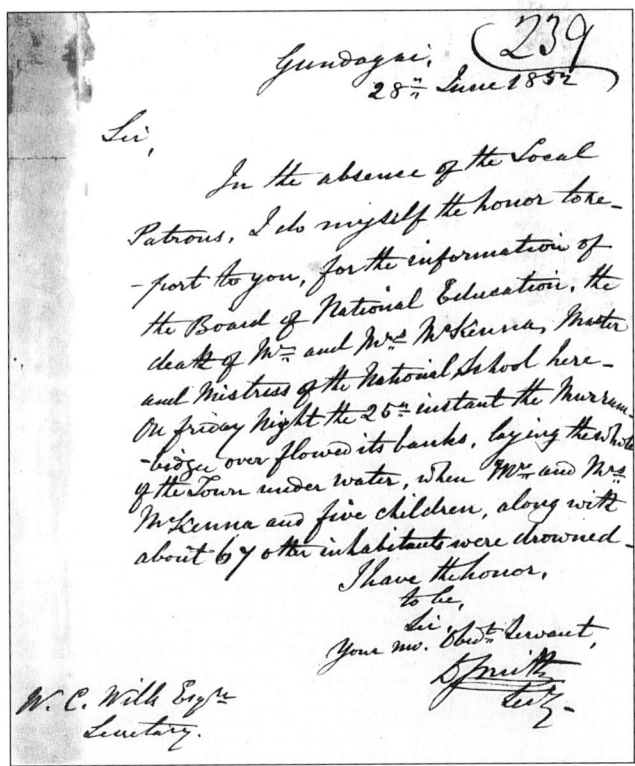

Letter reporting the drowning of the Gundagai teacher, Joseph McKenna, and his wife on 25 June 1852 (Archives Office of NSW ref: 1/387 Board of National Education, Miscellaneous letters received 1852)

15

The Elements

Storms

Grafton National School blown off its floor and foundations

On 20 January 1856 Alfred Lardner, secretary of the local patrons of the school at Grafton, reported to the Board of National Education:

It is my painful duty to state for your information that the School-house at North Grafton was blown down by a storm of wind and hail surpassing in violence anything I have ever experienced during a residence of 20 years in this Colony, on the evening of Thursday the 17th. Fortunately the children (96 in number) had left the room half an hour previously or the consequences might have been too awful to contemplate ...

The School house stood in a very exposed situation near the River—there was nothing for ¾ mile to check the fury of the storm—and only 16 feet wide, was not calculated to afford much resistance to the storm—the hailstones which were from 1 to 2 ½ inches in diameter, broke the four large windows in front in a moment—the wind rushed in, and finding no exit, lifted the place up from its foundations, and blew it over, shattering it much in its fall. The foundations and floor remain uninjured and unmoved from their place ... The Cottage and outbuildings are only slightly injured in the roof and windows—they being much wider and less lofty in proportion than the school.[1]

Cave Point Provisional School blown down by a gale

On 10 March 1896 Inspector Board sent a telegram to the chief inspector concerning the school at Cave Point (later Fingal Head): 'Cave Point School building erected by the residents was blown down by a gale on Monday'.[2]

Burringbar weathershed scattered far and wide by a gale

On 1 July 1929 Lindsay Hamilton, the teacher at Burringbar Public School near Murwillumbah, reported that

the weather shed was blown down by a gale on Saturday night the 29th instant. [This was the second time that this had happened.] Some idea of the force of the wind may be gained, when I say that several sheets of iron were carried a quarter of a mile away and lodged on a hill, two pieces of hardwood, 16 ft long by 4" x 2" were dropped in a field 100 yards distant. Much of the iron and timber will be of no further use as they are too badly broken and bent.[3]

Flood

James Dennis and his family almost afloat in Ulmarra School building

James Dennis was the head of Ulmarra (later Ulmarra East) Public School on the Clarence River in 1890. On 9 April of that year he reported:

The heavy rains that have prevailed since Christmas caused frequent freshes in the river, but on Sunday 9th March news was received of a higher rise than usual up the river. Next day the water came roaring over the bank. All communication between the school and the river bank was now cut off, and it was impossible to estimate the probable rise. However, we felt no alarm at the school, since the highest known flood, that of 1887, had barely reached the level of the house-floor, while in the school there were ten inches to spare. On Tuesday morning when we got up the water covered the lower part of the playground, and during the day stole rapidly up the slope. In the afternoon I began to pack up my furniture, books, &c., raising them three feet higher than any known flood. By this time the water was creeping up the door-step, and as it seemed likely to come into the house during the night, I removed the family to the school. To do this I had to take them out through a window and over a fence, and carry them 20 to 30 yards through the water. To go out through the door and the gate would necessitate wading through water four feet deep. I now packed up the school material ... When the water came into the school, blackboards were placed across the desks for the children to lie on. But as the water kept on rising at the same rate—about four inches an hour—I set to work to erect a platform by placing forms together on the top of the desks. I climbed up the windows and cut off the cords to lash the forms together, so as to form a sort of raft if it should be necessary. It was now nearly midnight, and the water still rose at the same alarming rate; hour by hour I watched it as it stole upwards. Mosquitoes made the children restless, and they had to be constantly watched to keep them from falling into the water. Outside the constant bellowing of cattle and squealing of pigs made a hideous din, mingled every now and then with the report of guns fired as distress signals. When daylight came there was nearly four feet of water in the school, but from that time it rose much more slowly. One press had capsized with all that it held, and forms and chairs were floating about the school, and amongst them, the table which fortunately remained upright and preserved the books lying on it. Towards midday the lower part of the forms we were on buoyed up, and the upper end was held firm only by our weight. One inch more would cover the forms altogether; I therefore thought it was time to leave ... Putting my head out of the window I cooeed till a boat came, and we all got out through the window. This was on Wednesday; the water was not out of the school till Saturday. Then we came home in a boat and were landed on the doorstep.[4]

Not surprisingly, James Dennis applied to be moved after this experience from the Clarence district, with its 'trying climate and frequent floods',[5] where he had taught since leaving the training school nine years earlier.

Floods mean Herons Creek School children unable to attend because of lack of lunches

There was no school at Herons Creek Provisional School near Kendall from 5 to 9 March 1894. Teacher Robert Dennis wrote:

Monday & Tuesday were very wet & although it cleared considerably on the remaining 3 days, the children were unable to attend on account of floods and the absence of food of a suitable nature for lunches, it being impossible to obtain flour from the stores or elsewhere at any price.[6]

Colin McKinnon and William Bondfield and the smell of dead fish at Swan Bay School

In May 1904 Colin McKinnon, the teacher at Swan Bay Public School on the Richmond River, closed the school temporarily, with the approval of Inspector Cornish, because of 'the pollution of the river through the wholesale destruction of fish'.[7]

In November 1917 this problem recurred.[8] The teacher at this time, William Bondfield, who had already sent a telegram about the matter of dead fish near the school, wrote to the chief inspector on 30 November 1917:

Owing to the fact that countless numbers of dead fish accumulated at the head of Swan Bay, and in close proximity to the school—the school-room is no longer (for the time being) in a healthy location. The wind wafts through and about the premises after passing across the festering fish: the result is unbearable and, I am sure is not sufficiently good to be regarded as safe.

This is not the first such occasion—in May 1904 the school was closed for two weeks or a little more—from the same cause.

It is hard indeed to believe that such a quantity of mullet, eels, and eel-tail catfish could be found gathered together as a harvest for the 'Grim Reaper'. Only those who actually see the sight or

Kurrara (later Banora Point) Public School, c.1910 (From Kurrara-Banora Point Primary School Centenary 1893–1993)

come in contact with the frightful stench can grasp the situation.

All this is caused by the recent flood. The waters inundated pasture lands heavily coated with grass and having lain for a few days the submerged grass ferments or decays—then the river lowers and the swamps pour out their filth—black—foetid and poisonous. The unfortunate fish in the bay were hemmed in and finding their way to the Bay's head were impounded and finally succumbed to the poisoned water ...

Some parents have already withdrawn their children from school—others have signified their intention of doing so—wishing by meeting to have the action taken by the Department of Education.

Personally, I shall have to remove my family or run the risk of typhoid or some fever. I suggest that the school be closed for a fortnight.[9]

In fact the school did not close completely. On 6 December 1917 Bondfield, to whom the Department had given no assistance (and no disinfectant) to deal with the problem, wrote:

The school has been kept in operation although the attendances were very, very low. During part of the time, sulphur had to be burned in the school-room to enable us to keep at work ... At the present moment the smell is in evidence but the fish are sinking and having suffered the worst stages—we are able to endure the modified

remnant, if it does not get worse.[10]

Dead cattle at Kurrara Public School

Following an unfavourable report on Kurrara (later Banora Point) Public School by the government health officer, the secretary of the Parents and Citizens Association, I. W. Helmsing, wrote to local member of parliament, Raymond Perdriau, in October 1922:

I would like to point out to you that after the flood experiences on the Tweed last year, dead cattle in an advanced state of decomposition were lying around the school for days.[11]

Dust

Dust at West Wyalong

On 10 December 1894 (although he mistakenly dated the letter 1895) the head of West Wyalong Public School, Thomas Thompson, applied for a pupil-teacher to be appointed to the school from the beginning of 1895.[12] By this time there were well over 100 children in the school and Thompson noted that 'the present average would be greater but for the presence of an epidemic of sore eyes'.[13] Thompson himself had sandy blight which caused him so much pain that he was away from school on 11 and 12 December 1894 and over three years later, in applying for removal for himself and his family he wrote that 'the glare, and the constant dust has affected the eyes of all of us'.[14]

Inspector Thomas was not pleased with the way that Thompson sometimes ordered what the inspector considered excessive amounts of material for the increasing number of pupils. In December 1898 Thompson, having been asked to explain the 'apparently excessive wear and tear'[15] on materials, had each of his teachers give an account of why the reading books lasted such a short time. (Reading was being taught in the shed at this time because the school was overcrowded.) Violet Hancox, the pupil-teacher who had been appointed at the beginning of 1895, wrote:

The constant dust of the playground and hardly a day passes without a duststorm sometimes so bad that one cannot see the children destroys the books ... In the hands of such young children, with lessons twice a day, these frail books do not seem to last long, notwithstanding my care. The school has been so full, that at least two rows of seats cannot place the books on the desks during reading lessons, and the hands of the children, in this hot weather, damp with perspiration, seem to make the leaves go very quickly.[16]

Inspector Thomas accepted the explanations and the school was able to be supplied with more reading books.[17]

Fire

Yarrowitch Public School burns down—local woman suspected

A new teacher, Gertrude McGrath, arrived at Yarrowitch Public School near Walcha in mid-January 1898.[18] She had been at the school less than a fortnight when it burnt down on the night of Friday 28 January.[19] There was some local feeling that the fire was the result of carelessness although Gertrude McGrath had not lit a fire or even a match there.[20] Following a police investigation, Sergeant Edwards of Walcha police wrote to police Superintendent Garvin that he was of the opinion

that [a local woman] is the person who set the school on fire, in the first place she is a woman of very bad character, she also has a seperation [sic] from her husband and has been for the past six months residing with her mother about 2 miles from her old home, which is about 200 yards from the

The Yarrowitch Public School building c.1913. This building was erected in 1898 to replace the one destroyed by fire. The flat area on the right side of the photograph was dug out by the older boys in their lunch breaks. (NSW Dept of School Education)

school; but on the night of the fire she was at her husbands place, and the only reason she can give for being there is that she was on her way home riding, and wanted to feed her horse. She states that … what she saw of the fire was from her bedroom window. She states she did not go outside. Several people are of the same opinion as the sergeant, but can give no reason. only that she is a very bad character, also very spiteful, and that she dislikes the present teacher.[21]

Although a reward of £25 was offered, the proven cause of the fire was not found.[22]

Boys responsible for destructive fire at Plunkett Street Public School

On 22 December 1911 Plunkett Street Public School at Woolloomooloo was extensively damaged by fire. The next day, 23 December, the *Sydney Morning Herald* reported:

It is … believed that the work was done by boys.

The first item of evidence in support of this supposition is the story of Mr Frank Hall who lives near the school.

I had just come off my duty on the trams, and was lying down' he told a 'Herald' reporter, 'when I heard that the school was on fire. I live only a few yards away, and was down in a minute, and believing that the gates would be shut, jumped over the side fence. I saw four lads there, two in the yard and two getting out of the window. One of them turned to me and offered me a handful of compasses, and when I asked him where he got them, he seemed to realise that I was not one of his pals. He took to his heels before I could grab him, and he was off like a shot …

As the motor engines of the Fire Brigade descended the steep slopes of the surrounding hillsides, it seemed as if they were running into a living sea, so dense was the crowd of children all about the burning school-house. Many expressed a heartfelt wish that the outbreak had occurred in school times, and not as at present, during the holidays. It is also interesting to note that many of the boys that swarmed about the engines as soon as they drew up, and who willingly gave information, knew very well that the fire had broken out in the main building and numerous other details of the outbreak that proved to be, not as is usually the case with the rumours that

Class at Plunkett Street Public School, c.1910 (NSW Dept of School Education)

Furniture saved from the fire of unknown origin which almost destroyed Rylstone Public School on 6 August 1925 (NSW Dept of School Education)

circulate at every fire, vague and inaccurate, but surprisingly near the actual state of affairs.

Five boys were convicted of the crime, four being released on probation.[23]

Megalong Subsidised School building destroyed by fire

On Monday 16 August 1937 the Megalong school building, which at that time was being used for a Subsidised School (i.e., not a government school) taught by Patrice Grady, was totally destroyed by fire. The police report stated that it had been a 'One roomed building, constructed of wood with iron roof. Old and out of repair. Value approximately £10'.[24]

On 24 August 1937 Patrice Grady reported:

I made a fire in the school in the morning & before leaving at 3.30 p.m. swept the fire to the back of the fire-place as usual. At 4.15 p.m. Mr. T. Cowing informed me that the school was alight. Two men and myself went down, but found that nothing could be done. All the school materials were destroyed.[25]

Cane broken in two by fire-lighting boys at Dumbleton Public School

In the early hours of 30 September 1937 there was a fire at Dumbleton (later Beverly Hills) Public School. The police report on the matter stated:

Drawers in the school had been broken open, and the cane had been taken out of one, broken in two and left on the table. Jars of flowers had been upset and thrown out of the window, but so far nothing is found to be stolen. As the result of our inquiries we are satisfied that it was boys responsible for the offence.[26]

16

Dangers

Teacher dies down shaft at Pipeclay Creek

Frederick White, a married man who was the teacher at Pipeclay Creek (later Buckaroo) Public School near Mudgee, closed the school as usual on Friday evening 5 June 1874[1]. On Tuesday 9 June the chairman of the local school board wrote to the Council of Education:

I beg to inform you that no traces [were found] of Mr White at the school at 12 o'clock on Monday the 8th June. The Local Board has closed the school and [is] waiting for advice for what to do respecting the school. Search has been made but [there is] no account of Mr White whatever.[2]

The *Sydney Morning Herald* of Friday, 19 June 1874 (p. 5), carried the following report:

Mudgee, Thursday:

Yesterday an inquest was held at Pipeclay Creek, on the body of Frederick White, the master of the Public School. He had been missing for a fortnight and was found in a shaft fifty feet deep, with his neck and a leg broken. Verdict, accidental death.

In 1963 John L. Tierney (who wrote under the pen name Brian James) noted that local oral sources of information on this event had told him that 'Fred White was confronted by other dangers than those of "mine shafts". He fell down that "mine shaft" in Sapling Gully very late at night, and after a convivial evenings [*sic*] at "Fredericksburg"—the Bucholtz home.'[3]

Big blackbutt tree threatens school, pupils, and teacher sleeping in the school

On 17 January 1893 Robert Dennis, the 21-year-old[4] first teacher at Herons Creek Provisional

Herons Creek Provisional School teacher Robert Dennis's sketch, (17 January 1893), showing the leaning blackbutt tree threatening the school building (Herons Creek School File [Archives Office of NSW ref: 5/16264])

School near Kendall, wrote to Inspector Nolan:

There is a large 'Black butt' tree between 100 & 150 feet in height and a girth measurement of some 18 ft or so in dangerous proximity to the school house. It has a very uncanny lean in the direction of the school and what causes it to be more dangerous than it otherwise would be, is the fact of the butt being completely eaten out by bush fires leaving only a shell to sustain the whole weight of the tremendous upper growth, especially when there is any strong wind blowing. The only wonder to me is, that it has not fallen before. Any how, if it were to fall now, while the pupils were at their lessons, there would be no escape and I would not be at all surprised if the result were attended with serious loss of life, as the upper branches would certainly strike the building.

I asked a resident if it is possible to fall the tree in question 'off the school'. He says it can be done but a very calm day will have to be selected for the work. I do not know how much it will cost but will you authorize me to get some one to fall it. I can assure you it is necessary.[5]

On 6 February Dennis wrote to Inspector Wright:

Yesterday I rode to Laurieton and saw Mr Laurie [and] explained everything. He could not give the advice required. Mr Laurie said that every precaution had been taken to clear any timber which appeared to endanger the school, before the building was erected, but the fact stands nevertheless that this tree is particularly dangerous and the only way I can account for it is that the tree in question has acquired the lean since the school was finished. Mr Laurie said further that if I were right to get the services of Mr J. Brown today and fall it without further delay.

I called on Mr B. on my way home & he agreed to be at the school this morning early, which he did & brought the necessary tools with him. Brown asked my permission to fall 3 or 4 small trees as they were likely to cant the big one on to the school as it fell. This permission I gave him and he fell them. He then erected a platform around the big tree and got 2 friends to help him with the 'crosscut saw' and to drive the wedges. I let the children out when he told me viz: 3.25 p.m. as I understood he was going to start work in earnest. He asked my opinion, I repeated what Mr Laurie said. He had another look at the tree & the lot of them said the task was a difficult one and finally decided to have nothing to do with it without the presence of Mr Laurie or some other responsible person, else a written authority to exonerate everyone from blame in the event of it coming on the school. Mr Brown is a practical man, and as Mr Laurie said 'If Joe Brown can't fall it off the school no-one can' you will see the work is difficult. In falling it there is a chance of throwing it off the school by some system of wedging but should it fall itself nothing is more certain than the school being completely smashed if nothing worse happens.

I may state that when Brown fell one of the trees it struck against the large one & knocked off a limb from it, Brown called my attention to the rottenness of it. I trust, Sir, you will do your best to help me in the matter, as I have to sleep in the school being unable to obtain lodgings at any of the residents' houses. I enclose a rough drawing to give an idea. It is not exaggerated in any particulars.[6]

Another possibility Dennis drew attention to was that the tree could fall onto the main road and have to be cleared from it.[7] The records do not show whether or how the worrying blackbutt was eventually removed.

Incomplete clearing of school ground leaves lances for children to fall or walk on

When members of the local school board visited Karangi Provisional School near Coffs Harbour in February 1895 they reported on the clearing of the ground:

We found that some work in the way of clearing off the ground round the school had been done but the condition of the ground is dangerous for children to walk on, owing to the numerous small brambles and trees which covered the ground being cut down about a foot from the ground, representing thousands of lances on which the children might at any time fall'.[8]

Teacher shooting the wildlife at Possum Creek accidentally shoots himself dead

Eighteen-year-old John Howes, who was the adopted son of Mr R. H. Howes of Prince Alfred Hospital in Sydney,[9] took up his first appointment at the newly established Opossum Creek Provisional School at Possum Creek near Bangalow after Easter in 1899. He spent his spare time shooting the abundant wildlife but accidentally shot himself dead on 14 August 1899.[10]

Tree falls on new school building at Bagawa

In a storm near Coffs Harbour on the night of 1 June 1903 a tree fell on the new Bagawa (later Nana Glen) Public School building and six trees fell on the school fence. Teacher Henry Masters noted: 'Delay in repairing the building will cause serious damage to wood-work, and render $1/3$ of the school practically useless during wet weather'.[11]

* * *

17

Animals

Henry Lawson and the goanna at Eurunderee Provisional School

In 1876 Henry Lawson was a foundation pupil at Eurunderee Provisional School near Mudgee. In his

ANNEX TO APPLICATION FOR ESTABLISHMENT OF A PUBLIC SCHOOL

AT *Eurunderee*

First page of annex to application for a Public School at Eurunderee, listing Henry Lawson as a prospective pupil, (20 July 1877). Eurunderee School was already in operation as a Provisional School, with Henry Lawson in attendance and John Tierney as teacher at the time this application was made. (Eurunderee School File [Archives Office of NSW ref: 5/15856])

'Fragment of Autobiography' Lawson recalled:

Amongst the scholars was a black gohanna [*sic*]. He lived in a dead hollow tree near the school and was under the master's immediate protection. On summer days he'd lay along a beam over the girls' seats, and improve his mind a little, and doze a lot. The drone of the school seemed to be good for his nerves …

Sometimes, when the master's back was turned for a minute or so, one of the boys would cry suddenly: 'Girls, the goanna's fallin'.' And then you'd hear the girls squawk. One form of alleged punishment in the Old Bark School was to make a bad boy go and sit with the girls. I was sent there once, by mistake. I felt the punishment, or the injustice of it keenly; but I don't remember that I minded the girls.[1]

Snakes

A black snake in the rafters at Dungarubba Creek Provisional School

In 1892 Julia Maclean, a 20-year-old city girl in charge of the school at Dungarubba Creek (later Dungarubba) Provisional School near Woodburn, complained to a visiting member of the school board about a large black snake in the rafters of the school.[2]

Reptiles such as death adders in the playground at Yamba Public School

The playground at Yamba Public school was ploughed and levelled to remove the undergrowth and ferns in 1897 after Inspector Lobban, who had received complaints from parents, wrote that 'this undergrowth is a great cover for reptiles such as death adders which are known to be plentiful in that part of Yamba'.[3]

Snakes in the playground at Brunswick Heads

The teacher at Brunswick Heads Public School, Fred Fordham wrote to the Department in September 1928:

Scrub is growing rapidly, whilst ferns and grass provide a harbour for snakes. During the last season four snakes were killed in the playground, whilst another was killed in the manual room.[4]

Mice

Mice destroying the books at Fernleigh Public School

The teacher at Fernleigh Public School near Ballina, John Schuback was supplied with a book press and other new furniture for the school after he reported on 10 July 1899:

The present supply consists of five desks (one insufficient) and they are old and of 'bush make'.

Abermain Public School fertilizer team, 1917 (From the Education Gazette, *1 May 1917)*

There is no book-press ... and the mice are destroying the books. The table is also an old one of 'bush construction'.[5]

Horses

Loss of a valuable horse at Coorabell

In 1920 Donald Macrae, the teacher at Coorabell Public School near Bangalow, wrote to the inspector about the need for a horse paddock at the school. Macrae, who suffered from intestinal trouble and therefore needed to drink milk, wrote:

To me both a horse and cow are absolutely necessary. Through having no place to run a horse, I was compelled to let him stray on the road, with the result that I lost him and there appears no hope of recovering him. He is a very valuable horse and his loss is felt.[6]

Goats

Jennings locality swarming with goats

In 1891 at Jennings Public School near the Queensland border north of Tenterfield the teacher, Walter Dalton, reported that 'Not withstanding that a 3 railed fence has been erected around the school grounds at this place—the goats—this locality swarms with them—have begun to make the school and weathershed their homes, both inside and underneath'.[7]

Flocks of goats at Eringonia

In July 1892 Inspector John Smith noted of Eringonia (later Enngonia) Public School, 70 miles north of Bourke, that 'there are flocks of goats there and a post and railed fence would not keep them out'.[8]

Goats take possession of buildings at Yamba Public School

In 1895 a wire mesh screen was added to the weathershed at Yamba Public School after Inspector Lobban wrote:

The village is infested with goats, and in wet weather the verandas of the Teacher's residence and the weathershed are taken possession of by these animals which are at all times a nuisance.[9]

Garden at Chakola Public School near Cooma, 1920 (NSW Dept of School Education)

West Wyalong goats eating pupils' dinners

After an attack on West Wyalong Public School's closets by vandals in 1901 Inspector Connelly wrote:

It seems to me very desirable to place palings round the two-rail fence which surrounds the West Wyalong School ... Unless fenced the goats would play havoc with young trees.[10]

The Department considered that this work might be undertaken when funds were available. The fence, however, had not had palings added by September 1905 when the West Wyalong Progress Association wrote to the Minister requesting that this be done as 'it is a common occurrence for the children to lose their dinners through the goats having the free run of the playground'.[11]

Teacher shoots goats at New Vale Public School

The teacher at New Vale (later Zig Zag) Public School near Lithgow, Robert Dennis, wrote in 1907 that for two years he had

had endless trouble with a couple of goats and a horse ... They live 150 yds from the playground,

where I have endeavoured to grow trees for the past 3 years (I have just planted them for the 4th time) and these wretched animals have each time destroyed them. Last year the children made gardens and it was quite a common thing to see those goats destroying the work of the boys.[12]

Trouble with the goats continued. In May 1908 the superintendent of school agriculture, who had visited the school, wrote to the Department urging that the fence around the one acre school site be wire-netted because 'the neighbours (miners) keep a number of goats and calves which are allowed to roam at large'.[13] He went on to say that 'the teacher has shot the goats two or three times but the practice is pernicious and might lead to serious consequences'.[14] On this latter statement, above the words 'shot the goats' a perhaps alarmed departmental official has pencilled 'how many' on the file.[15]

Cattle

Wild cattle break into playground at Martins Creek

In 1894 the inspector asked Daniel Carter, the teacher at Martins Creek Provisional School,

Hannam Vale Provisional School, 1907 (Teacher Bertha Smith right, Kate Redman left); building erected in 1905 (From Hannam Vale Public School Centenary 1892–1992)

whether it was true, as had been reported by a resident, that wild cattle were being driven past the school endangering the children because they had access to the school ground.[16] In May 1894 Carter replied:

The fence is in very bad repair now, causing it to be utterly useless. Wild cattle are often driven along the road, which passes the door, by Vacy butchers and also others who have selections in this direction. Mr Martin's bullocks have broken through the playground when being driven along the road.[17]

Cattle at Possum Creek leave school in a filthy condition

George McDonald, the teacher at Opossum Creek Public School at Possum Creek near Bangalow, wrote in 1901 that 'At present the cattle camp around the school and in the verandah leaving the place in a filthy condition. They also make it very muddy in wet weather.' [18]

Cattle annoying lady teacher at Hannam Vale

Bertha Smith was the teacher at Hannam Vale Public School near Kendall in 1908 when local resident James Buttsworth wrote to local member of parliament, Robert Davidson:

Now as I daresay you know the school ground is for the most part surrounded by a reserve & cattle & horses have made it a common camping ground & make a nice mess all round the school. Besides the teacher & pupils have gone to a lot of trouble in making a garden, fencing it round with poles, planting flowers, vegetables & other things but the cattle cannot be kept out & are continually annoying the teacher, who is a lady.[19]

Cow droppings on school steps and verandah at Coorabell

In 1936 Nicholas Lennon, the teacher at Coorabell Public School near Bangalow, wrote:

I find it necessary to have the cow-droppings cleaned from about the school building (and on one morning from the school steps and verandah) on very frequent occasions. I would say that this happens on at least 3 days weekly.[20]

Pigs

Pigs come to the school door at Clunes

In 1890 Charles Howard, the teacher at Clunes Public School near Bangalow, reported to Inspector McLelland that pigs belonging to local residents Smith and Walker 'cannot be kept off the School ground, nor will the owners secure them, They actually come to the School doors, The boar is the worst. Will you be so good as to compel the owner to keep them off.' [21] McLelland reported to his superior officer that 'It will be at once apparent how great a nuisance to the teacher and his family must be a herd of pigs running, all day long, over the grounds'.[22] Howard was authorised to take legal proceedings if the nuisance continued.[23]

Pig pens too close to the school at Kurrara

When Inspector Henry visited Kurrara (later Banora Point) Public School on 14 May 1913 he saw that pig pens were being constructed (owner Mrs McAdoo) about 25 yards from the school building.

Although he wrote to Mrs McAdoo asking that the pens be moved further from the school, this was not done and they were completed and occupied by pigs in about July of that year. Following further notices to Mrs McAdoo from Tweed Shire Council, the pigs were eventually removed on 12 September, after having been in the pens for about two months.[24]

Dogs

Numerous dogs an intolerable nuisance at Martins Creek

In 1924 Thomas Dibden, the teacher at Martins Creek Public School near Paterson, successfully requested a paling fence around the school residence because 'I do not know of any place, as closely settled as this, where dogs are so numerous. Despite all our protests, where owners are known, these pests invade the premises, even the kitchen and pantry. They also befoul and scratch up the garden; and are altogether an intolerable nuisance.' [25]

Gardening at Lakemba Public School (From Report of the Minister of Public Instruction, *1910, p. 87)*

Rabbits

Rabbits alive and dead under Ivanhoe Public School building

In 1892 the teacher at Ivanhoe Public School, Frederick Long, made a successful application for some means of protection of the school building from rabbits. He wrote:

The rabbits are continually burrowing under the school. Lately I have filled up several holes. Some of these rabbits die underneath the boards, & the smell arising from the decaying bodies is most disagreeable.[26]

Dead rabbits under Ganmain Public School force teacher and pupils to vacate premises

The teacher at Ganmain Public School near Coolamon, Bryan Dale, reported in 1907 on

the intolerable nuisance and danger of typhoid or other diseases arising from the stench of dead rabbits beneath the school floor. Several children are away sick and so deadly is the smell that yesterday and today we were obliged to vacate the school.[27]

Rabbits and hares eating everything green in Badgerys Creek Public School garden

On 18 October 1915 the teacher at Badgerys Creek Public School, James Neville, made a successful request for the Department to supply wire netting to enclose the school garden. He wrote that

At present the garden is open to hares and rabbits, and during certain periods of the year, they become very troublesome eating almost everything green. This greatly impedes the successful working of the garden and disheartens the children.[28]

Frogs

Frogs in the water supply at St Ives

The first head teacher of St Ives Public School, George Bolus, reported in 1893 that he had had the school tank thoroughly cleaned because of the bad taste of the water and that 'in the tank were found four years' accumulation of sediment and a dead frog, doubtless the cause of the bad taste'.[29]

Bird life

Ducks and fowls at Kiama prevent floral culture

The superintendent of school gardens visited Kiama Superior Public School in June 1892 and reported that

The playground of this school is less than one acre. Owing to the number of cottages surrounding the grounds it is over run with the ducks and fowls of the neighbours. Therefore there is very little chance of doing any floral culture until these defects are remedied.[30]

Birds in the water at Ivanhoe

William Lewington, the teacher at Ivanhoe Public School in 1898, reported in October of that year that the water from the school tank 'is at present in a very bad state, owing to small birds being in it, in a putrified [sic] condition. They have very probably got in by floating off the roof down the spouting.'[31]

Forty fowls in Burringbar teacher's garden

In 1916 head teacher of Burringbar Public School near Murwillumbah, Edward Hayes, successfully applied for wire netting to enclose his garden. He wrote: 'I have no fowls, yet as many as forty daily from neighbouring residences take complete charge of our gardening operations'.[32]

Window broken by jackass (i.e., kookaburra) at Lismore High School

The head of Lismore High School, Malcolm Mackinnon, wrote in 1927: 'I have to report that three windows ... were broken by the storm on Sunday 13th Nov. & another by a laughing jackass the next day'.[33]

Jackass (i.e., kookaburra) crashes through window at Hannam Vale Public School

On 1 July 1935 teacher Stephen Collier, heading his report 'Strange bird accident', described an unusual happening at Hannam Vale Public School near Kendall. He wrote:

At 3.35 this afternoon, just as the children had marched out of school, a Jackass crashed through the lowest right hand 12" x 10" thick pane of the window, shattering the glass into more than a thousand pieces. Fragments of glass were scattered over 9 dual desks, and some pieces hit the opposite wall 18 ft. away.

The Jackass was stunned, a piece shaved off its beak and a couple of small cuts on its head. We could find no reason for the accident. I took the Jackass to the house and a quarter of an hour later it flew away and joined its mates.[34]

Swooping magpie causes boy to die by inhaling a pea at Campbelltown

In 1954 at Campbelltown a young boy (who was reported by the Department to be not a pupil of Campbelltown Public School) died as a result of inhaling a pea. In a rider to his report on this death the Coroner wrote on 19 November 1954:

I believe the Primary cause of [the boy's] death was the terrifying experience and fright he received by a Magpie swooping down over his head ...

I am of the opinion that all School Teachers should warn School Children, especially the Kindergarten classes of the danger of these birds especially at this time of the year ...

Parents would be well advised not to send their children to school without hats ...

And in the case of the young Kindergarten pupils they should be accompanied by an adult ... or in a group, not to be allowed to walk to or from school alone.[35]

Ants

Ants in school lunches at St Ives

In 1926 secretary of the Parents and Citizens Association at St Ives Public School, George Gaukrodger, wrote that 'A luncheon cupboard is badly needed ... Recently lunches were uneatable owing to ants.'[36]

Assorted fauna

Assorted fauna at Wyrallah and Tucki Tucki Public Schools

In 1890 John Horton, the teacher at Wyrallah Public School, wrote:

Dingoes, wallabies, bandicoots, native-cats, opossums, and in the summer months huge carpet snakes pay us nightly visits; a good paling fence would at least keep some of the foregoing from under the residence.[37]

At nearby Tucki Tucki Public School in 1907 teacher Gaisford McCurdy, who was considered by Inspector McCoy to have the best school garden in the district, complained that his teaching of agriculture was difficult because the adjoining school paddock was

densely covered with Lantana which harbours bandicoots and other marsupials which destroy the growing plants. In fact, of late some of the plots have been divested of everything that was growing in them.[38]

White ants

White ants in possession at Burringbar

On 1st June 1901 Inspector Cornish reported with regard to the Burringbar Public School building (built in 1893 and moved in 1895):

Not a very costly, or in any way a symmetrical looking structure was built, and the whole of the material being pine, the white ants have now full possession of it. The majority of the lining boards, the studs and window sashes are riddled with these destructive insects, and portions of the building can scarcely hold together. Half of one window has completely fallen out through the depredations of the ants, and the teacher has temporarily nailed up a board to exclude the rain. It is only 8 ft high to the wall-plate, is neither ceiled nor lined, so that it must be exceedingly oppressive inside during summer time. The structure is beyond repair and a new school is absolutely necessary as soon as possible.[39]

A local resident, W. L. Murphy, had earlier written to the Department that the old school was 'only hanging together and as the song says, lets in both the sunshine and rain'.[40]

Fear of boys falling into W.C. at Macarthur Public School

The teacher at Macarthur Public School near Gravesend, Mary Fearby, wrote a report on white ants at the school in 1915. Among the damage they had caused was that the 'top seat in Boy's [*sic*] W.C. [water closet] has been badly eaten away by [them], & unless something is done immediately, I fear there may be an accident of a disagreeable character at no very distant date'. [41]

Inspector fears collapse of Buxton Public School building during inspection

In September 1915 Inspector Thomas reported on the Buxton school building near Picton:

I inspected this school last week, and found that the condition of the building from the ravages of white ants was much more serious than I thought ... A very violent gale was blowing at the time of my visit and I was afraid, at times, that the building would collapse, as much of the framework (studs and plates) has been weakened, in addition to the destruction of the weatherboard and lining.

I beg to suggest that the white ant specialist be instructed to report upon the matter, and to express a definite opinion as to whether it is practicable to remove the damaged portions, and renew with sound material. If such is not practicable, I am afraid that a new building will be necessary.[42]

Teacher's boot almost goes through wall at Tregeagle

The teacher at Tregeagle Public School near Lismore in 1917, David Grierson, wrote: 'By appearances I think the white ants are in the school room. I happened to tap the bottom board on the northern wall today and my boot almost went through it.'[43] Despite numerous treatments, white ants continued to destroy the school and in 1930 local member of parliament, William Missingham, wrote of the white ant problem that 'if this is not attended to, the white ants will remove the school in a short time'.[44]

Danger of Nana Glen Public School building falling on the children

It had been planned to erect a new building for Nana Glen Public School near Coffs Harbour but in July 1929 Inspector Lewis was notified that the new building must stand over for the present. Repair work was done, however, after Lewis wrote to the chief inspector:

I would like to point out that over two years ago Mr Inspr. Lee found that the present building was urgently in need of repairs but considered that these would probably prove too costly to be worth while as the school is in quite an anomalous position etc.

As the school is in danger of falling on the children owing to the timber being eaten away by white ants, I strongly recommend, if the decision not to remove the school is irrevocable, that the white ant expert (accompanied by a carpenter) be sent to apply some remedial measures as soon as practicable.[45]

18

Vandals and Tramps

Berrigan Provisional School verandah used as shelter by tramps

In March 1892 Berrigan Progress Association, through its secretary, A. Hiddle, unsuccessfully applied to have the Department fence the Berrigan Provisional School ground. Hiddle wrote that 'at present it is a refuge at night for the tramps, who sleep on the verandah. At noonday the sheep, goats, etc. seek the same refuge much to the annoyance of the children and teacher.' [1] Trouble with tramps continued at Berrigan with the inspector writing in 1894 that

the adjacent land is much used as a camping ground by travellers who make free use of the school water and even sleep and eat on the school verandah. The teacher and a resident member of this school board both assert that the premises are frequently left in a filthy condition by tramps.[2]

Tramps at Buxton

W. Greetham, secretary of the Buxton Progress Committee, wrote to local member of parliament, William McCourt, on 6 November 1895 requesting that the Buxton Provisional School near Picton be fenced

to make it safe from travellers as it is fortunate it has not been burnt down as they carry bushes to make their beds on and camp and some of them climb over the gates at the back and sleep in the

Berrigan Public School, 1909, building completed 1898 (NSW Dept of School Education)

verandah and they use the water that should be in there for the use of the school. Several times the tank has been empty and they have to go a considerable distance for water and [this] has caused a good deal of annoyance to the teacher.[3]

No fence was erected, however, as Inspector Johnson wrote that 'a fence would not keep out the tramps or prevent them from taking the water'.[4] The school's problems with tramps were still continuing in 1907 when the then teacher, Carlisle Parker, successfully applied for repairs to a window as, he wrote: 'It is now an easy matter for travellers to unlock the windows and get into the School to camp'.[5]

New Vale Public School locality infested with larrikins

In 1900 the teacher at New Vale (later Zig Zag) Public School near Lithgow, Robert Dennis, wrote of a broken window at the school which had been broken when he came to the school that 'this is the work of larrikins who infest the locality'.[6]

Lead from school roof stolen for fishing· sinkers at Brunswick Heads

Inspector Cornish reported in April 1902 that at the then closed school building at Brunswick Heads, 'Stealing the lead off the school roof has ... recently taken place by persons requiring "sinkers" for their fishing tackle'.[7]

Mothers anxious about tramps and snakes at Burraneer Bay

In October 1904 the inspector reported on the fact that some children, who lived closer to Lilli Pilli, had to walk through bush to Burraneer Bay Public School. He wrote that

By means of cart tracks through the thinly timbered bush, the children from all the outlying places can reach the School within a journey of 1° mile ... The Mothers are naturally anxious about their children, (especially their girls) having to travel through the bush, on account of tramps and snakes. All the homes are close together at both places, and the children go in companies to the School, and thus protect each other.[8]

Vandalism at Numulgi looking like the work of a madman

Numulgi Public School near Lismore was broken into and vandalised in June and July 1911. The hands of the clock were twisted round each other. The girls' sewing was soaked with ink, library books were splashed with sulphuric acid, a window was broken, and some records were disfigured with ink. Teacher William Miller reported that this was not an isolated incident. He wrote: 'for the last 3 months, at intervals, outrages have been perpetrated in this locality—viz. separators damaged, cream spilt, harness cut to pieces, gear of bullock team stolen'.[9] After his investigations at the school and in the locality, the inspector noted that 'some of the work looks like that of a madman e.g., cutting of harness, poisoning animals, sawing the shafts off a buggy etc—The police say they know who the perpetrators are but in the absence of any direct evidence, they are unable to make an arrest. Apparently they are doing their best to secure the necessary evidence.'[10]

Travellers camping on Nana Glen Public School verandah

On 10 February 1916 Henry Dale, the teacher at Nana Glen Public School near Coffs Harbour, wrote to the inspector:

At present the verandahs [of the school] are frequently made use of as camping places by travellers, whose careless use of fire constitutes a grave danger, especially in such dry seasons as we have lately experienced.[11]

Tramp uses school records as a pillow at Five Mile Tree

In 1925 Arnold Quarmby, the teacher at Five Mile Tree Provisional School near Crookwell, wrote that

on returning from vacation I discovered records and other material piled in a corner evidently having been used as a pillow by some tramp or traveller. The two middle sheets of roll were torn out and blowing about the floor ... I did not report the matter as I knew nothing could be done to trace the intruder.[12]

Tuggerah Public School, c.1910 (Copy held by NSW Dept of School Education)

Tramps habitually camping at Herons Creek Public School

During the last weekend of August 1931 Herons Creek Public School near Kendall was forcibly entered and, as teacher Raymond Fuller reported:

All presses and drawers were forced open, and books and other materials scattered freely around the rooms. There was no money in the building, and nothing of any value was taken, but a window pane was broken, two padlocks and press lock were destroyed, a cricket shield damaged, and two holes cut in a water tank with an axe ... I have no idea of the person responsible for the damage.[13]

The inspector commented: 'There is no vested residence at Heron's Creek, the teacher resides half a mile away, and tramps have at times used the verandah'.[14] Constable Thomas Gunther of Kew police station reported that on hearing of the offence he 'immediately went to Herons Creek and commenced inquiries. Quite a number of tramps had passed through the village during the weekend. I telephoned all surrounding stations and interviewed many of the tramps'.[15] No charges were laid in this case.

In December 1931 Fuller wrote again to the inspector:

I wish to again report on the undesirable practice so common at this school of travellers making use of the building for camping purposes. Being situated on the main road, tramps are always camping on the verandah. Fires are lit close to the building and I frequently pick up live matches on the verandah. The place is often left in a dirty condition with papers, tobacco and cigarettes strewn about, while during wet weather the floor is left covered with mud. Candles are frequently used and the remains left about on the floor, while filthy writings and drawings are made on the walls.

During week ends children's gardens are frequently damaged, pot plants destroyed and vegetables stolen. I have done all I can to prevent this practice but as there is no residence, and I do not live near the school, I cannot prevent people camping there. There is a grave risk of fire owing to the careless way matches are dropped and fires left burning. I have burnt the grass back from the building and rendered it as safe as possible under the circumstances.[16]

19

Pupils

Pupils kept at home to hunt off the cockatoos at Tucki Tucki

In May 1868 teacher Frederick Miller, in the course of explaining a fall in attendances at Tucki Tucki (later Wyrallah) Public School near Lismore, wrote:

Another reason is that most of the Parents of children being farmers are dependent on their crops of maize for a living and that the cockatoos being such a pest and source of great loss they are obliged to keep the children at home to hunt these birds off their crops.

As soon as the fine weather sets in and the maize crops are gathered I am sure that the school will be greatly increased in attendance.[1]

Father Curran flogs pupil in Dubbo Public School playground

In December 1883 the teacher at Dubbo Public School, James Butler, who was himself a Catholic, wrote to Inspector Johnson:

I have the honour to acquaint you that, on the 17th inst., the Revd. Mr. Curran, Teacher of the R. C. School in this town, <u>rode</u> most furiously into the playground of the Public School in pursuit of a pupil who, he said, had insulted him ... he rode like one 'possessed' after a lad named Rossiter, making violent efforts to strike him with his riding whip. The scene in the playground was most disgraceful; in fact, so keenly have I felt the humiliation of witnessing the demon-like conduct of the Revd.

Swimming class for pupils of Dubbo Public School, 1921 (NSW Dept of School Education)

Gentleman, that I have determined to pass him in future without the slightest sign of recognition.[2]

Assistant Inspector Fletcher investigated the matter and reported on 5 January 1884:

As Father Curran was riding along the street and past the school, some one, or more, of the boys, who were in the playground, exclaimed 'Oh! here's Father Curran—We shall have currants for the Christmas pudding'—or something to that effect. Mr. Curran, riding up to the fence, called to the teacher, and said 'These boys of yours are very insulting, Mr. Butler', whereupon Mr. B. asked him to name any of the offenders and they should be promptly punished. But, with the remark 'Oh! I don't know their names', he was riding off, when he caught sight of one of the supposed offenders, and, quickly turning his horse round, rode furiously into the school yard, scattering the lads, and (as related in the teacher's letter) chasing one in particular ...

It is very doubtful whether the lad (Rossiter) singled out by Father Curran, was one of those who made the alleged remarks at all. But, though the boy's father is a Protestant, the mother is a Roman Catholic, and the boy was, till very recently, a pupil in the local Roman Catholic School, of which Father Curran is the Head Master, but from which he (Father Curran) lately dismissed him.[3]

Larrikin pupils throw blue metal at teachers at Plunkett Street Public School

In 1890 the head of Plunkett Street Public School at Woolloomooloo, George Metcalfe, wrote of the way he had found the school on his arrival at the beginning of the year:

I found the pupils larrikins of the worst type, in school they threw acorns and Moreton Bay figs about, also pencils and even books or ink-wells. Outside the school, they threw blue metal at the windows and at the teachers.[4]

Early in the year Metcalfe wrote of the worst act of larrikinism yet reported at the school:

The school premises are being damaged by a gang of larrikins, they call the teachers names, come into the school-yards, howl and yell like wild beasts, throw horse dung in at the windows and doors, and worse than all, they pelt the teachers and the buildings with blue metal.

This afternoon the premises were in a state of siege, being assailed by a gang of about 25 half-clad urchins of the lowest type. They pestered the Girls' School, to such an extent that the pupil teacher could not give her lesson, on Mrs Tuckett going out to see who they were, she was nearly struck on the head with a stone. They came onto the porch, and rang the bell, they threw stones into the Boys' School one of which struck the top of a desk with great force, while the children were sitting in their places.[5]

New Vale applicants for an Evening School not serious enough

An application for an Evening School at New Vale (later Zig Zag) near Lithgow in March 1893 gave as prospective pupils 25 young miners and railway workers. The inspector successfully recommended that the application be declined for the following reasons:

1. I do not believe that the applicants would attend regularly, and from their character, I am of opinion that the affair would quickly develop into a 'smoke club'.
2. There is a brewery (which is working night and day) within 70 yards of the school-house and I feel satisfied the applicants would be found there oftener than at the school.
3. The teacher [20 year-old Herbert Bayliss] is too young and too inexperienced to conduct, with any success, an institution of this kind, and particularly to deal with miners and young men of that class. I am afraid he would be the pupil as often as the master.
4. I do not believe in the earnestness of the applicants and give this among other reasons. There is a well-conducted School-of-Arts in Lithgow only one mile, or one mile-and-a half distant from the homes of the majority of these young men and yet, from one year's end to the other, the face of one of them is never seen inside its walls. This fact is, I think, significant.[6]

Pupils pulling maize too busy to enrol in new Stockinbingal Public School

Stockinbingal Public School near Cootamundra opened in March 1894 and a few weeks later, on 12 April teacher Alfred Kendall wrote to the chief inspector that 'There are still about 10 pupils whose names are not enrolled—they are busy maize pulling'.[7]

Burringbar pupil buys a knife with money intended for a cricket ball

At Burringbar Public School near Murwillumbah in 1897 teacher Frederick Clarke encouraged the school's boys, who had been using a cricket ball belonging to the Burringbar Cricket Club, to obtain their own ball. Trouble ensued when one of the boys used money he had been paid, which some believed to have been for the purpose of buying a cricket ball, to buy a pocket knife for himself. Because much local ill-feeling occurred over this matter, an inquiry was held by Inspector Board at which the 13-year-old reported:

I remember the boys arranging to buy a cricket ball; they said they would all help. A gang of cane cutters told me that if I carried their mail for them they would give me something for myself and I said I would give it towards buying the ball if the others would help me. When I brought the half crown to the school the others said they would not give anything; [three boys] told me that. I bought a knife with the money. Mr Clarke said I would be getting 2 years for gathering money under false pretences.[8]

Pupils continually slipping down in the mud at Medowie

On 14 August 1899 the teacher at Medowie Public School, Sara Cole, reported that

in wet weather the ground around the school, being of a <u>very</u> greasy nature, becomes almost unsafe to walk upon after a little traffic so that pupils are continually slipping down in the mud. A few loads of sand would remedy this evil.[9]

John L. Tierney remembers his Eurunderee Public School days

John L. Tierney (1892-1972), who wrote under the pen name Brian James, was a pupil at Eurunderee Public School near Mudgee from 1899 to 1907. In his reminiscences of Eurunderee School he wrote:

In the main all writing and figuring were done on slates. Cleaning of slates was done, in theory, with

Gardening at Greenwich Public School, early 1900s (NSW Dept of School Education)

Playing hockey at Coreinbob Provisional School near Wagga Wagga, c.1920s (NSW Dept of School Education)

wet sponges or rag, but in practice the operation was performed by spit and elbow. This was frowned on and checked as filthy, and stern punishment was meted out to those caught. But the practice flourished none the less. Anyway, germs hadn't yet been invented and no one died, as far as was known, from indulging in the insanitary method.

Pen and ink work was reserved for the copy books and the exercises were done at home. Ink was contained in small crockery wells—four of them to a desk, where they fitted into round apertures in the wood. It was part of the monitors' duties to see that the ink wells were kept supplied from the stone jars. Certain boys with sadistic leanings used to drown flies in the wells ...

A brief word on the games we used to play. Of the organised games of more modern times we knew nothing. Perhaps our numbers, about 40 or so, and isolation would have made these difficult to arrange. Anyway, our love of activity, no small ingenuity, and the high spirit of adventure gave us no still and idle moments in play periods. There was always something, and the variety of games was extensive. I will however only mention a few of the team games.

Football, apart from punting and long kicking, was not played—disparities in size and the want of proper team numbers rules [sic] it out: there were only twenty boys in the school. But cricket could be played short teamed—and was. The pitch was a level patch in the old Bismarck Lane. Stumps were homemade, of pine saplings, bats were of a cheap kind— sometimes these were homemade too—and the ball

was one called a composition. Much cheaper than leather. But a lot of fun was knocked out of cricket just the same; though I fail to recall any Bradmans being produced by our form of cricket.

Faster, nippier, more exciting and joyful was hockey—or the way we played it. Admittedly the finer rules that govern the game were not followed, or even known. The hockey field was an area on the rather rough and rocky end of the playground. When finance permitted we used a composition ball—which was not up to the savage beating it got. So a substitute was found in an empty two pound golden syrup tin. These tins cost nothing, and were plentiful. After a few minutes play the tin became a lethal missile and worth dodging in its flight. When the tin was reduced to a roundish piece of jagged metal, about the size of a hen's egg, a replacement by a new tin took place.

The sticks cost nothing as they were suitable suckers from ringbarked white box trees. Where a sucker joins the parent tree there is a flat sided lump. With a little trimming it was made into an ideal hockey stick.

Such absurd rules as forbidding the raising of the stick above shoulder level, or offside, and so on were entirely ignored. After 'Hockey one, hockey two, hockey three', the fierce game was on. Often the wretched tin, now reduced to a size suitable for long flight, would zoom and shriek the full length of the field at 60 miles and hour. The only attempt to stop it, seldom successful, was to hook at it cautiously, at safe distance. Goalie simply fled, making only a token effort to stop it. Strangely enough, no one was killed, or even badly hurt, apart from black hummocks on shins and ankles: anything smaller than a turkey's egg was not deemed worthy of any notice. One thing it did for me, and others, was to inculcate a strong faith in miracles.[10]

Impudent pupils at Buxton

In March 1910 Hilton Newnham, the teacher at Buxton Public School near Picton, gave the cane to two boys at the school for insolence. The father of one of the boys lodged a complaint and Inspector Cornish conducted an inquiry at the school on 24 March 1910. He reported:

There are 4 boys at the Buxton P S ... who have a most impudent manner in their actions & speech, quite noticeable at the Inquiry—they have given the Teacher a great amount of trouble for some time past. On 16th March, as the children were marching into School, the lad ... amused himself by moving along in

PEDAGOGUE: "What is meant by a mental occupation?"
PUPIL: "One in which we use our minds.".
PEDAGOGUE: "And a manual occupation?"
PUPIL: "One in which we use our hands."
PEDAGOGUE: "Now, which of these occupations is mine? Come, now, what do I use
          most in teaching you?"
PUPIL (readily): "Your cane, sir."

(From The Bulletin, *15 September 1883, p. 18)*

a crouching posture; the Teacher told him to straighten himself. He did so by adopting an extreme opposite attitude, throwing back his head & stiffening his body & legs very rigidly & taking up a double-quick step. The Teacher, regarding this as gross insolence, brought the cane down on his shoulders 2 or 3 times. (In my opinion he deserved it.)

In school, the confederate boys then set about obstructing and annoying the Teacher, and this culminated when [two of the boys] openly contradicted the Teacher several times. Mr Newnham finally dealt 2 or 3 strokes with the cane on [one boy's] back. After school, the boys decided to make a raid upon the Teacher, but desisted as they approached the School from the Street ...

In my opinion, the lads were troublesome & impudent to the Teacher, and set such an example in the School likely to lead to serious results. It is not the first time that the Teachers at Buxton have been subjected to vexatious complaints to the Minister, and some of the boys at the school now appear to regard the Teacher as a butt for rudeness and annoyance.

There is no evidence to show that the Teacher used excessive Corporal Punishment, and I recommend that he be wholly exonerated.[11]

Shy girl sent home for giggling

In 1915 an inquiry was being held into teacher John Lewis's running of Moonahcullah Aboriginal School near Deniliquin. (Lewis was, incidentally, the first known Aboriginal teacher in a New South Wales government school.) Parents made written statements for the inquiry and a parent, who was a rabbiter, signed his mark to the statement that

my daughter was 7 years when she came into school one day Mr Lewis made the other children laugh at her, another time he dragged her to the school door, left her outside it and told her to go home to her father and mother, each time because she giggled being shy.[12]

Pupils steal stamps from West Wyalong Public School

A police report, which was dated 4 April 1919, on the theft of postage stamps from West Wyalong Public School, stated:

Sometime after Mr Larcombe the Head Teacher at the P.S. here returned off Christmas holidays and opened the School he reported that during his absence the School was entered through a fan light, and was thoroughly ran sacked and a quantity of O.S. [On His Majesty's Service] postage stamps taken. In the course of my inquiries and investigations I went to [a father's] residence, and when questioning [this father's son] I saw a postage stamp stuck on the wall of the house, and eventually the boy ... admitted that he entered the School and took the stamps from there, but as there was holes in them he did not think they were of any value, so he and other boys stuck them to their legs, trees, fences, etc. and what they did not use that way they tore up and destroyed.

Some few days after this interview with the boy an attendant arrived and took him away to Gosford Home.[13]

Pupils walking through mud up to their boot tops to Willala Provisional School

In August 1920 Frank H. Barwick of Uplands, secretary of Willala Provisional School's Parents and Citizens Association, wrote to the Department renewing a previous request by the association for a new school building at Willala near Boggabri. He noted that the present building

has been removed from the original and other sites to the present one. It is altogether too small, dilapidated and insanitary. Neither teacher or children have a fair opportunity of showing their best work under existing conditions. At present they have to walk through mud to their boot tops to get to the school door [a six-year drought having broken—this drought had been in progress since before the school was placed on low ground], and with wet feet all day and no provision for warmth, colds are prevalent. Some of these children have to ride or drive three, four, and up to over six miles in their wet shoes after school. A new building erected on higher ground is urgently required.[14]

In September 1920 the teacher at the school, William Fletcher wrote that 'the parents have

Weighing and measuring at Blackfriars Public School, 1923 (NSW Dept of School Education)

become alarmed as one child died, another had a narrow escape and another left to visit the doctor this morning'.[15] Fletcher noted, however, that the school could not be blamed for these illnesses.

Horner's love novels at Tullamore

In 1937 a mother whose daughter was in the 7th Class at Tullamore Public School complained that the teacher, Jack Pauling, did not teach the post-primary pupils properly. She wrote that 'Pauling is very fond of hearing his own voice and reads books to the children while they play in their seats'.[16] Answering the accusations against him, Pauling wrote that '[This mother's] daughter confined her time to reading Horner's love novels and when these were confiscated and she was debarred from reading them she left in the middle of the second term'.[17]

20

Pupils at Inspection

Good rapport between pupils and teacher at Spring Valley

On 23rd February 1865 Inspector Thomas Harris visited Spring Valley National School near Collector where the teacher was Thomas Bonynge. Harris reported:

The conduct of the pupils is good. They are rather shy, but well-behaved & attentive, and apparently they have great confidence in their Teacher ...

The teacher of this school is not a very intelligent and well-informed man, but he is very respectable, painstaking and well-conducted. His unassuming manners, and diligent attention to his school duties have, I am told, secured to him the confidence & respect of all the residents. The Local Patrons are very desirous that he should remain in his situation.[1]

Calabash pupils take fright at sudden appearance of Inspector Lawford

In 1888 Calabash Provisional School near Marengo (later Murringo) was inspected by Lancelot E. Lawford who was not pleased with the children's progress or with anything else about them. Teacher Ellen Brennan was called on to explain. On 22 August she wrote to the chief inspector

with regard to the defects shown at the inspection of the above school on the 8th instant, I have the honour to state that Mr Inspector Lawford having come into the school room quite unexpectedly and suddenly, the children consequently became alarmed also confused and nervous, as most of them are very young, and being reared in the bush are unaccustomed to strangers, therefore they are

Cricket at Edith Public School, 1910 (NSW Dept of School Education)

very shy and dull, particularly in the presence of the Inspector of whom they are very much afraid. On the other hand, he (Mr Lawford) having spoken a little passionately to them [he had called them 'dirty little pigs' for spitting on their slates and he had told them that they answered like parrots], they became flurried and quite incapable of answering questions in arithmetic, grammar, and other subjects which at other times they find no difficulty in answering.[2]

Pupils' poor performance at inspection blamed on poverty

Medowie Public School was inspected on 18 June 1896 and Inspector Kevin found the proficiency of the pupils very unsatisfactory. In explanation teacher Sara Cole wrote:

I have the honor to state that the low attainments of the pupils at the recent examination are attributable to
1 the fact, that the <u>five weeks</u> immediately preceeding [sic] the Inspection, were unusually wet and stormy ones, and
2 on account of the inability of the mothers through poverty—the majority of them being wives of miners who are on strike, or away in other colonies seeking work—to provide their children with warm clothing and ensure their regular attendance.[3]

Of this explanation Inspector Kevin wrote:

It seems to me that Miss Cole is not thorough enough in her work, for she does not make the pupils do <u>their</u> share of the instruction. No doubt, as she states, she has had drawbacks, but a little energy in the teaching would improve matters.[4]

A trick question from the inspector at Numulgi

On 12 March 1897 Peter Board inspected Numulgi Public School near Lismore and was not happy with the work of the teacher, Benjamin Edwards, who was subsequently called upon to explain why Inspector Board had found his methods of instruction 'superficial and mechanical' and why the results were unsatisfactory in most subjects. Edwards protested that this was not so. Among his reasons for rejecting Inspector Board's verdict was the following instance from the inspection:

Second class were rigidly inspected in multiplication tables and answered satisfactorily. Then came what in my opinion was unfair. They were asked 'What two numbers multiplied together make 54' All hands were up and the reply naturally elicited was 'six nines'. This was not allowed on the grounds that it represents six numbers.[5]

Inspector Board's response to Edwards's defence was:

My remark that the methods of instruction were superficial and mechanical was an inference, not from an isolated instance such as Mr Edwards quotes, but from the insufficient degree of mental culture shown by the classes and evident fact that proper means had not been taken to make the instruction permanent in its results.[6]

Eglinford pupils are like a herd of wallabies

Inspector Kevin reported after his inspection of Eglinford (later Congewai) Public School near Cessnock in 1897 that '<u>The pupils appeared to me a herd of wild young wallabies</u>, and it was most difficult of keep them quiet at times'.[7]

Chief Inspector Frederick Bridges wrote to Inspector Kevin that 'Such language as that underlined where you say that the pupils appeared to you 'a herd of wild young wallabies' should not be introduced into official correspondence'.[8]

Wall stained by pupils' dirty feet at Burraneer Bay

On 25 February 1898 the inspector visited Burraneer Bay Public School in its new building and teacher Charles Coombs was called upon to explain the inspector's observation: 'Wall stained on two sides of interior by dirty feet of pupils'.[9] In his explanation Coombs wrote:

These stains are owing to the newness & softness of paint on the walls during the first three weeks of use. Many children attend school barefooted, & the dust from their feet makes a smudge that will not wash off. The walls are painted the same light colour all round & the least mark made on them while the paint was so new & soft, remained.

Pruning lesson at Castle Hill Public School, early 1900s (NSW Dept of School Education)

There is no gangway at each end of desks, so that children sitting so close to walls had disfigured them with their feet before I became aware that any special attention was necessary to protect them.[10]

Inspector Lawford calls without warning at Wandook School

In December 1902 the teacher at Wandook (later Mundiwa North) Provisional School near Deniliquin, Ellen May Perrin, wrote a lengthy defence of herself and her pupils as reported upon by Inspector Lawford after his inspection of the school on 4 December. She wrote that

the children were scared and I have much pleasure in explaining how it happened. I was talking to one of my pupils sitting on the end of a form explaining a sum with my back towards the door & suddenly I half turned to speak to a child when I thought I saw someone behind me. I looked & there stood a man & Mr Lawford is so tall & I am very nervous & if I get a fright like that I am all of [a] tremble that day & the children also got such a start that they did not know what they were doing when being examined. Neither myself nor the children heard any trap stop and as the school is on a main road & bad looking men in shearing time call to ask the road to different stations we were scared. The Monday before Mr Lawford came a respectably dressed man called in a gig to ask the way to Jerilderie & as I did not know I asked one of the boys to explain to him & he was very uncivil to the boy.

When I saw Mr Lawford I was about to order him out or ask what [he] wanted. I said 'Good morning' to him to see if he would let me know what he wanted & a thought struck me that it was the Inspector Mr Lawford because I had word from him asking the best way to reach my school. So I asked him if he were Mr Lawford & he said Yes. No one knows what I went through that day & all that night for days after if anyone spoke to me suddenly I gave such a jump. Well, I got very excited & nervous & when I was asking the questions in some of the Oral lessons I do not know what I said. The report of my school was fair according to the way the children worked but it was not fair to me because I have nearly killed myself working at this school. Every night I go home worn out my head aches & I ache all over. I do nothing but work all day long & then I get this report. It is too bad. People out here tell me to take it easy not to work so hard.

I'll get no thanks for it, but I really thought I would get a splendid report If the children had not been so excited, I would have got a good report. I never saw them so bad ... At the distribution of Prizes yesterday I did feel happy. The Mayor Mr. Kelly & Rev. R. Welsh (Presbyterian) & others spoke so nicely about the way I have come out to this school under all kinds of difficulties,—taking no notice of the weather & commenting on my pluck at attacking the journey out through swamps all last week in rain & storm just to reach the children at my school & taking no consideration whatever of my health ... [The parents] asked Mr Kelly (Mayor of Deniliquin) to present me with [an] 18 carat gold Bracelet which was given to me by the children that I taught for a Christmas box for taking such an interest in them. I value this very highly as most of the farmers around my school are very poor receiving relief from the Government on account of the prolonged drought. When they gave me the present they said that they wish it had been a better year & they would have given me something more expensive. I got the letter from the department to explain the reason that I got such low marks the day before & I was just thinking of giving up teaching but since Friday I am satisfied that I can teach. The parents were very thankful to me on Friday even if I did not get a good report. The people are very kind to me out here & treat me as a child & talk to me as if I were a child & help me all they can & the children take such an interest

in their work & next Inspector's report will be very different from the last. The day Mr Lawford was at my school it was a stormy day, we were caught in a storm going home & my best pupils were not at school. To explain how the children love going to my school. A family of 4 come 12 miles daily if it is wet they will try to persuade their mother to let them come. It is the greatest punishment they can get at home to be made to stay home from school, I have heard this from several parents. I hope this letter will explain matters.[11]

Unmoved by Ellen Perrin's letter, Inspector Lawford wrote that 'There is not much in this explanation. I recommend that the Teacher be informed that far better work must be shewn at the next inspection.'[12]

Karangi pupils' farm work detracts from schoolwork

Early in 1903 Inspector Richard Henderson inspected Karangi Public School near Coffs Harbour under teacher Flora Maclean. Henderson was not pleased with the pupils' performance and in explanation Flora Maclean wrote that there had been sickness among the pupils and, in addition, that 'this is a dairying district and owing to the scarcity of grass lately, many of the children have been absent during the forenoon, minding cows in the cultivation paddocks'.[13] Defending herself

Yeoval Public School, 1930 (NSW Dept of School Education)

against charges of her pupils' poor performance again in April the next year, Maclean wrote that

the majority of the parents of my pupils are dairying, and their children have to help with the cows and feed pigs before they start for school which all of them seldom reach before noon. When they do arrive, they are too tired to properly study and during the summer months many of them do not do any home lessons, the excuse being that they have too much else to do.[14]

Untuneful pupils at Kurrara Public School

In December 1904 the teacher at Kurrara (later Banora Point) Public School, Christopher McCallum, had occasion to defend himself against criticisms of his teaching made by Inspector Cornish. He wrote:

It's all very well for Mr Cornish to say 'look at other schools where they can have concerts etc. I could give a nice concert with 20 pupils with voices like locusts!

I have done my best in Reading & Dictation but one cannot beat Nature. Mr Cornish came the day after the Show, when I had 17 present, & I will defy any Teacher in the Commonwealth to teach 7 of them Reading & Dictation. They have their father's and mother's monotonous way of speaking & I cannot break them off it.[15]

Boys gathering locusts at Bagawa Public School

When Bagawa (later Nana Glen) Public School near Coffs Harbour was inspected on 20 November 1908 the inspector was not pleased. He wrote:

The discipline is faulty. Many of the pupils were observed to copy during the Arithmetic and Dictation tests, while throughout the inspection

they showed themselves to be illmannered and noisy. During the recess more than half the boys left the playground without the Teacher's authority and scoured the adjacent bush in search of 'locusts' turning up fully ten minutes late with a number of these creatures in their pockets to add to the already unnecessary noise and disorder. These boys too included some of the oldest lads attending. During the five years of my inspectorship I have not visited so badly disciplined a school.[16]

In his explanation, teacher John Roach wrote:

I was very much upset owing to the biggest boy ... inducing a number of his fellows to accompany him in search of 'locusts' that had just made their appearance in the bush near the school, and were consequently late in their ranks after recess. I might state that these lads were interested in locusts etc at the time as a few days previous to the inspection I had given a 'Talk' on Insect Life.[17]

Grinning boy upsets inspector

Woodport Public School near Erina was inspected on 11 May 1910 by Inspector Walker, who had quite a few criticisms to make of teacher William King's teaching and running of the school. One aspect criticised was the lateness and general demeanour of the pupils. In explanation of this King wrote:

The second day of the inspection was Market Day in Gosford, and a number of the older children were kept to pack fruit and vegetables for market. Most of those who were late came into the lines before the children were marched into school. The only thing I saw, or heard about, that had the appearance of disrespect, was a boy having a grin on his face when he was spoken to by the Inspector. I do not think he means any disrespect, it is a silly habit he has. He has not been in the district very long. As a rule, it is easy to control the children.[18]

21

Pupils Travelling to School

John Middenway gets pepper in his eyes on the way to Fort Street Public School

John Saunders Middenway, who was born in 1855, attended Fort Street Public School as a pupil. Many years later he wrote:

I recall a practical joke played upon me one morning while on my way to Fort St. from the home at the northern end of Dowling St. A lad introduced me to a Chinese whistle as he called it. It was a clay pipe with a cork inserted in the bowl in which were two small holes in the side towards the stem. I was instructed to blow hard, which I did, and received a puff of pepper in my eyes. I returned home howling to my mother. Recovering later I determined to balance matters by passing it onto someone else. I procured a larger pipe, made larger holes, filled it with pepper and set out in search of a victim. This chanced to be Dave Roberts ... I spent the next few weeks dodging Mrs Roberts.[1]

Wyrallah Evening School pupil is attacked with a bottle

In May 1888 John Horton, the teacher at Wyrallah Evening School near Lismore, wrote in explanation of why he had closed the Evening School there in the first week of that month:

some of the young men on their way home had a fight in which one youth Edward Jenner got his face cut open by a bottle. This created an ill-feeling among them, and on Friday evening 4th May several of them signified their intention of not attending any more, partly because of the fight, and partly on account of the distance and bad roads.[2]

Means of conveyance for children at Mulwee Provisional School, Port Stephens

In 1899, before the new school building opened at Mulwee Provisional School, Port Stephens, resident Samuel Lilley wrote to his local member of parliament, R. A. Price, with requests concerning the new building, one of which was:

The fencing should also be done as most of the children will have to travel long distances (will ride). And in one case the child is a cripple And his father intends to get a little trap for his children to come to school and as the fencing timber is upon the ground almost, it can be done very cheap.[3]

Travelling arrangements for Kuring-Gai children attending Berowra Public School

On 15 November 1903 Owen McGrail, the officer in charge of Kuring-Gai (then 'Kuring Gai') railway station, wrote to the Minister:

Kuring Gai is a new crossing Station opened at a point about midway between Colah & Berowra Platform on the North Coast Line. Berowra is the nearest school and the [McGrail and Wall] children (8 in number) attend there the road is a very isolated one, no house between there & Berowra and the road is frequented by many very undesirable looking tramps as the name is generally applied to them. I have asked for Train service but only half could be allowed because this place is not put in for Stoppages as far as I know at present. The trains that I asked for were 4.22 pm returning 10 a.m. going out to school but unfortunately the [Railway] Department will not agree to the stoppage of that Train but in lieu of this they are

Pupils of Koribar Public School near Nabiac. This photograph, by teacher Arnold Weber, appeared in the Report of the Minister of Public Instruction, *1912, with the caption: 'As a result of the work of the Gould League of Bird Lovers, the destruction of bird-life has dwindled nearly to vanishing point'.*

allowed to travel by Goods Train a.m. out of here 7.30 a.m. thus leaving them 2 hours very nearly to wander about [the] bush or roads before school opens ... They are all Female Children & from accounts in [the] papers from time to time I would prefer letting them go unschooled than perhaps have them murdered along the road.[4]

The Department forwarded McGrail's request to the Office of the Railway Commissioners but they decided that 'the circumstances do not warrant the stoppage of the important train in question [the 9.05 a.m. train from Sydney]'.[5]

Inspector Blumer wrote:

The school is less than half a mile from the Railway station in rather a lonely spot. The Teacher, who lives close to the Station, is quite willing for them to wait at his house ... I recommend that Mr McGrail be informed that nothing further can be done by this Department to remedy the inconvenience his children are necessarily subjected to.[6]

Log crossing to Bagawa Public School

Before a new building was provided for Bagawa (later Nana Glen) Public School near Coffs

Harbour on another site early in 1903, the inspector wrote that access to the school required most users

to cross either the Orara River or Bucca Creek, the only means of crossing being a log ... during wet seasons, the school has been frequently closed for days even weeks, on account of the inability of teacher or pupils to reach it. In damp weather the logs are very slippery and dangerous.[7]

Grass up to children's necks at Kurrara Public School

Kurrara (later Banora Point) Public School was closed for two days in November 1903 because of heavy rain. Teacher Christopher McCallum wrote: 'Children cannot be expected to attend on such wet days, for they all have a long way to walk and wet grass up to their necks in places'.[8]

Cronulla conveyance coach capsizes on the way home from Miranda

In 1907 Cronulla pupils were being conveyed to Miranda School. Many Cronulla parents who were not happy about the children travelling by coach agitated for a school at Cronulla. (Cronulla School opened in 1910.) Forwarding to the Minister a petition with 22 signatures on 2 August 1907, Charles McAlister of Cronulla Beach wrote on the subject of a school at Cronulla to local member of parliament, Frederick W. A. Downes. McAlister pointed out that

a serious accident happened to the 2 horse coach with the children returning from school on 31st July. At the large Culvert near Hotel and before the driver reached the high portion—the horses shied and capsized the Coach over a 2 ft bank. Slight grazes and fright were the worst but the parents are quite upset and several of the children will not be sent for a time.[9]

Digging out the pupils of Macarthur Public School

Teacher Mary Fearby at Macarthur Public School near Gravesend successfully applied on 23 November 1917 for sanctioning of the closing of the school on account of

threatening weather and dangerous creeks. On Monday 19th Nov. some children crossing a creek containing drift, or (as they call it) quicksand. 2 boys bogged deeply—one to his neck and the other to his waist. The girls returned home, got shovels & dug them out, far too muddy & wet to come to school.[10]

Pupils get wet feet opening the horse paddock gate at Stockinbingal

On 30 November 1917 B. Wintenden, secretary of the Stockinbingal Farmers and Settlers Association, wrote to the Department requesting a new gate for the school's horse paddock, writing that

this paddock is used by a number of children whos [sic] distance from the school makes it necessary for them to either ride or drive ... often the gateway is six inches deep in water, The present substitute for a gate is so delapidated [sic] that the children can not open or shut it without getting their feet wet, and thus having to remain wet footed dureing [sic] the whole of the day.[11]

Parent praises ponies so quiet that pupils can dismount by sliding over their tails

In 1921 Inspector Fraser wrote of Billinudgel Public School near Brunswick Heads:

During my inspection of Billinudgel the horses, cattle and dogs in [the] school grounds called for a serious talk with the teacher. Manifestly, horses, cattle and dogs at large in the playing area

Conveyance of children to Miranda Public School from Sylvania, Port Hacking and Cronulla (Report of the Minister for Public Instruction, *1908, opposite p. 10*)

Kerry and Co. *Off to School* 1893–1910; gelatin silver photograph, 15.9 x 20 cm *(The Art Gallery of New South Wales)*

constitute a danger to the pupils that could not be allowed to continue. I made an appeal through teacher and children to the parents to fence off a portion of the grounds for the pupils' horses; and instructed the teacher to take the necessary steps to prevent cattle and dogs from entering the grounds during school hours.[12]

On 12 May 1921 Edith Flood of New Brighton, Via Billinudgel, wrote her opinions on this matter to local member of parliament, George Nesbitt:

Would you be kind enough to approach Mr Mutch, Minister for Education, on behalf of country children whose only means of attending school is per medium of a quiet old family horse. On the occasion of Mr Frazer's [sic] last visit of inspection, the order was given that no horses are to be allowed in the school playground. This regulation is causing great hardship to parents & children, especially to those children who have long distances to travel to school and creeks to cross en route.

No doubt the regulation is intended in the interests of, and with regard to the safety of the children while at play, but the parents should be given credit for having enough common sense to deter them from sending their children to school on vicious horses. You, who know this country district so well, must, many times, have seen as many as three children being conveyed to school on the back of one quiet kindly old horse and again as many as six or seven packed into a sulky with a child driving. Now, owing to this drastic regulation, all of these children have to walk three or four miles or more, or else stay at home. In wet weather, some, having creeks to cross, in which the old horse is knee deep in running water, have to miss perhaps two weeks schooling or even more. Then the attendance inspector pays a call and wants to know the reason why.

The playground would cease to be a playground in this paspalum country if the horses were not there to keep down the grass, and some of the farmers' children have no play time except what they get at school. I read most of the papers but have never yet read of a child being injured in a school playground by a 'school' horse. Many of the children dismount by sliding down over the horse's tail.

Coreinbob Subsidised School near Wagga Wagga, c.1925 (NSW Dept of School Education)

The parents can be trusted to see to it that the children do not run any unnecessary risks, and in a playground as large as that at Billinudgel school, there is absolutely no danger to the children, as the horses (about three in number) retire to the far side as soon as the school comes out to play.[13]

Horse severs pupil's toe on the way home from Wyrallah Public School

Two girls aged about 10, one of whom was Isa Paisley, were riding home from Wyrallah Public School near Lismore in about 1930. As was usual they were barefooted and, when Isa's companion dismounted to pick something up off stones on the side of the road, her horse trod on her bare little toe, severing it. The toe jumped around on the stones until its owner caught it and wrapped it in a handkerchief to take with her, then the girls resumed their ride home.[14]

Falls from horses at Megalong

Reporting on Megalong Provisional School's attendance on 11 August 1939, teacher Laurie Steeper wrote that the low average attendance was partly because 'two long-distance riders have been absent many weeks on account of having been involved in accidents while riding home'. One of these was probably a pupil who fell off his pony and dislocated his arm, after which he and another sibling walked the nine miles a day across hilly country.[15]

22

Pupil-Teachers and Students-in-Training

Conscientious pupil-teachers at Ballina and Woodburn

The head of Ballina Public School in 1885, Charles Smythe, in filling in the Department's form on which 'The Teacher ... will state everything within his knowledge calculated to influence the Minister in estimating the value of the Pupil-Teacher concerned', wrote of probationary pupil-teacher, William Bourke, who lived with Smythe's family, that 'he is of strictly moral character has no associates beyond my own family' and that 'he spends all his leisure time in studying'.[1]

In the same year, the head teacher of Woodburn Public School, Peter Van Epen, wrote of his pupil-teacher, Jessie Miller, that 'Her leisure time is occupied with home study, or an occasional walk in the environs with the teacher's daughter'. He also wrote that she 'associates with no questionable characters' and that 'she spends her Saturdays and Sundays at her Parents' home'.[2]

Instruction for pupil-teachers at Wagga Wagga School, c.1899 (Copy held by NSW Dept of School Education)

Agnes Archbald standing third from right, wearing a black dress, c.1908 (Photograph courtesy of Hazel Eaton)

Agnes Archbald lacking in animation and energy

Fifteen-year-old Agnes Archbald became a pupil-teacher at Kogarah Superior Public School in October 1891.[3] On 25 January 1892 Inspector Skillman wrote of her: 'This probationer displays so little animation or energy that it is doubtful whether she will ever become an efficient teacher'.[4] On the same day the head of the school and the infants' mistress commented on Agnes Archbald's 'rather monotonous voice'.[5] One attribute her superior officers were prepared to grant her was her honesty. Having been sick for about a week in June 1892 and not having produced a medical certificate for this absence, the head of the school wrote: '[Archbald] states that no medical man was in attendance on her, but I think it most unlikely that she would attempt to shirk her duty'.[6]

Part of the reason for Archbald's lack of zest may well have been her three mile walk to and from school. In June 1892 she asked to be moved from Kogarah school to Rockdale or Arncliffe as 'My parents reside at Lady Robinson's Beach between Rockdale and Arncliffe and it is necessary for me to leave home shortly after 7 a.m. and [I] do not return till dark'.[7] In explanation of her failure at examination she wrote in February 1893 that 'the long distance I have to walk daily prevents me from doing justice to my studies. I try my utmost to prepare the lessons which are set for me.'[8]

Despite this unpromising beginning, Agnes Archbald remained a teacher and taught at different schools including Arncliffe and Rockdale. She eventually gaining a 3A classification in 1923 and retired in January 1935.[9]

William Sheehy in need of careful management

Joseph Finney, the head of Fort St Practising School, in his report in December 1894 on student-in-training, William Sheehy, wrote of him that

'It is notorious that Mr Sheehy wants careful management'.[10] Finney described Sheehy's habits and manners as 'Peevish—Mr Sheehy has been a difficult student to manage. His conduct has been reported on adversely by several of the masters.'[11]

Earnest Ernest Moloney at Wyalong Public School

In January 1895 the head of Wyalong Public School, John Anstey, filling in the required form on his pupil-teacher, 18-year-old Ernest Moloney, wrote of Moloney's conduct out of school: 'Extremely well conducted, rarely out of doors, leisure time spent in study'.[12]

Two successive troublesome pupil-teachers at Richmond Superior Public School

William Bowles was appointed as pupil-teacher to Richmond Superior Public School in 1896, having previously been at Wisemans Ferry Public School. On 4 November head of the school, James Collins, wrote to Inspector Pitt at Parramatta:

I desire to call your attention to the fact that Mr Bowles, pupil-teacher at [Richmond] school is repeatedly late for his lessons, and he is besides extremely negligent in preparing lessons. When he entered on duty in this school in April last, I found he had none of this year's work prepared, and could not do the first exercise in Latin. In order to make up for his deficiency I have been giving him extra lessons ever since in the subjects he is most backward in; but it is exceedingly annoying to me to find him making no effort himself; but; on the contrary, he is wilfully negligent, and very often late. I wish therefore to be relieved from all responsibility in the event of his failure, which is inevitable by his present conduct.[13]

Things had not improved a month later when Collins wrote of Bowles on 3 December:

I have ascertained that he keeps very bad hours, that his associates are very objectionable, and I have been informed that he frequents the hotels. I have recently observed him under the influence of liquor myself. Under such circumstances, it is impossible for him either to be punctual, or to be diligent in his studies.[14]

On the advice of Inspector Pitt that he should resign rather than be dismissed, Bowles resigned from the end of January 1897, writing that he had

Richmond Superior Public School, 1909 (NSW Dept of School Education)

'been offered a position far more suitable to me than teaching'.[15]

Bowles was succeeded at Richmond School by Leslie Thomas Stewart who was not an improvement on Bowles and who was said by James Collins to have given him 'more trouble than assistance'.[16] Stewart began his short career as a pupil-teacher at Richmond School in February 1897. He lived with his parents out of Richmond and rode in to school each day. On 5 March, Collins wrote:

From the date of his entry upon duty till the present time his conduct about the school, and his neglect of duty have given me great annoyance.

His usual excuse for failing to do home lessons, was that he suffered from [a] 'bad head' which incapacitated him from work. On one occasion, about a month ago, after a week of continued negligence, I sent for his father and explained the boy's neglect of duty to him. The father also informed me that he [presumably the boy] had frequently been afflicted by a bad head ...

Parents have on two occasions complained of the language he has used in the playground and this I called his father's attention to.

I have cautioned him against undue familiarity with the school boys, and have seen him soon afterwards wrestling with them in the playground.

I cannot conscientiously recommend his being retained as a teacher, and from his general conduct I think he never intended to remain. He says he has a position in Sydney to which he is going.[17]

Stewart resigned in April 1897 with the Department making the resignation effective from the end of March. As his reasons for resignation he gave the following:

Blackfriars Superior Public School, 1913 (NSW Dept of School Education)

1st That the distance intervening between my home and the school is too great to traverse every day (viz 9 miles).

2nd That I find that the class entrusted to my charge is too great for a probationer to handle ... the roll call being 63 and the average daily attendance being 57.[18]

23

Parents

Parent Samuel Lilley, teacher Frederick Spinney and Inspector John Kevin

On 4 October 1899 parent Samuel Lilley wrote as the representative of the Swan Bay Progress Committee to local member of parliament, Richard Price, about the newly erected school building for Mulwee Provisional School, Port Stephens:

You are aware that I am now living here and so soon as I came I at once set to work to get a school erected but ... the ground has not been sufficiently cleared to make the building safe or [to make] the childrens and teachers lives [safe].[1]

Inspector John Kevin wrote of this request:

The writer of this letter draws very largely upon his imagination. He had nothing to do with the establishment of the school beyond signing the formal application, as all the trouble fell to my lot. The ground about the school has been cleared a chain wide under my own supervision, and there are <u>no</u> dangerous trees in close proximity to the building.[2]

Lilley wrote again about the dangerous trees on 8 January 1900, saying that a recent storm had demonstrated their dangerousness. Inspector Kevin again stated that there were no dangerous trees and added: 'I might mention that Mr Lilley represents no committee of any kind. He is a mere busybody'.[3] Despite this, the 18-year-old teacher of the school, Frederick Spinney, was asked by the Department for his opinion on whether there were dangerous trees. In reply he wrote on 5 March 1900: 'The inspector had the ground cleared in the first case and Lilley's interference is not called for'.[4] Inspector Kevin added to Spinney's report his own note to the chief inspector:

For your information. I have already reported in these terms, and why my word was not at once taken seems very strange. Is an Inspector's report to be rejected, and the impudent and mendacious statements of a busybody accepted as trustworthy? The Dept. does not know the character of the individual who writes these letters.[5]

In April 1900 teacher Frederick Spinney was asked to explain his poor performance when the school had been inspected shortly before. It was pointed out to him that 'though the school has now been opened nearly six months the pupils do not appear to have made any progress'.[6] In his defence Spinney wrote that 'none of my pupils had been to school before and consequently knew absolutely nothing. Also they are of an extremely shy disposition'.[7] Inspector Kevin did not accept this explanation and Spinney was warned that if the pupils' attainments had not improved at the next inspection the question of dispensing with his services would have to be considered.[8]

Spinney's pupils' attainments had not improved noticeably by his next inspection in 1901. Inspector Kevin wrote on 8 May 1901 that

this is poor work for a young man full of lusty life and with some experience in teaching ... The plain fact is—he is lazy ... In addition to this, the scholars are hardly out of sight on Friday afternoon before he is driving furiously home to Bishop's Bridge—36 miles distant—and he does not get back till school time on Monday morning—wholly unfit for work I should assume.[9]

A related matter concerned the non-attendance at the school of Samuel Lilley's children (Lilley was parent of one child and guardian of two others at the school). On 16 May 1901, after being visited by the police on the matter of non-attendance, Lilley wrote again to member of parliament, Richard Price, saying that Spinney was the reason he would not send the children to school and making many allegations against Spinney as a teacher, among the mildest of which were:

The first day of opening the school.

Lesson draw monkeys Second day do the same if they could not draw monkeys they were told to draw him the teacher as ugly as they could. The teacher amuseing [sic] himself reading novels, singing songs and smokeing [sic] in the School.[10]

Fights were also said to have occurred at the school as a result of a boy bringing a pair of boxing gloves to school.

Referring to Lilley's letter, Inspector Kevin wrote on 24 May:

There is probably some truth in this man's statements, but as he must have got what he says second-hand and garbled, and as his own character is so bad the charges must be received with great caution. Mr Spinney is undoubtedly indiscreet, foolish and heedless and behaves at times like one bereft of his senses; but age and experience of the world are likely to cure this in time.[11]

The Department required Inspector Kevin to conduct a formal inquiry into the allegations made by Lilley and on 19 June he reported:

I visited this place yesterday to hold an inquiry but the complainant's [Lilley's] conduct was so bad that nothing could be done. He was dictatorial, un-reasonable, and insulting; had no witnesses to call, and when he learnt that I had sent the defendant [Spinney] a statement of the charges that he might prepare his defence, he rushed out of the school in a rage and I saw no more of him. He wanted me to take his complaints without qualification, and there and then condemn the teacher unheard. In all my experience I never had to deal before with such an unmitigated blackguard.[12]

Rather than being dismissed as had been threatened, Spinney was severely reprimanded and moved to Carrabolla Provisional School near Muswellbrook from which, Inspector Kevin noted with satisfaction, 'it will be impossible for him to go home except in the vacations'.[13] Spinney, who was reprimanded again in May 1902 for closing Carrabolla School without authority, resigned from that school in October 1902.[14]

Coorabell parent goes to the lock-up because of overcrowded school

In September 1902 Arthur Ball who had been agitating for a school at Myocum near Bangalow, wrote to local member of parliament, R. D. Meagher, concerning Coorabell Public School which the Myocum children attended:

You have no doubt heard that Mr Wallis, one of our most respected citizens, has already not only undergone the disgrace of being summoned to the police court but actually went through the degradation of being confined in the lock up because he kept his children home feeling that the overcrowding was a constant menace to their health.[15]

Quarrymen and farmers do not mix at Martins Creek

In 1926 teacher Thomas Dibden, the head of Martins Creek Public School in the Hunter Valley, reported that 'The local Parents and Citizens' Association has apparently lapsed ... It is very difficult to form such an assocn. at Martins Creek. Quarrymen and farmers do not mix too well.'[16]

The adverse effects of poetry and singing at Billinudgel Public School

In March 1929, David Grierson, the teacher at Billinudgel Public School near Brunswick Heads, in the course of defending himself against a complaint by a mother, wrote that this mother

has written at different times, once to request me not to teach [her children] poetry as it excited them, and again a few days ago saying 'I want you to cease giving my children singing lessons as they are not adapted for it and it does them more harm than good'.[17]

Delusion of duplications at Narrabeen Public School

On 18 November 1946 the mother of a pupil at Narrabeen Public School wrote to the Department:

I am afraid there is something very wrong going on in the public schools to-day and the teachers, as a whole, that I have had dealings with concerning ... my child, now nearly eight years are not all equal to the high standard I have always been used to ... This appears to be due to the changeing [sic] around of teachers who resemble one another and teach the same class in the same name. These could be sisters. These have the opposite ideas. For instance one teacher will prove [my son] a good scholar and another will put him in the worst block without any known reason to the child. When the other Miss Godfrey returns she puts him in his former seat once again. These things continue in numerous different ways.

I am positive I have seen three teachers in the name of Godfrey teaching second class this year (Narrabeen).

Last year I witnessed two teachers called Miss Simon. [My son] used to describe them as the big one and the little Miss Simon.

Again at Narrabeen North Infants I witnessed more than one teacher in the name of Wetherell ...

I have had advice as to where these teachers have gone to (or some of them) and why; and I certainly do not hold with these arrangements.

These things are very confusing to young children and when things are not quite right it is difficult to describe which one does right and which does wrong ...

A couple of weeks ago [my son] came home and complained of being approached by a woman in the playground who accused him unfairly of having broken and entered a ladie's [sic] house and having stolen a wristlet watch. This woman resembled my cousin ... but was taller and wore dark rimmed glasses with a rim of white on the frames also.

I went to the school about it and Miss Godfrey without question dominated the child and kept repeating in a firm voice 'No strange woman came to the school yesterday. There was no strange woman came to the school yesterday now was there?' She turned and repeated to me several times at intervals '[Your son] is telling you tales as no strange woman was in the playground yesterday'.

[My son] thinks Miss Godfrey altered during the day after the visitor had gone and the other Miss Godfrey replaced her.[18]

Inspector Harrie Barlex concluded on 12 December that this parent was 'labouring under a delusion of duplications'.[19]

24

Inspectors

Bernard McCann drowns and is succeeded by Thomas Harris [1]

Bernard McCann (born c.1831) came to New South Wales from Ireland as a teacher with the Board of National Education in 1856.[2] He became an inspector in 1859 and on Saturday 22 October 1864, at the age of about 33, he was drowned while returning to Goulburn from duty when he tried to cross the flooded Wollondilly River at Rossi's Crossing near Goulburn with his horse and buggy.[3] His body was recovered a week later.[4]

In February 1865 William Dwyer, the inspector for the western district, referred to 'the sudden and melancholy death of Mr. McCann in the midst of his labours, and just as I was entering his district'.[5]

McCann was succeeded at Goulburn as inspector for the southern district by English-born Thomas Harris (1824-68) who had trained as a teacher in Glasgow, and who had entered on duty as a teacher with the Board of National Education in 1855.[6] Harris arrived in Goulburn to take up his appointment as McCann's successor on 10 January 1865.[7] In his diary he recorded that he 'attended sale for purchase of a horse' on 19 January[8] and on the next day he listed the Board of Education articles left for him by McCann's widow.[9]

In the report of the National Board of Education for 1865 Harris wrote:

The schools with which I have had to deal for administrative purposes are scattered over an area of about 40,000 square miles, embracing three geographical regions, namely, the Coast District, south of the Clyde River; the Southern Table Land, south of the River Abercrombie; and that portion of the Inland Plains of the Colony situated in the valleys of the Murray and Murrumbidgee. The school at Wentworth, near the mouth of the Darling, is the most remote from my station [Goulburn].

The number of schools in operation in the district at the end of 1864 was thirty-five ... At the end of 1865, the number of schools in the district receiving aid from the Board was forty-four ...

It was my intention, as indicated in my programme for the year, to visit each school at least twice; the first time, to ascertain its material condition, to notice the means employed for the instruction of the pupils and the formation of their habits, to observe the methods of teaching adopted, and to make such suggestions to the teacher and local patrons as the circumstances might require. During the second visit, I proposed to test the results by searching examinations of the classes, and also to conduct the annual examination of teachers. From the fact that, during the last half of the year, the travelling allowance was withheld, I was enabled to visit most of the schools but once. From the same cause, the examinations of teachers, except those in the neighbourhood of Goulburn, had to remain in abeyance ...

The distance travelled during the year, in the discharge of my duties, was 2,154 miles.[10]

Some of the hazards of travel for Harris at this time are indicated by the following notes in his diary:

Saturday, 25th [March 1865]: Conferred with some

parents of pupils attending the Bega School—started for Narrira—lost for three hours—remained at Brogo Farm until Sunday, 26 instant.[11]

Saturday, 1 April [1865] Horse being unable to go further, travelled by Coach to Goulburn'.[12]

Thursday 15th [November 1866] ... engaged in searching for my horse which had strayed.[13]

In the course of his duty, Harris had occasion to praise some teachers such as James McNab and Mary Doubleday at Pyree National School near Kiama which he inspected on 26 May 1865. Of their school he wrote:

The spirit of work and intelligent enquiry are the characteristics of the school. The Teachers rule most effectively and without apparent effort. The result of the discipline of this school is seen in the good conduct of those who have recently left the school, several of whom I met.[14]

On the other hand he had occasion to make the following observation of Bombala National School which he inspected on 26 and 27 March 1866:

Mrs Hopkins [the teacher's wife] spends much of her time in the school. Her influence upon the girls would be better if her style of dress and general deportment were less showy.[15]

Of Taralga National School, which he inspected on 22 February 1866, he noted:

Mr Rich, by dissolute habits in times past, injured his reputation in this place. The Local Patrons wrote in complaints against him. The pupils are tolerably clean and tidy. They are very shy, their conduct may be described as that of mere submission, there is neither [illegible word] nor disorder among them. There seems to be but little sympathy between master and pupils ...

From the condition of the school, if the teacher had not already tendered his resignation I should have suggested his removal. He informed me that his term of office would end on the 31st April, instant.[16]

Harris's health did not last in his demanding work as inspector of schools. On 10 July 1865 he wrote that 'As I am suffering from a very bad boil, I am

Bombala Public School, c.1890s (NSW Dept of School Education)

unable to sit, and for some days shall be quite unable to travel'.[17] He was confined to his office and on 17 July 1865 he wrote of this time, which he spent writing reports, that 'During the week I have been so indisposed as to be unable to sit. That which I considered to be a boil is a stubborn carbuncle. My Medical Attendant is of opinion that I shall be unable to ride during this week.'[18]

In the first six months of 1866 he made the following entry in his diary fifteen times: 'sick, incapable of work'.[19] On 22 May 1866, successfully applying for leave to visit Sydney for treatment (while there he worked on writing up his reports), he wrote:

For some months now I have been troubled with a soreness in the roof of my mouth which during my late illness has resulted in an ulcer that prevents me from taking solid food and causes an impediment in my speech.[20]

On 24 October 1867 he wrote:

With reference to the arrears of my reports and other official matters I have the honor to assure the Council that, whilst I much regret their existence, they have accumulated from circumstances, to a great extent, beyond my control; One of which is the fact that for some time past from weak sight I have found it very difficult to write by artificial light, I will do my utmost to clear them off at once.[21]

On 4 November Harris listed his work for the whole of the week and added the note: 'During the whole week I have been so unwell as not to be able to perform other duties'.[22] His distance travelled for the week ending 11 November 1867 was 74 miles.[23]

Because of his illness, Harris was moved to Sydney in November 1867 and died there on 1 April 1868.[24]

William McIntyre is subjected to 'hardship, exposure and slavery'

William McIntyre (1830-1911) came to New South Wales from Northern Ireland in 1856 as a teacher with the Board of National Education.[25] In 1861 he was appointed inspector of the northern district which at that time comprised the entire colony north of the Hunter Valley and which had Armidale as its base.[26] In 1863 McIntyre's horses were swept away in a flooded river and he almost drowned.[27] As was the case with all inspectors, his work entailed the setting up and supervision of schools and in carrying out this work he travelled about 150,000 miles in the colony and made arrangements for the opening of about 100 new schools.[28] The *New South Wales Education Gazette* of 1 October 1903, (p. 122) reported:

With a splendid physique, robust constitution, and a happy temperament, he was just the man to select for pioneer work ... He was prompt to keep any appointment made and often travelled through flooded country to be present at meetings arranged for in connection with the establishment of schools. Some of his experiences in travelling between Armidale and the coast are of a thrilling character. He was an excellent horseman, and his horses were staunch and strong. He rode one horse and led

Inspector William McIntyre (From the New South Wales Educational Gazette, *1 August 1901, p. 50)*

another, which bore the 'saddle bags' for the tour. He found it a good plan to change horses at intervals.

Of Wardell Provisional School on the Richmond River, McIntyre wrote in the 1867 *Report of the Council of Education* (p. 41):

Owing to the state of the wind and tide in the river, I could not reach this school on the day fixed for its inspection, until after the pupils were dismissed, and as I was not aware of its existence prior to the date of my visit, my engagements would not permit me to delay another day to examine the pupils.

Of his district generally, he wrote in the same report (p. 41):

To some of the schools convenient to my station, I paid several incidental visits on the Council's business; but owing to the extent of country over which my duties call me, including the districts of the Tweed, Namoi, Peel and Liverpool Plains, several places where schools were required could not be visited. During the year I travelled about 3,500 miles.

In his *Australian Dictionary of Biography* entry on McIntyre, Bruce Mitchell writes: 'In 1869 he [McIntyre] wrote that he had "grown grey in the service" and that his constitution had been "partially ruined by hardship, exposure and slavery" '.[29] McIntyre retired in 1902, noting on his retirement that he had 'good reason to be very thankful to a kind of providence for the frequent protection from dangers of flood and field which he had to encounter'.[30] He died at Glebe in 1911 aged 81.[31]

Alexander Lobban assesses educational needs on Don Dorrigo Plateau

Alexander Lobban (1843-1919) was an inspector of schools in New South Wales from 1883 to 1910.[32] Late in 1890 a petition from local residents at Dorrigo requested the provision of education for

Inspector Alexander Lobban, c.1890s (NSW Dept of School Education)

their children. Lobban, then the district inspector at Grafton, was asked to report on this petition but on 17 November he wrote:

As the Dorrigo is on the Northern tableland, it properly forms part of the Armidale District. I therefore recommend that this Petition be referred to the District Inspector at Armidale.[33]

The district inspector at Armidale, John Bradley, however, did not see Dorrigo as part of his territory and on 24 November 1890 he wrote to the chief inspector, John Maynard:

To avoid further delay in this matter I have sent to Mr D. Coghlan Form of Application for the appt. of an Itin. Tchr with necessary Directions as to filling up of the form. As no postal address appears on the petition, I have sent one form by way of Grafton Road and another via Fernmount on the Bellenger [sic], which I believe is the nearest postal township.

As to the district in which the locality concerned is situate, I beg to state that Mr Lobban is in error in saying that the 'Dorrigo' lies on the Northern Table-land. It constitutes a secondary or 'false' table-land N. of the Macleay Range immediately at the head of the Bellenger [sic]; and in the old days, when I worked the whole of the Northern District, I could reach it in about 3 hours from Fernmount or Boat Harbour.

My nearest schools—Bell Flat & Wirrialpa H. T. [Half-Time] (which I consider should be in Grafton Dist.) are some 40 miles distant by an exceedingly rough track.

The Dorrigo 'Cedar Scrub' is in the Grafton Electorate, and whatever Inspr. visits the Bellenger [sic] can take this charge with least personal inconvenience, and most saving to the Dept. Mr D.C.I. [deputy chief inspector] McIntyre from his own experience should be able to confirm my statements.[34]

Inspector Lobban, now accepting responsibility for the area although he was still not happy about doing so, reported to Chief Inspector Maynard on 10 December 1890:

I have arranged my programme for next year so that

I shall do the Bellenger [sic] Circuit in February.

Will you kindly inform me if it will be necessary for me to visit Dorrigo before that time. I am still of opinion that with my staff of Inspectors, I should not have any of the new schools on the Table Lands—real or 'false'—added to my list.

I can arrange to visit the Dorrigo when at Bellengen [sic] in February or if it be necessary to go sooner I shall take the Grafton Road to Armidale and follow the cedar waggon tracks along the Table Land.[35]

Thus, early in 1891 Inspector Lobban visited the Don Dorrigo region. The following, which he titled 'Reminiscences', is in his 1891 diary although he wrote it after this time:

Early in 1891 the educational wants of the children on the Don Dorrigo Plateau was [sic] brought under the notice of the Department of Public Instruction, and it fell to my lot to enquire into the matter— At that time the roads in the Clarence and Bellenger [sic] Districts was [sic] about the worst I had seen in New South Wales—There was practically no made road between the Clarence and the Bellenger [sic]. Between Fernmount and Bellingen there was a large stretch under water, and the mud was so soft that it was almost impossible to get over it at all. It was in the midst of this quagmire that I first met a gentleman who in after years was in truth a guide, philosopher and friend to me—Mr W T. Matthews, J.P.

I confided to that gentleman, on this occasion, my intention of visiting Don Dorrigo, and sought his advice as to the best course for me to pursue in order to obtain the information needed. I had driven to Fernmount; but as there was no road up to the Dorrigo, Mr. Matthews offered to go with me; and advised me to have a horse saddled and bridle for the trip. I have often thought that a good example of 'Faith' is seen when a stranger follows a guide through country unknown to him, with the utmost confidence that the desired goal would be safely reached—Hence I cast myself unreservedly on my guide and felt that he would pilot me safely through the primeval forests of Don Dorrigo. He informed me that there was an almost perpendicular mountain named Fassifern to ascend, on foot—leading our horses—It was a warm February morning, and I was just recovering from a severe attack of influenza. When we got half-way up this rock, my breath failed, and we both sat down for a rest. Alas! and alack! my horse heaved a sigh which burst the saddle girth, and off fell saddle and appendages, and slid down the hill many feet. I felt that I could never carry it up the steep, but my friend who had many times negotiated the pinnacle was soon in pursuit of the receding saddle and in due course after, [sic] mending the girths, had it again fastened on the horse. We then continued our ascent, and when we reached the summit I was almost breathless and my throat was so dry that it ached—There were a great many splendid cedar logs on the level space at the top of the hill, and Mr Matthews explained to me that they had been cut in the brushes and were drawn to that point from which they were rolled down the 'Fassifern' to the level below, from which they were drawn to Bellingen (which at that time was called Boat Harbour) and sent to Sydney—

On reaching the tableland one's interest was immediately arrested. Miles of densely timbered country lay in front with only cedar-getters' dray tracks through it. It was a magnificent stretch of most valuable timber—cedar, 'Rosewood', and lordly pines, whose moss grown branches pro- claimed their antiquity. Rivulets of crystal water were frequently seen. We rode on several miles through the level tract of unique brush country and at length came upon green slopes of very lightly timbered country leading down to the Beilsdown and its tributaries. It was strange how suddenly the brush stopped and the grass commenced. The edge of the black forest seemed as regular, as the edge of the standing lucerne beside a mown field—I was filled with admiration, and, seized with a desire that all my friends in the Education office should see this remarkable region. We had some further miles to ride before we came to the settlement on the Beilsdown which consisted of two families—The children under 14 years at these two homes numbered exactly 12. These homes were on the un-timbered country and I was struck with the very fine potatoes that were growing there.

We next went on to Coghlan's Plains, past the Beilsdown Water fall which at that time was a feature of great interest to stray visitors. This 'plain' is so called because it [is] grassed country without trees. In the locality we saw all the children up to 14 years of age—and they numbered 14.

Inspector Bertie Harkness in a T-model Ford outside Euabalong Public School, 1917 (NSW Dept of School Education)

After passing the Beilsdown, rain began to fall, and my companion said that we should next proceed to 'Little' plain (I think):—At all events to a plain where a hospitable welcome would be vouchsafed to us and a comfortable night's lodging. Our tracks lay through a dense growth of magnificent timber— Such pines as I had never seen elsewhere, and past some wonderful cedar trees. Just at even-tide we drew up at the home of Mrs Hewett of whose kindness I have still a grateful remembrance. At this settlement there were 15 children ranging from infants to the age of 15 years. Mrs Hewett's home was romantically situated on the table land looking down on the Little Murray at its base. There I saw magnificent quinces growing.

Next day we further explored this rich and interesting district and called at all the homes which we had not visited on the previous day. We found 37 children scattered over Don Dorrigo at the Three Centres, over 20 of them were of school age, And it was at first proposed to appoint an itinerating teacher; but the proposal fell through. The first school under the Department was opened in a temporary building provided by Mr McDougall, at the plain where a Government cedar plantation had been tried and failed, and [when] settlers from the South Coast and elsewhere began to select on the Dorrigo, another school was opened at Beilsdown, a new building in the meantime having replaced the temporary structure near McDougall's place—I visited the region many times afterwards, both from Tyringham and Bellingen, and was always impressed with the wonderful possibilities of the place.

It may be mentioned here that all the rivers and rivulets draining the Dorrigo are affluents of the Clarence and its tributaries.

———

I shall always remember with pleasure my first two days on the Dorrigo, and the delightful companionship of my excellent guide.

When I next visited this region some two years later an excellent road had just been completed to the top of the table land, and I had the pleasure of driving the first buggy up the new road, and to celebrate the event when I reached Beilsdown, I gave the oldest man I saw and the youngest child a ride in my buggy.[36]

Glossary of Terms Used

ABORIGINAL SCHOOL 1880-1968 An elementary school dating from 1880 in which enrolment was restricted to Aboriginal children. Most Aboriginal Schools were Provisional Schools and were staffed until the 1940s or 1950s by untrained teachers. In 1968 the few remaining Aboriginal Schools were converted into ordinary Public Schools.

BOARD OF NATIONAL EDUCATION 1848-1866 Body responsible for government schools in New South Wales.

CLASSES OF PUPILS
1848-1904 Classes 1 to 5
1904 'New Education' introduced
   Infants: Kindergarten (where available)
           Class 1
   Primary: Classes 2 to 5
   Super-Primary: 6 and 7

CLASSES OF SCHOOLS AND CLASSIFICATION OF TEACHERS For much of the period dealt with in this book the classes of schools and the required matching classification of teachers were as follows:

Class of school or department	Teacher's classification
1	1A
2	1B
3	2A
4	2A
5	2B
6	2B
7	3A
8	3B
9	3C
10	3C

The highest class of school was 1 and the highest class of teacher was 1A. In a grade below 3C was the lowest grade, probationer. No grading was given to pupil-teachers.

CORRESPONDENCE SCHOOL, THE 1916-90 A school providing primary and secondary education by correspondence lessons.

COUNCIL OF EDUCATION 1867-80 Body responsible for government schools in New South Wales.

DEPARTMENT OF EDUCATION The Department of Public Instruction replaced the Council of Education on 1 May 1880. It gradually became known as the Department of Education and in 1915 the Minister gave instructions for the Department to be known as the Department of Education; legislative sanction for the change did not come until 1957. The name of the Department of Education was changed to the Department of School Education on 13 December 1989.

DEPARTMENT OF PUBLIC INSTRUCTION - see DEPARTMENT OF EDUCATION

EVENING PUBLIC SCHOOL 1880-1915 A school which first emerged in 1880 to provide an elementary education for persons over 14 years of age who had previously received no education, or very little. Evening Public Schools offered young men (very few females were ever enrolled) two hours of instruction three nights a week. They were usually conducted in the local Public School building by the headmaster or another competent teacher. Most of them were poorly attended and short-lived and they were rapidly replaced from 1911 with Evening Continuation Schools.

FEES see SCHOOL FEES

FORAGE ALLOWANCE An allowance paid to teachers, particularly teachers of Half-Time and House to House Schools, for whom travel to school was necessary.

HALF-TIME SCHOOL 1867-1950 An elementary school which emerged in 1867 to cater for children in areas of scattered population. The 1866 Act provided for the appointment of itinerant teachers, and during 1867 and 1868 teachers were in charge of up to seven 'stations'. From 1869 each teacher visited only two stations, and the schools became truly Half-Time. The attendance of at least 20 children was required, in two groups of 10 or more. In 1898 the required attendance was reduced to 16, and by 1908 no fixed number was required.

HIGH SCHOOL 1883- A secondary school, first established in 1883 but a very small part of the education system until the re-organisation of secondary education after 1910.

HOUSE TO HOUSE SCHOOL 1881-1923 An elementary school which emerged in 1881 to cater for sparsely populated areas unable to be reached by other types of schools. The typical House to House School was composed of two or more teaching stations several miles apart, where children were gathered and visited by the itinerant teacher. Despite the name, a significant minority of House to House Schools with only one teaching station operated up to 1900. The teachers were on the whole untrained or of the lowest classification, instruction was confined to basic subjects and no school buildings had to be erected. The last so-called House to House School closed in 1923, but Ivanhoe Travelling School operated until 1949 in the same manner as the old House to House Schools.

LEAVING CERTIFICATE 1913-66 Examination at completion of the full course of secondary education.

NATIONAL SCHOOL 1848-66 All schools operated by the Board of National Education were called National Schools. They were renamed Public Schools in 1867.

NEW SYLLABUS Syllabus issued by the Department in 1904 and re-issued in 1905 in an amplified form. The *Report of the Minister of Public Instruction* 1904, p.16, states:

The syllabus, besides providing for a progressive course of instruction, is designed to give practical application to the principle of the correlation of subjects of study, to make 'the self-activity of the pupil the basis of school instruction,' to bring the work of the teacher into closer touch with his home and social surroundings, and to make the school a powerful agent in the intellectual, moral, and social development of the child.

PARENTS AND CITIZENS ASSOCIATIONS Parents and Citizens Associations began to emerge in 1905, usually to raise funds for educational needs, to bring the school and parents into closer contact, and to consider issues relating to the welfare of the school. At first they were called Parents Unions but by 1908 the term Parents and Citizens Association had become general.

PATRONS 1848-67 The Board of National Education managed each school in co-operation with a group of local patrons. Each school was required to have at least three local patrons from different religious denominations. Patrons were expected to meet at least monthly and their duties included supervising school buildings, fixing the rate of school fees, and reviewing complaints by parents.

PRIMARY FINAL 1930-1943 Examination at the completion of the primary course.

PROBATIONARY PUPIL-TEACHER A newly-employed pupil-teacher on probation prior to appointment as pupil-teacher.

PROMOTERS Local residents (usually about three in number) who took a prominent role in the setting up of an individual school. One of the promoters was nominated by the inspector as the person with whom the Department would correspond about the matter of setting up the school.

PROVISIONAL SCHOOL 1867-1957 An elementary school which first emerged in 1867. A Provisional School could be established in areas where at least 15 children, but fewer than the 25 required for a Public School, could be expected to attend. Parents provided the building and furniture, while the Council of Education or later the Department of Education paid the teacher and supplied books and equipment. During the 1880s the minimum number of children required was reduced to 12; from 1898 the minimum was 10, and from 1945 it was nine. After 1882 there were provisions for the Department to provide all or part of the cost of buildings, but well into the twentieth century parents often met most of the cost. The schools were generally staffed by untrained teachers or by teachers of the lowest classification. Gradually they became in effect simply small Public Schools, and in November 1957 the remaining ones were converted to Public Schools.

PUBLIC SCHOOL 1848- The basic elementary school in the New South Wales education system, known as National Schools from 1848 to 1866 and as Public Schools since 1867. Originally the attendance of 30 children was required for the establishment of a school, but this was reduced to 25 in 1867 and 20 in 1880; in 1957, when Provisional Schools were converted to Public Schools, the minimum figure was reduced to nine. Until 1875 parents had to pay one-third of the cost of buildings, but the Council of Education and then the Department have since met the total costs. Until the 1880s there were no government secondary schools, and no official post-primary courses in Public Schools. But the 1880 Act recognised the presence at school of numbers of children who had completed the primary course, by providing for the establishment of Superior Public Schools with primary and post-primary courses, and for separate High Schools. After 1913 many Public Schools incorporated one or more distinct secondary departments or 'schools'. The modern development of High Schools has meant that, with some exceptions like the Central Schools, most Public Schools now offer only the primary course.

PUPIL-TEACHERS 1851- *c*.1908 Trainee teachers who began their course between the ages of 13 and 16; during school hours they taught a class full-time, and for an hour or so each day, out of school hours, they were instructed by the head of the school.

QUALIFYING CERTIFICATE 1911-1922 Examination to mark the end of the primary course.

QUARTERLY RETURN A return which was filled in quarterly by the head of the school giving enrolment and attendance and also information on other matters.

SCHOOL BOARDS 1867- *c*.1905 School boards were constituted under the *Public Schools Act, 1866*. Each board was to consist of at least three local people appointed by the Council of Education and was regularly to visit, inspect and report on the school under its charge. School boards had similar managerial and supervisory roles to those of the earlier local patrons.

The *Public Instruction Act, 1880* reconstituted school boards to make them responsible for all government schools in a prescribed district. The boards were retitled district school boards and were to consist of no more than seven local representatives. Their functions were no different from those of the earlier boards. From the 1890s district school boards tended to become responsible for small districts or even a single school.

SCHOOL CLASSES see CLASSES OF SCHOOLS AND CLASSIFICATION OF TEACHERS

SCHOOL FEES
1848 the Board of National Education recommended that school fees should range from 1 penny to 1 shilling per child per week; the local school board to set the rate.
1853 the Board of National Education recommended a minimum of 3 pence per child per week; any amount above this to be decided by the local school board.
1867 the Council of Education recommended that local school boards set fees according to local economic conditions. Generally the fees ranged between 6 pence and 1 shilling per child per week, with reductions for members of one family.
1880 the *Public Instruction Act* reduced primary school fees to 3 pence per child per week with a maximum of 1 shilling per family per week.
1883 High School fees set at 2 guineas (£2 2s.) per child per quarter, increased to 3 guineas in 1893.
1906 Primary and Superior Public School fees abolished from 8 October 1906.
1911 High School fees abolished from 1 January 1911.

1923 High School fees of 2 guineas per quarter reintroduced from 1 January 1923, subject to a means test.
1925 High School fees abolished

SUBSIDISED SCHOOL 1903-89 A school designed for localities where the minimum attendance required for even the smallest type of government school could not be obtained. While the Department paid a subsidy for each pupil, parents were totally responsible for providing the school building and the teacher; often, however, Subsidised Schools were permitted to use former government school buildings. The last Subsidised School, Hatfield, became a government school in 1989.

SUPERIOR PUBLIC SCHOOL 1881-1931 A Public School officially recognised from 1881 as providing both primary and post-primary education. Pupils who had completed the primary course studied subjects like mathematics and languages which were also taught in High Schools. Because they charged considerably lower fees, the Superior Public Schools were able to compete more than effectively with the early High Schools. From 1913 Superior Public Schools were reorganised, being restricted to offering two-year vocational courses—commercial, home science or junior technical. An individual school could provide one or more of these, but smaller Superior Public Schools, generally in the country, offered a modified composite course. By 1925 there was a less rigid vocational emphasis, the courses had been extended to three years and students could sit for the Intermediate Certificate examination. Although the schools were still officially known as Superior Public Schools, it was common for the names of the distinct secondary 'schools' operating under the same roof as the primary school to be used: in one context a school might be described as a Superior Public School, and in another as a Junior Technical School. After 1931 the term Superior Public School was abandoned, super-primary schools being known only by the names of the courses offered.

TEACHER CLASSIFICATION see CLASSES OF SCHOOLS AND CLASSIFICATION OF TEACHERS

TRAVELLING SCHOOL 1908-49 A school similar to a House to House School catering for small, scattered groups of children. There were only three such schools, the first opening in 1908 and the last closing in 1949. The early teachers used a horse-drawn van which served if necessary as the schoolroom, but the later teachers used their vehicles only as their means of transport, teaching in the various houses in exactly the same manner as house to house teachers had done.

Notes

The following abbreviation is used in these notes:

AO NSW   Archives Office of New South Wales

1 REASONS FOR WANTING A SCHOOL
1. Terara-Underbank, Miscellaneous Letters Received 1867, Council of Education (AO NSW ref: 1/755 Vol. 21).
2. Eurunderee School File (AO NSW ref: 5/15856).
3. Newrybar School File (AO NSW ref: 5/17133).
4. Bungawalbyn School File (AO NSW ref: 5/15165).
5. Buxton School File (AO NSW ref: 5/15218).
6. Badgerys Creek School File (AO NSW ref: 5/14748).
7. Mulwee School File (AO NSW ref: 5/16999).
8. Cave Point School File (AO NSW ref: 5/15344).
9. Macarthur School File (AO NSW ref: 5/16671).
10. Tullamore School File (AO NSW ref: 5/17898).
11. Willala School File (AO NSW ref: 5/18117).
12. Medowie School File (AO NSW ref: 14/7683).

2 LOCATION DIFFICULTIES
1. House to House Schools Subject File (AO NSW ref: 20/12752.A).
2. Warge Rock School File (AO NSW ref: 5/18026).
3. Ibid.
4. Ibid.
5. Bribbaree School File (AO NSW ref: 5/15082).
6. Ibid.
7. Ibid.
8. Ibid.
9. Macarthur School File (AO NSW ref:5/16671).
10. Ross Hill School File (AO NSW ref: 5/17522).
11. Teachers' career records, NSW Dept of School Education.

3 TEACHERS' TRAVEL
1. Teachers' career records, NSW Dept of School Education.
2. Eringonia School File (AO NSW ref: 5/15828).
3. Ibid.
4. Ibid.
5. Swan Bay School File (AO NSW ref: 5/17728).
6. Narara School File (AO NSW ref: 5/17052).
7. Megalong School File (AO NSW ref: 5/16810).
8. Ibid.
9. Teachers' career records, NSW Dept of School Education.
10. Megalong School File (AO NSW ref: 5/16810).
11. Teachers' career records, NSW Dept of School Education.
12. Ibid.
13. Bagawa School File (AO NSW ref: 5/14749).
14. Teachers' career records, NSW Dept of School Education.
15. Cabbage Tree Island Aboriginal School File (AO NSW ref: 5/15225).
16. Ibid.
17. Ibid.
18. West Wyalong School File (AO NSW ref: 5/18216).
19. Ibid.
20. Argyle East School File (AO NSW ref: 5/14674).
21. Ibid.
22. Teachers' career records, NSW Dept of School Education.
23. Wandook School File (AO NSW ref: 5/18014).
24. Ibid.
25. Ibid.
26. Fernleigh School File (AO NSW ref: 5/15883).
27. Ibid.
28. Teachers' career records, NSW Dept of School Education.
29. Tiri School File (AO NSW ref: 5/17855).
30. Ibid.
31. Ibid.
32. Willala School File (AO NSW ref: 5/18117).
33. Ibid.
34. Ibid.
35. Ibid.
36. Ibid.
37. Ibid.
38. Ibid.
39. Teachers' career records, NSW Dept of School Education.
40. Mulwee School File (AO NSW ref: 5/16999).
41. Ibid.
42. Ibid.
43. Ibid.
44. Ibid.
45. Ibid.
46. Ibid.
47. Teachers' career records, NSW Dept of School Education.
48. Ibid.
49. Tullamore School File (AO NSW ref: 5/17898).
50. Ibid.
51. Gulargambone Aboriginal School File (AO NSW ref: 5/16180).
52. Training School—Wagga, Miscellaneous Letters Received 1868, Council of Education (AO NSW ref: 1/792 Vol. 58).
53. Tumbulgum School File (AO NSW ref: 5/17904).
54. Ibid.
55. Ganmain School File (AO NSW ref: 5/15959).
56. Heads of school cards, NSW Dept of School Education.
57. Teachers' career records, NSW Dept of School Education.
58. Tregeagle School File (AO NSW ref: 5/17884).

59. Ibid.
60. Kurrara School File (AO NSW ref: 5/16518).

4   ETON-HARROW TRAVELLING SCHOOL
1. Ashley Freeman, 'The House to House and Travelling Schools of New South Wales 1880-1949', M Ed thesis, University of New England, Armidale, 1986, p. 250.
2. Ibid., p. 258.
3. *Government School of New South Wales 1848 to 1993*, NSW Dept of School Education, 1993, p. 65.
4. Teachers' career records, NSW Dept of School Education.
5. Ibid.
6. Ibid.
7. *Government Schools of New South Wales 1848 to 1993*, NSW Dept of School Education, 1993, p. 65.

5   ACCOMMODATING THE TEACHER
1. Copies of Official Correspondence and Official Diaries of Thomas Harris, Inspector of Schools, Southern District (Goulburn) 10 Jan 1865 - 21 Nov 1867 (AO NSW ref: A5014 Vol. 1, pp. 42, 46).
2. Codrington School File (AO NSW ref: 5/15427).
3. Ibid.
4. Herons Creek School File (AO NSW ref: 5/16264).
5. Heads of school cards, NSW Dept of School Education.
6. Wedallion School File (AO NSW ref: 5/18064).
7. Ibid.
8. Ibid.
9. Ibid.
10. Teachers' career records, NSW Dept of School Education.
11. Ibid.
12. Medowie School File (AO NSW ref: 5/16807).
13. Ibid.
14. Ibid.
15. Teachers' career records, NSW Dept of School Education.
16. Buxton School File (AO NSW ref: 5/15218).
17. Ibid.
18. Ibid.
19. Ibid.
20. Ibid.
21. Ibid.
22. Ibid.
23. Ibid.
24. Ibid.
25. Ibid.
26. Ibid.
27. Ibid.
28. Ibid.
29. Ibid.
30. Hannam Vale School File (AO NSW ref: 5/16232).
31. Ibid.
32. Ibid.
33. Heads of school cards, NSW Dept of School Education.
34. Hannam Vale School File (AO NSW ref: 5/16232).
35. Ibid.
36. Ibid.
37. Ibid.
38. Ibid.
39. Ibid.
40. Ibid.
41. Teachers' career records, NSW Dept of School Education.
42. Ibid.

43. West Wyalong School File (AO NSW ref: 5/18217).
44. Heads of school cards, NSW Dept of School Education.
45. *Government Schools of New South Wales 1848 to 1993*, NSW Dept of School Education, 1993, p. 134.
46. Miranda School File (AO NSW ref: 5/16867).
47. Ibid.
48. Teachers' career records, NSW Dept of School Education.
49. Miranda School File (AO NSW ref: 5/16867).
50. Five Mile Tree School File (AO NSW ref: 5/15899); and Teachers' career records, NSW Dept of School Education.
51. Five Mile Tree School File (AO NSW ref: 5/15899).
52. Willala School File (AO NSW 14/7933).
53. Ibid.
54. Ibid.

6   TEACHERS' LIVING CONDITIONS
1. Training School—Wagga, Miscellaneous Letters Received 1868, Council of Education (AO NSW ref: 1/792 Vol. 58).
2. Tarlo-Ulmarra, Miscellaneous Letters Received 1869, Council of Education (AO NSW ref: 1/826 Vol. 92).
3. Wyagdon-Young. Misc., Miscellaneous Letters Received 1872, Council of Education (AO NSW ref: 1/926 Vol. 194).
4. Boro-Burrawang, Miscellaneous Letters Received 1870, Council of Education (AO NSW ref: 1/841 Vol. 109).
5. *Longman Dictionary of the English Language*, Longman, Harlow, Essex, 1984, p. 1801.
6. Teachers' career records, NSW Dept of School Education.
7. Henry Havelock Ellis, *My Life*, William Heinemann Ltd, London, 1940, p. 118.
8. Ibid. pp. 119-122.
9. Ibid. opp. p. 120.
10. Teachers' career records, NSW Dept of School Education.
11. Derry School File (AO NSW ref: 5/15690).
12. Ibid.
13. Derry School File (AO NSW ref: 5/15690).
14. Ivanhoe School File (AO NSW ref: 5/16371).
15. Stockinbingal School File (AO NSW ref: 5/17682).
16. Kiama School File (AO NSW ref: 5/16465).
17. Teachers' career records, NSW Dept of School Education.
18. Heads of school cards, NSW Dept of School Education.
19. Burraneer Bay School File (AO NSW ref: 5/15189).
20. Ibid.
21. Teachers' career records, NSW Dept of School Education.
22. Tuckaburra School File (AO NSW ref: 5/17893).
23. Teachers' career records, NSW Dept of School Education.
24. Eringonia School File (AO NSW ref: 5/15828).
25. Ibid.
26. Botany School File (AO NSW ref: 5/15037).
27. Botany School File (AO NSW ref: 5/15038).
28. Thone Creek School File (AO NSW ref: 5/17830).
29. Ibid.
30. Ibid.
31. Ibid.
32. Ibid.
33. Ibid.
34. Ibid.
35. Ibid.
36. Teachers' career records, NSW Dept of School Education.
37. Ibid.
38. *Government Schools of New South Wales 1848 to 1993*, NSW Dept of School Education , 1993, p. 44.
39. Teachers' career records, NSW Dept of School Education.

40. Byabarra School File (AO NSW ref: 5/15219).
41. Ibid.
42. Ibid.
43. Teachers' career records, NSW Dept of School Education.
44. Byabarra School File (AO NSW ref: 5/15219).
45. Teachers' career records, NSW Dept of School Education.
46. Byabarra School File (AO NSW ref: 5/15219).
47. Ibid.
48. Martins Creek School File (AO NSW ref: 5/16785).
49. Teachers' career records, NSW Dept of School Education.
50. Kurrara School File (AO NSW ref: 5/16518).
51. Berrigan School File (AO NSW ref: 5/14900).

7   SCHOOL COMMUNITIES
1. Copies of Official Correspondence and Official Diaries of Thomas Harris, Inspector of Schools, Southern District (Goulburn) 10 Jan 1867-21 Nov 1867 (AO NSW ref: A 5014 Vol. 1, pp. 134-5).
2. Teachers' career records, NSW Dept of School Education.
3. W. H. Wilde, *Courage a Grace: A Biography of Dame Mary Gilmore*,
   Melbourne University Press, 1988, p. 50.
4. Ibid.
5. West Wyalong School File (AO NSW ref: 5/18216).
6. Ibid.
7. Ibid.
8. Ibid.
9. Ibid.
10. Stockinbingal School File (AO NSW ref: 5/17682).
11. Ibid.
12. Ibid.
13. Ibid.
14. Heads of school cards, NSW Dept of School Education.
15. Berowra School File (AO NSW ref: 5/14898).
16. Ibid.
17. Ibid.
18. Ibid.
19. Ibid.
20. Ibid.
21. Ibid.
22. Ibid.
23. Ibid.
24. Ibid.
25. Ibid.
26. Ibid.
27. Ibid.
28. Ibid.
29. Ibid.
30. Ibid.
31. Teachers' career records, NSW Dept of School Education.
32. Ibid.
33. Buxton School File (AO NSW ref: 5/15218).
34. Ibid.
35. Ibid.
36. Ibid.
37. Ibid.
38. Ibid.
39. Ibid.
40. Teachers' career records, NSW Dept of School Education.
41. Buxton School File (AO NSW ref: 5/15218).
42. Teachers' career records, NSW Dept of School Education.
43. Burringbar School File (AO NSW ref: 5/15196).

44. Ibid.
45. Ibid.
46. Ibid.
47. Hannam Vale School File (AO NSW ref: 5/16232).
48. Tullamore School File (AO NSW ref: 5/17898).
49. Miranda School File (AO NSW ref: 5/16867).
50. Ibid.
51. *Miranda Public School 100 Years 1893-1993*, p. 24.
52. Miranda School File (AO NSW ref: 5/16867).
53. Ibid.
54. History of Miranda School written by Dept of Education, 1958.
55. *Miranda Public School 100 Years 1893-1993*, p. 24.
56. Ibid.
57. Miranda School File (AO NSW ref: 5/16867).
58. Miranda School File (AO NSW ref: 14/7696).
59. Ibid.
60. Ibid.
61. Ibid.
62. Ibid.
63. Ibid.
64. Ibid.
65. Ibid.
66. Ibid.
67. Ibid.
68. Willoughby School File (AO NSW ref: 14/7933).
69. Ibid.

8   ISOLATION
1. Teachers' career records and heads of school cards, NSW Dept of School Education.
2. Warner School File (AO NSW ref: 5/18030).
3. Ibid.
4. Ibid.
5. Ibid.
6. Ibid.
7. Teachers' career records, NSW Dept of School Education.
8. Irrawang School File (AO NSW ref: 5/16366).
9. Teachers' career records, NSW Dept of School Education.
10. Macarthur School File (AO NSW ref: 5/16671).
11. Ibid.
12. Ibid.
13. Ibid.
14. Ibid.
15. Ibid.
16. Willala School File (AO NSW ref: 5/18117).
17. Teachers' career records, NSW Dept of School Education.
18. Willala School File (AO NSW ref: 5/18117).
19. Five Mile Tree School File (AO NSW ref: 5/15899).
20. Teachers' career records, NSW Dept of School Education.

9   TEACHERS' EXTRA DUTIES
1. John Warren Middenway, note on 'Memoirs of John Saunders Middenway', copy held in historical resources of NSW Dept of School Education.
2. Teachers' career records, NSW Dept of School Education.
3. John Saunders Middenway, 'Memoirs of John Saunders Middenway', copy held in historical resources of NSW Dept of School Education, pp. 24-5.
4. *Status Quo*, MCMLIX, publication on schools in the Ballina Inspectorate and their origins, Education Week, 1959. Richmond River Historical Society. Schools Folder No. 1 A-K.

5. *Government Schools of New South Wales 1848 to 1993*, NSW Dept of School Education, 1993, p. 108.
6. Swan Bay School File (AO NSW ref: 5/17728).
7. Teachers' career records, NSW Dept of School Education.
8. Wyalong School File (AO NSW ref: 5/18215).
9. Ibid.
10. Ibid.
11. Ibid.
12. Ibid.
13. Ibid.
14. Ibid.
15. Ibid.
16. Teachers' career records, NSW Dept of School Education.
17. Medowie School File (AO NSW ref: 5/16807).
18. Ibid.
19. Ibid.
20. Ibid.
21. Teachers' career records, NSW Dept of School Education.
22. Heads of school cards, NSW Dept of School Education.
23. Teachers' career records, NSW Dept of School Education.
24. Conversation on 8 July 1994 with Warwick Franks, Charles Sturt University, Mitchell, an editor of the forthcoming *Oxford Companion to Australian Cricket*.
25. Teachers' career records, NSW Dept of School Education.
26. White Cliffs School File (AO NSW ref: 5/18100).
27. Ibid.
28. Ibid.
29. Ibid.
30. Teachers' career records, NSW Dept of School Education.
31. Letter held in historical resources of NSW Dept of School Education.
32. Willala School File (AO NSW ref: 14/7933).
33. Ibid.
34. Ibid.

10 DEFICIENCIES IN SCHOOL BUILDINGS

1. Richmond North School File (AO NSW ref: 5/17476).
2. Copies of Official Correspondence and Official Diaries of Thomas Harris, Inspector of Schools, Southern District (Goulburn) 10 Jan 1865 - 21 Nov 1867 (AO NSW ref: A 5014 Vol. 1, p. 401).
3. Copies of Official Correspondence and Official Diaries of Thomas Harris, Inspector of Schools, Southern District (Goulburn) 10 Jan 1865 - 21 Nov 1867 (AO NSW ref: A 5014 Vol. 1, pp. 215-6).
4. Training School—Wagga, Miscellaneous Letters Received 1868, Council of Education (AO NSW ref: 1/792 Vol. 58).
5. Wyrallah School File (AO NSW ref: 5/18228).
6. Ibid.
7. Teachers' career records, NSW Dept of School Education.
8. Bourke School File (AO NSW ref: 5/15043).
9. Codrington School File (AO NSW ref: 5/15427).
10. Wooram School File (AO NSW ref: 5/18208).
11. Nurung School File (AO NSW ref: 5/17195).
12. Wyalong School File (AO NSW ref: 5/18215).
13. Ibid.
14. Letter held in historical resources of NSW Dept of School Education.
15. New Vale School File (AO NSW ref: 5/17147).
16. Ibid.
17. Ibid.
18. Bagawa School File (AO NSW ref: 5/14749).
19. Miranda School File (AO NSW ref: 5/16866).
20. Ibid.
21. Ibid.
22. Ibid.
23. White Cliffs School File (AO NSW ref: 5/18100).
24. Ibid.
25. Ibid.
26. Ganmain School File (AO NSW ref: 5/15960).
27. Billinudgel School File (AO NSW ref: 5/14924).
28. Ibid.
29. Ibid.
30. Ibid.
31. Ibid.
32. Ibid.
33. Dungay Creek School File (AO NSW ref: 5/15760).
34. Teachers' career records, NSW Dept of School Education.
35. Collins Creek School File (AO NSW ref: 5/15445).
36. Teachers' career records, NSW Dept of School Education.
37. Tullamore School File (AO NSW ref: 5/17898).
38. Ibid.
39. Ibid.
40. Duncans Creek Lower (AO NSW ref: 5/15754).
41. Five Mile Tree School File (AO NSW ref: 5/15898).
42. Gladesville School File (AO NSW ref: 5/16003).
43. Austral School File (AO NSW ref: 5/14736).
44. Ibid.
45. Cabbage Tree Island School File (AO NSW ref: 14/7365).
46. Ibid.
47. Erskineville School File (AO NSW ref: 5/15831).
48. Brunswick Heads School File (AO NSW ref: 5/15134).

11 RESIGNATION FOLLOWING INSPECTION

1. Copies of Official Correspondence and Official Diaries of Thomas Harris, Inspector of Schools, Southern District (Goulburn) 10 Jan 1865 - 21 Nov 1867 (AO NSW ref: A 5014 Vol. 1, pp. 93-5).
2. Mount Victoria School File (AO NSW ref: 5/16972).
3. Helen Gibson, 'A Teacher to Remember', *Inside Education*, NSW Dept of Education, July 1973, pp. 26-7.
4. Teachers' career records, NSW Dept of School Education.
5. Dungay School File (AO NSW ref: 5/15760).
6. Ibid.
7. Ibid.
8. Ibid.
9. Ibid.
10. Ibid.

12 DIFFICULTIES IN SUPPORTING DEPENDANTS

1. Parramatta - Raymond Terrace, Miscellaneous Letters Received 1874, Council of Education (AO NSW ref: 1/975 Vol. 247).
2. *Sydney Morning Herald*, 12 June 1874.
3. Maclean School File (AO NSW ref: 5/16680).
4. Teachers' career records, NSW Dept of School Education.
5. Kogarah School File (AO NSW ref: 5/16493).
6. *New South Wales Educational Gazette*, 1 September 1894, p. 76.
7. Ibid.
8. Ibid.
9. Ibid.
10. St Ives School File (AO NSW ref: 5/17568).
11. Ibid.
12. Teachers' career records, NSW Dept of School Education.

13. Wyalong School File (AO NSW ref: 5/18215).
14. Ibid.
15. Ibid.
16. Ibid
17. Ibid.

13 TEACHERS' UNUSUAL BEHAVIOURS
1. Copies of Official Correspondence and Official Diaries of Thomas Harris, Inspector of Schools, Southern District (Goulburn) 10 Jan 1865 - 21 Nov 1867 (AO NSW ref: A 5014 Vol. 1, p. 126).
2. Brushgrove - Camperdown, Miscellaneous Letters Received 1868, Council of Education (AO NSW ref: 1/771 Vol. 37).
3. Branxton-Campbelltown, Miscellaneous Letters Received 1869, Council of Education (AO NSW ref: 1/806 Vol. 74).
4. Ibid.
5. Ibid.
6. Ibid.
7. Boro-Burrawang, Miscellaneous Letters Received 1870, Council of Education (AO NSW ref: 1/841 Vol. 109).
8. Ibid.
9. Ibid.
10. Ibid.
11. Ibid.
12. Teachers' career records, NSW Dept of School Education.
13. Ibid.
14. Ibid.
15. Ibid.
16. Ibid.
17. Merimbula-Mosquito Island, Miscellaneous Letters Received 1872, Council of Education (AO NSW ref: 1/911 Vol. 180).
18. Ibid.
19. Ibid.
20. Teachers' career records, NSW Dept of School Education.
21. Blayney-Bundywalla, Miscellaneous Letters Received 1873, Council of Education (AO NSW ref: 1/939 Vol. 208).
22. Clifford Turney, *William Wilkins, His Life and Work,* Hale & Iremonger, Sydney, 1992. pp. 233-5.
23. *Votes and Proceedings of the Legislative Assembly 1881*, Vol. 2, p. 1017.
24. William Wilkins, Report on Mrs Bardwell, Return to an order of the Legislative Assembly, 18 August 1881, p.4, in *Votes and Proceedings of the Legislative Assembly 1881*, Vol. 2, p. 934.
25. Ibid.
26. Ibid.
27. Ibid., p. 933.
28. Ibid.
29. Ibid.
30. *Votes and Proceedings of the Legislative Assembly 1881*, Vol. 2, p. 1033.
31. Ibid., p. 1017.
32. Teachers' career records, NSW Dept of School Education.
33. Ibid.
34. Ibid.
35. Ibid.
36. *Votes and Proceedings of Legislative Assembly 1881*, Vol. 2, p. 959.
37. Ibid.
38. Ibid., p. 937.
39. Ibid. pp. 933 ff.
40. Clifford Turney, *William Wilkins, His Life and Work,* Hale & Iremonger, Sydney, 1992. p. 234.
41. *Votes and Proceedings of Legislative Assembly 1881*, Vol. 2, p. 977.
42. Inspector's report on Girls' Dept, Redfern School, 1882 and correspondence on that report, *Votes and Proceed-ings of Legislative Assembly 1883-1884*, Vol. 7, p. 1050.
43. Ibid. pp. 1053, 1056.
44. Teachers' career records, NSW Dept of School Education.
45. Wandook School File (AO NSW ref: 5/18014).
46. Ibid.
47. Ibid.
48. Ibid.
49. Ibid
50. Ibid.
51. Ibid.
52. Ibid.
53. Ibid.
54. Ibid.
55. Ibid.
56. Ibid.
57. Ibid.
58. Ibid.
59. Ibid.
60. Ibid.
61. Ibid.
62. Ibid.
63. Ibid.
64. Ibid.
65. Ibid.
66. Ibid.
67. Ibid.
68. Ibid.
69. Ibid.
70. Ibid.
71. Ibid.
72. Ibid.
73. Ibid.
74. Ibid.
75. Ibid.
76. Ibid.
77. Ibid.
78. Ibid.
79. Ibid.
80. Ibid.
81. Ibid.
82. Ibid.
83. Ibid.
84. Ibid.
85. Teachers' career records, NSW Dept of School Education.
86. Wandook School File (AO NSW ref: 5/18014).
87. Helen Gibson, 'The Baron and the Bush School', *Education Gazette*, NSW Dept of Education, 1 August 1969, pp. 370-7 and 1 September 1969, pp. 438-43.
88. Ibid.
89. Wandook School File (AO NSW ref: 5/18014).
90. Ibid.
91. Ibid.
92. Ibid.
93. Teachers' career records, NSW Dept of School Education.
94. Dunvegan School File (AO NSW ref: 5/15769).
95. Ibid.
96. Ibid.

97. Teachers' career records, NSW Dept of School Education.
98. Ibid.
99. Warge Rock School File (AO NSW ref: 5/18026).
100. Teachers' career records, NSW Dept of School Education.
101. Warge Rock School File (AO NSW ref: 5/18026).
102. Ibid.
103. Teachers' career records, NSW Dept of School Education.
104. Warge Rock School File (AO NSW ref: 5/18026).
105. Ibid.
106. Ibid.
107. Ibid.
108. Teachers' career records, NSW Dept of School Education.
109. Warge Rock School File (AO NSW ref: 5/18026).
110. Ibid.
111. Ibid.
112. Teachers' career records, NSW Dept of School Education.
113. Ibid.
114. Glenellen School File (AO NSW ref: 5/16019).
115. Ibid.
116. Ivanhoe School File (AO NSW ref: 5/16371).
117. Ibid.
118. Ibid.
119. Ibid.
120. Ibid.
121. Teachers' career records, NSW Dept of School Education.
122. Overton School File (AO NSW ref: 5/17245).
123. Ibid.
124. Ibid.
125. Ibid.
126. Teachers' career records, NSW Dept of School Education.
127. Glenellen School File (AO NSW ref: 5/16019).
128. Ibid.
129. Teachers' career records, NSW Dept of School Education.
130. Burrumbuttock (East) School File (AO NSW ref: 5/15199).
131. Ibid.
132. Ibid.
133. Ibid.
134. Ibid.
135. Teachers' career records, NSW Dept of School Education.
136. Burrumbuttock (East) School File (AO NSW ref: 5/15199).
137. Letter, Dept to W. Small, 17 August 1900. Copies of letters sent by the Chief Inspector and the Under Secretary Dec 1896-1915, Vol. 407, p. 653 (AO NSW).
138. Teachers' career records, NSW Dept of School Education.
139. Ibid.
140. Ibid.
141. Ibid.
142. Crookwell River School File (AO NSW ref: 5/15571).
143. Ibid.
144. Ibid.
145. Teachers' career records, NSW Dept of School Education.
146. Kurrara School File (AO NSW ref: 5/16518).
147. Ibid.
148. Ibid.
149. Teachers' career records, NSW Dept of School Education.
150. Ibid.
151. Dumbleton School File (AO NSW ref: 5/15751).
152. Ibid.
153. Ibid.
154. Subsidised School Cards, NSW Dept of School Education.
155. Conversation with Ron Collins on 16 April 1994.
156. Ibid.
157. Ibid.
158. Teachers' career records, NSW Dept of School Education.
159. Kingswood School File (AO NSW ref: 5/16486).
160. Ibid.
161. Ibid.
162. Ibid.
163. Ibid.
164. Ibid.
165. Teachers' career records, NSW Dept of School Education.
166. Ibid.
167. St Ives School File (AO NSW ref: 5/17569).
168. Ibid.
169. Ibid.
170. Ibid.
171. Ibid.
172. Ibid.
173. Ibid.
174. Ibid.
175. Ibid.
176. Ibid.
177. Teachers' career records, NSW Dept of School Education.
178. Wyalong School File (AO NSW ref: 5/18216).
179. Ibid.
180. Ibid.
181. Ibid.
182. Teachers' career records, NSW Dept of School Education.
183. Narara School File (AO NSW ref: 5/17053).
184. Ibid.
185. Ibid.
186. Ibid.
187. Ibid.
188. Ibid.
189. Ibid.
190. Ibid.
191. Ibid.
192. Ibid.
193. Ibid.
194. Teachers' career records, NSW Dept of School Education.

14   REMOVALS

1. Tarlo-Ulmarra, Miscellaneous Letters Received 1869, Council of Education (AO NSW ref: 1/826 Vol. 92).
2. Ibid.
3. Teachers' career records, NSW Dept of School Education.
4. Ibid.
5. Bevendale School File (AO NSW ref: 5/14908).
6. Teachers' career records, NSW Dept of School Education.
7. Nurung School File (AO NSW ref: 5/17195).
8. Ibid.
9. Ibid.
10. Ibid.
11. Ibid.
12. Ibid.
13. Ibid.
14. Ibid.
15. Ibid.
16. Teachers' career records, NSW Dept of School Education.
17. Nurung School File (AO NSW ref: 5/17195).
18. Ibid.
19. Ibid.
20. Ibid.
21. Teachers' career records, NSW Dept of School Education.

22. Fern Glen School File (AO NSW ref: 5/15882).
23. Bungay School File (AO NSW ref: 5/15166).
24. Teachers' career records, NSW Dept of School Education.
25. Crookwell River School File (AO NSW ref: 5/5571).
26. Ibid.
27. Teachers' career records, NSW Dept of School Education.
28. Megalong School File (AO NSW ref: 5/16810).
29. Teachers' career records, NSW Dept of School Education.
30. Hurstville West School File (AO NSW ref: 5/16347), and Teachers' career records, NSW Dept of School Education.
31. Teachers' career records, NSW Dept of School Education.
32. Ibid.
33. Wilberforce School File (AO NSW ref: 5/18112).
34. Ibid.
35. Ibid.
36. Ibid.
37. Teachers' career records, NSW Dept of School Education.
38. Ibid.
39. Ibid.
40. Badgerys Creek School File (AO NSW ref: 5/14748).
41. Ibid.
42. Ibid.
43. Ibid.
44. Ibid.
45. Ibid.
46. Teachers' career records, NSW Dept of School Education.
47. Ibid.
48. Badgerys Creek School File (AO NSW ref: 5/14748).
49. Teachers' career records, NSW Dept of School Education.
50. Burringbar School File (AO NSW ref: 5/15196).
51. Ibid.
52. Ibid.
53. Ibid.
54. Ibid.
55. Ibid.
56. Ibid.
57. Teachers' career records, NSW Dept of School Education.
58. Wyrallah School File (AO NSW ref: 5/18228).
59. Teachers' career records, NSW Dept of School Education.
60. Ibid.
61. Ibid.
62. Ibid.
63. Ibid.
64. Herons Creek School File (AO NSW ref: 5/16265).
65. Ibid.
66. Teachers' career records, NSW Dept of School Education.
67. Ibid.
68. Willala School File (AO NSW ref: 5/18117).

15 THE ELEMENTS

1. Board of National Education records (AO NSW) cited in history of Grafton Public School written by Dept of Education, 1966.
2. Cave Point School File (AO NSW ref: 5/15344).
3. Burringbar School File (AO NSW ref: 5/15196).
4. Ulmarra School File (AO NSW ref: 5/17929A).
5. Ibid.
6. Herons Creek School File (AO NSW ref: 5/16264).
7. Swan Bay School File (AO NSW ref: 5/17728).
8. Ibid.
9. Ibid.
10. Ibid.
11. Kurrara School File (AO NSW ref: 5/16518).
12. West Wyalong School File (AO NSW ref: 5/18216).
13. Ibid.
14. Ibid.
15. Ibid.
16. Ibid.
17. Ibid.
18. Yarrowitch School File (AO NSW ref: 5/18257).
19. Ibid.
20. Ibid.
21. Ibid.
22. Ibid.
23. Plunkett Street School File (AO NSW ref: 5/17365).
24. Megalong School File (AO NSW ref: 5/16810).
25. Ibid.
26. Dumbleton School File (AO NSW ref: 5/15752).

16 DANGERS

1. Teachers' career records, NSW Dept of School Education; and Parramatta-Raymond Terrace, Miscellaneous Letters Received 1874, Council of Education (AO NSW ref: 1/975 Vol. 247).
2. Parramatta-Raymond Terrace, Miscellaneous Letters Received 1874, Council of Education, (AO NSW ref: 1/975 Vol. 247).
3. Tierney (1892-1972), who was in 1963 responding to an article which stated that Fred White had fallen down a mine shaft, explained that he placed the term 'mine shafts' in inverted commas because 'The term used invariably on alluvial diggings was 'diggers' holes' Not 'mine shafts'. (John Tierney, Addenda to Biography of John Tierney, 1963 Mitchell Library MSS 2721 Add on 1123 Box 2[6]]).
4. Teachers' career records, NSW Dept of School Education.
5. Herons Creek School File (AO NSW ref: 5/16264).
6. Ibid.
7. Ibid.
8. Karangi School File (AO NSW ref: 5/16420).
9. *Richmond River Times*, cited by *Northern Star*, 19 August 1899.
10. *Richmond River Times*, cited by *Northern Star*, 19 August 1899.
11. Bagawa School File (AO NSW ref: 5/14749).

17 ANIMALS

1. In *Henry Lawson: Stories, Poems, Sketches and Autobiography*, edited by Brian Kiernan, University of Queensland Press 1976, pp. 16-17.
2. *Status Quo*, MCMLIX, publication on schools in the Ballina inspectorate and their origins, Education Week, 1959. Richmond River Historical Society. Schools Folder No. 1 A-K, p. 15.
3. Yamba School File (AO NSW ref: 5/18232).
4. Brunswick Heads School File (AO NSW ref: 5/15134).
5. Fernleigh School File (AO NSW ref: 5/15883).
6. Coorabell School File (AO NSW ref: 5/15513).
7. Jennings School File (AO NSW ref: 5/16380).
8. Eringonia School File (AO NSW ref: 5/15828).
9. Yamba School File (AO NSW ref: 5/18232).
10. West Wyalong School File (AO NSW ref: 5/18216).
11. West Wyalong School File (AO NSW ref: 5/18217).
12. New Vale School File (AO NSW ref: 5/17147).
13. Ibid.
14. Ibid.

15. Ibid.
16. Martins Creek School File (AO NSW ref: 5/16785).
17. Ibid.
18. Opossum Creek School File (AO NSW ref: 5/17220).
19. Hannam Vale School File (AO NSW ref: 5/16232).
20. Coorabell School File (AO NSW ref: 5/15514)
21. Clunes School File (AO NSW ref: 5/15415).
22. Ibid.
23. Ibid.
24. Kurrara School File (AO NSW ref: 5/16518).
25. Martins Creek School File (AO NSW ref: 5/16785).
26. Ivanhoe School File (AO NSW ref: 5/16371).
27. Ganmain School File (AO NSW ref: 5/15959).
28. Badgerys Creek School File (AO NSW ref: 5/14748).
29. St Ives School File (AO NSW ref: 5/17568).
30. Kiama School File (AO NSW ref: 5/16465).
31. Ivanhoe School File (AO NSW ref: 5/16371).
32. Burringbar School File (AO NSW ref: 5/15196).
33. Lismore High School File (AO NSW ref: 5/16625).
34. Hannam Vale School File (AO NSW ref: 5/16232).
35. Campbelltown School File (AO NSW ref: 14/7369).
36. St Ives School Filc (AO NSW ref: 5/17569).
37. Wyrallah School File (AO NSW ref: 5/18228).
38. Tucki Tucki School File (AO NSW ref: 5/17893).
39. Burringbar School File (AO NSW ref: 5/15195).
40. Ibid.
41. Macarthur School File (AO NSW ref: 5/6671).
42. Buxton School File (AO NSW ref: 5/15218).
43. Tregeagle School File (AO NSW ref: 5/17884).
44. Ibid.
45. Nana Glen School File (AO NSW ref: 5/17047).

18 VANDALS AND TRAMPS
1. Berrigan School File (AO NSW ref: 5/14900).
2. Ibid.
3. Buxton School File (AO NSW ref: 5/15218).
4. Ibid.
5. Ibid.
6. New Vale School File (AO NSW ref: 5/17147).
7. Brunswick Heads School File (AO NSW ref: 5/15134).
8. Burraneer Bay School File (AO NSW ref: 5/15189).
9. Numulgi School File (AO NSW ref: 5/17192).
10. Ibid.
11. Nana Glen School File (AO NSW ref: 5/17047).
12. Five Mile Tree School File (AO NSW ref: 5/15898).
13. Herons Creek School File (AO NSW ref: 5/16265).
14. Ibid.
15. Ibid.
16. Ibid.

19 PUPILS
1. Training School—Wagga, Miscellaneous Letters Received 1868, Council of Education (AO NSW ref: 1/792 Vol. 58).
2. Dubbo School File (AO NSW ref: 5/15725).
3. Dubbo School File (AO NSW ref: 5/15726).
4. Plunkett Street School File (AO NSW ref: 5/17364).
5. Ibid.
6. New Vale School File (AO NSW ref: 5/17147).
7. Stockinbingal School File (AO NSW ref: 5/17682).
8. Burringbar School File (AO NSW ref: 5/15195).
9. Medowie School File (AO NSW ref: 5/16807).
10. John Tierney, 'Eurunderee School', in *A Brian James*

Miscellany, edited and published by A. J. H. Tierney, Epping, NSW, 1977, pp. 72, 74-6. Copy of 'Eurunderee School' held in historical resources of NSW Dept of School Education.
11. Buxton School File (AO NSW ref: 5/15218).
12. Moonahcullah Aboriginal School File (AO NSW ref: 5/16901).
13. West Wyalong School File (AO NSW ref: 5/18217).
14. Willala School File (AO NSW ref: 5/18117).
15. Ibid.
16. Tullamore School File (AO NSW ref: 5/17898).
17. Ibid.

20 PUPILS AT INSPECTION
1. Copies of Official Correspondence and Official Diaries of Thomas Harris, Inspector of Schools, Southern District (Goulburn) 10 Jan 1865-21 Nov 1867 (AO NSW ref: A 5014 Vol. 1, pp. 81-2).
2. Calabash School File (AO NSW ref: 5/15230).
3. Medowie School File (AO NSW ref: 5/16807).
4. Ibid.
5. Numulgi School File (AO NSW ref. 5/17192).
6. Ibid.
7. Eglinford School File (AO NSW ref: 5/15795).
8. Ibid.
9. Burraneer Bay School File (AO NSW ref: 5/15189).
10. Ibid.
11. Wandook School File (AO NSW ref: 5/18014).
12. Ibid.
13. Karangi School File (AO NSW ref: 5/16420).
14. Ibid.
15. Kurrara School File (AO NSW ref: 5/16518).
16. Bagawa School File (AO NSW ref: 5/14749).
17. Ibid.
18. Woodport School File (AO NSW ref: 5/18186).

21 PUPILS TRAVELLING TO SCHOOL
1. John Saunders Middenway, 'Memoirs of John Saunders Middenway', copy held in historical resources of NSW Dept of School Education, p. 14.
2. Wyrallah School File (AO NSW ref: 5/18228).
3. Mulwee School File (AO NSW ref: 5/16999).
4. Berowra School File (AO NSW ref: 5/14898).
5. Ibid.
6. Ibid.
7. Bagawa School File (AO NSW ref: 5/14749).
8. Kurrara School File (AO NSW ref: 5/16518).
9. Burraneer Bay School File (AO NSW ref: 5/15189).
10. Macarthur School File (AO NSW ref: 5/16671).
11. Stockinbingal School File (AO NSW ref: 5/17682).
12. Billinudgel School File (AO NSW ref: 5/14924).
13. Ibid.
14. Conversation with Isa McPherson (née Paisley), 6 February 1994.
15. Megalong School File (AO NSW ref: 5/16810).

22 PUPIL-TEACHERS AND STUDENTS-IN-TRAINING
1. Ballina School File (AO NSW ref: 5/14764).
2. Woodburn School File (AO NSW ref: 5/18178).
3. Teachers' career records, NSW Dept of School Education.
4. Kogarah School File (AO NSW ref: 5/16493).
5. Ibid.
6. Ibid.
7. Ibid.

8. Ibid.
9. Teachers' career records, NSW Dept of School Education.
10. Blackfriars School File (AO NSW ref: 5/14945).
11. Ibid.
12. Wyalong School File (AO NSW ref: 5/18215).
13. Richmond School File (AO NSW ref: 5/17472).
14. Ibid.
15. Ibid.
16. Ibid.
17. Ibid.
18. Ibid.

23 PARENTS
1. Mulwee School File (AO NSW ref: 5/16999).
2. Ibid.
3. Ibid.
4. Ibid.
5. Ibid.
6. Ibid.
7. Ibid.
8. Ibid.
9. Ibid.
10. Ibid.
11. Ibid.
12. Ibid.
13. Ibid.
14. Teachers' career records, NSW Dept of School Education.
15. Coorabell School File (AO NSW ref: 5/15513).
16. Martins Creek Parents and Citizens Association Files (AO NSW 20/12964).
17. Billinudgel School File (AO NSW ref: 5/14924).
18. Narrabeen School File (AO NSW ref: 14/7731).
19. Ibid.

24 INSPECTORS
1. For this entry on Bernard McCann and Thomas Harris I am particularly indebted to Les Barber, who, approximately a hundred years after they held the position, was their successor as inspector of schools at Goulburn (1957-9). The copies of Harris's official correspondence and official diaries used for this entry were entrusted to Les Barber's care and are, in 1994, at the Archives Office of New South Wales. A photocopied set of these two volumes is also held in the historical resources of the New South Wales Department of School Education.
2. John Dugdale, 'Inspectors of Schools in the State Education System of New South Wales, 1848-1971', PhD thesis, University of Sydney, 1990, p. A-6.
3. Ibid., and *Goulburn Herald and Chronicle*, 2 November 1864.
4. *Goulburn Herald and Chronicle*, 2 November 1864.
5. *Report of the Commissioners of Education in New South Wales* for the year 1864, p. 24.
6. John Dugdale, 'Inspectors of Schools in the State Education System of New South Wales, 1848-1971', Ph.D. thesis, University of Sydney, 1990, p. A-8.
7. Copies of Official Correspondence and Official Diaries of Thomas Harris, Inspector of Schools, Southern District (Goulburn) 10 Jan 1865-21 Nov 1867 (AO NSW ref: A 5014 Vol. 1, p. 2).
8. Ibid., p. 21.
9. Ibid., p. 16.
10. *Report of the Commissioners of Education in New South Wales* for the year 1865, p. 28.
11. Copies of Official Correspondence and Official Diaries of Thomas Harris, Inspector of Schools, Southern District (Goulburn) 10 Jan 1865 - 21 Nov 1867 (AO NSW ref: A 5014 Vol. 1, p. 109).
12. Ibid., p. 110.
13. Ibid., Vol. 2, p. 280.
14. Ibid., Vol. 1, p. 216-217.
15. Ibid., Vol. 2, p. 64.
16. Ibid., Vol. 2, p. 23-24.
17. Ibid., Vol. 1, p. 197.
18. Ibid., Vol.1, p. 225.
19. Cited by Les Barber, 'When times were certain long long ago'. Copy held in historical resources of NSW Dept of School Education.
20. Copies of Official Correspondence and Official Diaries of Thomas Harris, Inspector of Schools, Southern District (Goulburn) 10 Jan 1865-21 Nov 1867 (AO NSW ref: A 5014 Vol. 2, p. 71).
21. Ibid., Vol. 2, p. 531.
22. Ibid., Vol. 2, p. 542.
23. Ibid. Vol. 2, p. 549.
24. John Dugdale, 'Inspectors of Schools in the State Education System of New South Wales, 1848-1971', PhD thesis, University of Sydney, 1990, p. A-8.
25. Entry on William McIntyre by Bruce Mitchell in *Australian Dictionary of Biography*, Vol. 5: 1851-1890, Melbourne University Press, 1974, p. 167.
26. Ibid.
27. Ibid.
28. The *New South Wales Educational Gazette*, 1 August 1901, p. 51.
29. op. cit., p.167.
30. The *New South Wales Educational Gazette*, 1 August 1901, p. 51.
31. Entry on William McIntyre by Bruce Mitchell in *Australian Dictionary of Biography*, Vol. 5: 1851-1890, Melbourne University Press, 1974, p. 168.
32. John Dugdale, 'Inspectors of Schools in the State Education System of New South Wales, 1848-1971', PhD thesis, University of Sydney, 1990, p. A-32.
33. Beilsdown School File (AO NSW ref: 5/14850.3).
34. Ibid.
35. Ibid.
36. Diary of Alexander Lobban, 1890 to unknown year. A copy of this extract is held in the historical resources of the NSW Department of School Education. On the map Lobban drew of the district on 16 March 1891, not long after his visit, a resident with a name spelt 'Hewitt' lives at a spot close to the 'Bielsdown' River (the spellings Bielsdown and Beilsdown were interchangeable) rather than close to the Little Murray River (Beilsdown School File AO NSW ref: 5/14850).

Index